The Other Side of the Altar

The Other Side of the Altar

One Man's Life in the Catholic Priesthood

Paul E. Dinter

FARRAR, STRAUS AND GIROUX *New York*

Farrar, Straus and Giroux
19 Union Square West, New York 10003

Distributed in Canada by Douglas & McIntyre Ltd.
Printed in the United States of America
First edition, 2003

Library of Congress Cataloging-in-Publication Data
Dinter, Paul E. (Paul Edward)
    The other side of the altar : one man's life in the Catholic
priesthood / Paul E. Dinter.— 1st ed.
        p.   cm.
    ISBN 0-374-29966-8 (hc : alk. paper)
    1. Dinter, Paul E. (Paul Edward) 2. Catholic ex-priests—
United States—Biography. 3. Celibacy—Catholic Church.   I. Title.

BX4668.3.D56 A3 2003
282'.092—dc21
[B]

                                                2002032542

Designed by Cassandra J. Pappas

www.fsgbooks.com

1   3   5   7   9   10   8   6   4   2

In gratitude to
and
in memory of

DAVID JOYCE
(1959–1983)

and

DAVID ENTWISTLE
(1954–1993)

Contents

ℱoreword

THIRTY-NINE YEARS AGO, entering the major seminary, I reached for the brass ring of the Catholic priesthood. As prizes went back then, it seemed a rich and exotic one. It was September 1964, three months before Vatican II introduced English into the Mass and turned around the altar tables in Catholic churches. There were forty-two of us first-year philosophy students, most of us just turning twenty.

We thought of ourselves as John XXIII's boys. Elected in 1958, as we had entered high school, the amazing Papa Roncalli had called for an aggiornamento, or updating, of the all-too-medieval Catholicism that we (and our parents and their parents) had known all our lives. Though John had died just over a year earlier, Vatican II—"his" council—was about to begin its crucial third session. In the excitement the council had worked up among us, the labels "traditionalist," "conservative," or "progressive" meant little. The church was awaking from a four-hundred-year slumber, and we were going to be the ones doing the waking.

Less than four decades later, the prize is tarnished. A pall has descended over the priesthood as priest after priest has been accused of sexual abuse, and bishop after bishop, when not himself a perpetrator, has been revealed as a soulless bureaucrat oblivious to the pain of young victims, reckless about the fate of future victims, intent on saving the reputations of priests and the institutional church. Discredited and in despair, some priests have taken their lives. Catholics here and abroad—where sexual abuse has also been uncovered—have been as stunned as the general populace by the breadth and depth of the accusations, the seeming truth of too many of them, and the lengths to which supposedly good men have gone to keep them a secret. The bishops' efforts at their Dallas meeting in June 2002 to contain the damage might have put the fear of God into some wayward priests—while stranding others in a merciless limbo—but they most notably failed to police or to censure any of their own number. The reputation of the Catholic priesthood as a profession has plummeted.

This book is a story of the priesthood, a personal account over almost forty years about the celibate priesthood and about sexuality. It is a story that—it can no longer be denied—is not two stories, but one story: how the Catholic priesthood's efforts to control the moral terms of debate regarding the proper role of human sexuality have irrevocably collapsed, calling into question not only the priesthood's credibility, but its own self-understanding.

My story will, I hope, help to illustrate how the two plot lines have merged. It falls into four phases. Between 1964 and 1974, I finished college; began theological studies; took a year off from the seminary (during which I dated and taught high school); returned to the seminary; reluctantly but hopefully took on the burden of celibacy; was ordained first a deacon, then a priest; and was assigned to a parish and then reassigned as Catholic Chaplain at Columbia University. These were years when I was willing to tackle both the seminary and the diocesan administrations and still felt convinced that change was not only possible, but inevitable. In the decade and a half that followed, I was drawn into a full-time, challenging, and wonderfully rewarding ministry on campus, and also completed a doctorate in biblical studies. I was allowed to work at a remove from the archdiocese, which supported my budget and the campus ministry's expansion into community service work (to which I added my own personal involvement in peace activism).

But then John O'Connor became the Archbishop of New York, and his auxiliary bishop, Edward Egan, became my supervisor. Their agendas did not always overlap, but the strange chemistry between those two formidable churchmen combined to push me out of my position at Columbia in 1988. I then ended up spending most of a year on sabbatical in Rome.

Phase three began after I returned to New York. Weathering an accusation of disloyalty to Cardinal O'Connor, I received a temporary assignment, and when that ended, I was left to dangle in the wind. So I found space in a friend's rectory and did some college teaching while I filled in at various parishes on weekends for the next year and a half. During a final three-year teaching stint, individual and group therapy convinced me finally that celibacy had ceased to energize my participation in ministry; in fact, it was seriously crippling me. The physical, spiritual, and emotional loneliness was killing my spirit. I took a leave from the priesthood in 1993, and after eleven months, I resigned from the priesthood permanently—in August 1994, just thirty years after beginning to pack my trunk for the move to Saint Joseph's Seminary.

Phase four began when, by a bureaucratic miracle, I was canonically dispensed from the obligation of celibacy and was married in the same parish church where I had last celebrated Mass. All at once I became the stepfather of two young girls, struggled to find full-time work, and continued to go to church with my family on Sunday just as men of my father's generation before me had done.

Today I stand within the body of the faithful but outside the active priestly ministry for one main reason: I could no longer accept the hierarchy's spurious ideology of human sexuality and its failed moral teachings. Thirty years inside the club, during which I gave that teaching every benefit of the doubt—and as many years of monastic retreats and further study—failed to win my mind or heart or to convince me of the adequacy, either for priests or for laypeople, of the "official" teaching in the matter of sex.

But it is not enough to state this argument and expect to convince anybody who is not already convinced. So I have not tried to construct a treatise against Rome's one-eyed view of sexuality and the human condition. Many others have gone before me and documented Rome's heavy-handed efforts to block changes in outmoded teachings and to pack the college of bishops with "law-and-order" types. Instead, I wish to tell my story and to venture some reflections about my journey over four decades. If there are a few salacious details about the lives of priests, they are only a few—enough to tell the larger story. I was never an eyewitness to misdeeds, but I knew more than I wanted to know about sexual acting out among priests. What I missed for a long time was the hidden patterns at play. I need not rehash the news reports about the ways in which several hundred U.S. priests wove their webs of deceit to ensnare young innocents or normally insecure teenagers. But I hope to sketch out a more comprehensive portrait of the day-to-day world of the priesthood in which they could do so, then be ignored or passively condoned, and finally transferred to new assignments in which they could start up their sick drama yet again. I will do so by drawing on my own experience and that of other active and resigned priests, but I will do so in a way that seeks to be discreet yet truthful.

Everything in this book is true. But because I want to portray not the malfeasance or the sexual behavior of individuals but an entire subculture that lures unwary and sexually naïve boys and men into its web, I will speak anecdotally and employ some artistic license. Some of the characters, clerical and lay, have died; many are still alive. Some characters are composite figures and some bear fictitious names; others are woven so tightly into the historical record that they must be depicted as themselves.

My hope is that by writing personally and critically, reflecting on my own experience, I may say something to the church as a body and to the wider world as well—and justify my risking this effort. For while unsexing both men and women in the name of "perfect chastity" may guarantee institutional stability, the Catholic church and its leaders can no longer afford to sacrifice individual lives on the altar of its own self-idealization. Reading the "signs of the times" is not sixties fashion for religious trendiness, a marketing strategy to make unsavory demands palatable. It is a fundamental instinct of faith. And the times—they have a-changed. But it is not the "times" that have shriveled the promise of renewal of the church and the ministerial priesthood. Nor is it "tradition" that has reasserted itself to frustrate the aggiornamento at the heart of Vatican II. The villain is the priestly habit of dishonesty coupled with the ordained leadership's unwillingness to imagine a life in which sanctity and active sexuality cohabit and minister to each other.

Revaluing sexuality within the spiritual life of all humans—adolescents, the unmarried, the elderly, married couples, gay people, and even celibates—requires a supreme act of the religious imagination, indeed a religious awakening, that has thus far proved too daunting for most Catholic leaders. I hope to contribute to this awakening by telling the truth, as I know it, about life behind the Roman collar.

The Other Side of the Altar

One

Meeting the Mystique

OCTOBER 1954. The children of our parochial school are drawn up in front of the towering Victorian Romanesque church, clutching small American flags. We are an honor guard, awaiting the arrival of the archbishop. The parish my family belongs to—Our Lady of Mercy in Port Chester, New York—is celebrating its centenary. Unobtrusively, Francis Cardinal Spellman, barely taller than the fifth-graders, alights from a large black automobile, unrecognized except by one nun, who rushes out to kneel and kiss his ring. I remember noticing that he wore a frock coat over his clerical vest, though I would not have known what to call it at the time. He smiled warmly, waved with his right hand, then disappeared into the rectory. Soon after, the clerical procession behind a gold crucifix and candles began to wend its way through our ranks, down the walk and along the avenue, before turning into the church for the Solemn Pontifical Mass.

First came a dozen altar boys in their black cassocks, white surplices, and Eton collars sprouting white silk bows, then the priests similarly attired, but in Roman collars and their distinctive pom-pommed hats, carrying their black leather-bound breviaries.

Following them came the graying monsignori, papal chamber-lains in their purple mantellettas, looking very grand. Then be-decked in matching gold brocade vestments, walking in single file, the subdeacon, deacon, and celebrant for the occassion. Last of all, flanked by two deacons-of-honor, walked the cardinal, trans-formed from a village vicar to a scarlet-clad representative of His Holiness Pope Pius XII, the Vicar of Christ on earth. Filing through the arch of swords formed by the white-plumed Knights of Columbus, the procession disappeared up the stairs and through the portal of the church. Hurriedly dismissing us—only the older boys serving on the altar were allowed inside that day—the sisters scooted in the side entrance to be in place for the once-in-a-generation pontifical Mass that was about to take place.

Then as now, most American Catholics are born into Catholic families. My father's family were immigrants from Croatia, and once my mother migrated to Catholicism from Serbian Ortho-doxy, our parish church—Saint Mary's we called it—became the axis of our world outside the home. Centered in the uptown por-tion of an industrial village hugging the shores of the Byram River, on the border of New York and Connecticut, the parish and its school threw a thick cloak of Catholic parochialisms around us: daily catechism lessons, weekly Sunday Mass, monthly First Friday Mass, yearly festivals both in church and at school. We went to Saint Mary's for weekend dances and roller-skating parties, the Catholic Youth Program in the school basement and the dance classes in the auditorium, for CYP basketball games on winter Saturdays, the Saxers Little League in spring, and in sum-mertime for day camp, which was staffed by high school students and seminarians, students for the priesthood.

Of the host of parish activities, the Altar Boys Society claimed both my time and my longtime loyalty. Serving on the al-tar made for a strong identity marker—it rivaled playing on a parish team or singing in the choir—and gave a boy a leg up in the parish. Like all good clubs, altar boys firmed us into a group through regular meetings that initiated us little by little into shared mysteries—in this case, the mysteries of the altar. To keep the rank and file of altar servers trained and ready, the priest "moderator" met with the entire Altar Boy Society—fifty to sixty of us—every Saturday morning. Father Ed Brogan was a product of the wartime seminary, ordained the year I was born. He sported a crew cut, a chic semi-Jesuit cassock (flapped not buttoned in the front), and penny loafers, and he was the only priest we ever knew who smoked cigarettes. All of which labeled him very cool. Precisely at 9 a.m., he would call us to order and read out our weekly assignments. Then he would train us in the different levels of the job, rehearsing us in the church for Monday night novena prayers and benediction, Forty Hours devotion, First Friday Adoration, or Lenten Stations of the Cross—making sure to get us out by 10:00, when basketball started, over in the gym.

He also coached us in the most daunting task we faced, one that made or broke a career as an altar boy—committing the acolyte's Latin responses to memory. Recited aloud on behalf of the entire congregation (few of whom knew any Latin), the responses were secret passwords that led us into the inner sanctum of Catholic worship. Now that Latin is long gone here in the United States, it is easy to forget how fundamental it once was to the panoply and piety of Catholics. But because the average church member had no clue, being able to handle the Latin gave us entrée into the church's sanctuaries, where the laity literally were forbidden to set foot. Somewhat puffed up by our little knowledge, we were regularly coached on sacred decorum, yet the point never seemed to be prayer, much less comprehension, but speed and precision. The parish pastor, a regal man who had made it to general as a chaplain in World War I and who inspired a certain awe, was the fastest Latinist of them all. He was fussy as well, so with him your crisp Latin seemed on a par with personal sanctity.

Serving was part solemnity and part holy busy-ness—rushing into the sacristy at the last minute, vesting, passing the priest's inspection, reeling off the Latin responses (from *Ad Deum qui laetificat juventutem meam* on through the last *Deo gratias*, which followed the priest's dismissal, *Ite missa est*), all the while handling the complex rubrics of the Mass, then rushing out to the next activity. And yet somehow it all awakened me to matters of significance that lay beneath the words and gestures of the ritual drama. The catechism had us memorize definitions of the sacraments as "outward signs" that gave grace, so I guess we should have been looking for the inward potential in all the rituals. But most of the time, it was enough to do the externals well: we were assured that if they were well done, the sacraments "worked" and put good Catholics in that enviable locale called "the state of grace." Priests, above all, lived there at a spiritual address to which the post office did not deliver, but where brothers lived together in true unity. Or so it seemed.

Little by little, I was drawn into the world of these signs of grace and to the place where they were enacted. The massive brick and terra-cotta church that fronted Westchester Avenue across from the public library conjured a wider world for me. I went there for services—early and often as a server at the 7 a.m. daily Mass—but also to retreat for private prayer and a kind of mulling over things, like what would I do with my life? Because we were taught that the presence of the sacrament in the tabernacle made Catholic churches the antechamber to heaven, it seemed like Saint Mary's was a pretty good place to spend time alone. We were certainly encouraged to do so—"visiting the Blessed Sacrament" it was called, and it counted as a special act of devotion that would inevitably make us more spiritual and honest with ourselves. As altar boys, one of the duties we could draw was adoration, an entire hour spent in wordless attendance before the eucharistic Presence each first Friday of the month. The bonus: self-importantly walking out of class in the middle of the school day without Sister being able to object. The onus: boredom—a whole hour, kneeling or sitting, still and undistracted, observed by parishioners stopping by during the day for a spell of adoration and prayer.

Sometime in the course of my preadolescence, I decided I wanted to get good at this kind of time alone. I think I was testing myself, because I never really liked it much. But I became convinced that mastering it would allow me to ascend Mount Tabor, to make it in the world of spiritual men like Father Brogan. For I was being drawn to the men who moved in and out of the place of silence and signs that was my parish church and by the mystique that surrounded them. Maybe not early on by the pastor, who seemed too remote and august. But Father Hordern's wry smile and dry wit and Father Finnerty's mischievousness, coupled with his dutiful manner, projected an image of sturdy rather than dry sanctity. It was the thirty-something Father Brogan, though, who made the biggest impact on us. His youngish laughter balanced his no-nonsense approach to our altar duties, and both had a way of pulling us in and making us comfortable with him.

To the girls of the parish, the tall, vivacious, good-looking curate who also sang at parish functions pretty much fulfilled the Hollywood stereotype. But Father Brogan had depth, too. The word was out among the boys (and most adults as well) to avoid his confessional: he asked too many questions. But a lot of girls lined up there, spending five times as long as any of us boys kneeling at the grille in a holy tête-à-tête. You see, he spoke with you as an individual and took you seriously. Oddly enough, he did the same when he said Mass: he spoke the Latin Scriptures and prayers as if his uncomprehending congregation really could hear the message beneath the sheath of that obscure, ancient tongue. Long before I came to comprehend any Latin, I had developed an ear for the soft, Italian-accented language of prayer because Ed Brogan made it an instrument of communication. Nothing with him went by rote.

Father Brogan projected an image of being a priest that seemed to lie at the far horizon of a boy's aspirations. So when I felt it was time (I was twelve, but I know the idea had planted itself in my imagination from about the age of seven), I made a decision. I would go "public" about my desire to become a priest. I screwed up my courage and, still wet behind the ears—but before my first wet dream announced that adolescence had arrived—I took the risk, joining the queue outside his confessional one Saturday afternoon. It seems strange now that the most natural place to choose for sharing a confidence not related to sin would be the whispered darkness of the "box," but in those days the confessional was a private space where an almost teenage boy's most secret thoughts could be shared.

Situated in the back corner of the church, the confessional's two entrances to the right and left of where Father Brogan sat were fed by a single line down the side aisle. If the lines feeding the other priests' confessionals were like drive-through lanes at a fast-food franchise, his was like waiting for a table at Le Cirque. What's more, all the other sinners could see you waiting and stage-whisper, "How come you're waiting to see Brogan!?" So much for penitent anonymity! In fact, I never remember thinking that the priest on the other side of the veiled grill didn't know exactly who I was. On that day, I probably identified myself to Father Brogan, but I doubt I had to tell him who I was. He had been a fixture in my life since at least the second grade, so when he heard, "Bless me, Father, for I have sinned. It's a week since my last confession. I think I want to become a priest," he would have known who was speaking to him through the screen. I remember him responding warmly, but not urgently. Nor did he require me to do anything about my decision. More than any words, his reassuring tone stayed with me. It told me I hadn't done anything wrong, and I wasn't reaching too high. Still, I had crossed my private Rubicon and I left the church that afternoon feeling I had done something big.

Boys do not find it easy having an inner life, a fantasy world, in which they do not figure as sports heroes, cops, firemen, film stars, members of the military, or a little of each. My father, who had volunteered for naval service just as I was turning into a zygote, and so had left behind a pregnant wife and an infant daughter to ship out to the Pacific, modeled the action-figure version of manhood even when, back in civilian life, he was building a bread business. Because I never excelled at sports and was among the last kids picked when guys chose up sides, I had started to follow my sister's habit of reading, enjoying the demands that books made on my imagination.

The public library sat just across the avenue from our church, and its book-lined precincts felt almost as special. Getting my own library card and then watching it fill with the ink-stamped dates gave me a record of reading progress though I never caught up to my sister, who boasted that she had read every book in the children's section of the library before the eighth grade. Introducing me to historical persons and events, access to the library's treasures gave me an edge at school and filled in gaps left by our catechism lessons. Bible history in the sixth grade became one of my favorite all-time subjects, fitting events I had heard of in church into a wider picture. Like biblical tales, novels gave me space to imagine a bigger world than the modestly suburban one where we lived, and a life in that larger world more purposeful than my everyday one. My friend Johnny and I took to making up indoor games that echoed the historical adventures we got to see for twenty-five cents at the Saturday movies. Although he sang in the choir and connected with the mysteries of the altar from the faraway choir loft, we overcame the distance by our joint devotion to dramas, historical and spiritual, decades before *History's Mysteries* would become a successful TV formula.

This tale of a twelve-year-old's pursuit of lofty spiritual goals in the New York suburbs during the middle years of the twentieth century may strain credibility when measured by the worldly ways of today's preteens. But the truth is, I was far from alone. Back then young Catholic men in the thousands essayed a stint in the seminary if only to assure themselves that they were not cut out for the priesthood or the religious life, enrolling in high school or college seminaries in historically high numbers. Most young men who did so gained approval for trying, and there was little stigma attached to withdrawing at an early age. And in the years before the parochial high school system expanded, parents knew a bargain when they saw it: the subsidized education in the prep seminary could well lead to the college career that few of them had enjoyed. So their sons were responding not only to the pull of the priestly mystique but also to the frequent push of significant adults who had much to gain from their reaching so far upward. Boys throughout the 1940s, 1950s, and into the 1960s who conceived a vocation to the priesthood for themselves in pre- or early adolescence did so in circumstances not very different than my own. One friend who informed his parish priest of his willingness to attend the minor seminary was told, "You've made me the happiest I have ever been in my life." Being made to feel that special—it was not the style our fathers had followed with us—could help a young man jump through a lot of hoops in the course of his growing up.

Another colleague, whom I'll call J.T., excelled at school and at basketball, but he did not feel that he had hit his stride until he made the move into the minor seminary. When he first made his decision known, his parish priest, another Irish-American, by the name of Father Grogan, flung open the ample black confessional cape J.T. was wearing and closed it around him to signal his inclusion in the sacred circle of regard for men called to the cloth. With his new identity, even playing basketball took on new purpose; he watched the girls at courtside cheering him and the other guys on court, and thought what dull lives girls led. Sideline spectators, girls tended to be seen merely as nonboys. In the idealized male world of the aspirant priest, a boy's identity was defined not by how you stood vis-à-vis young women or even how other guys accepted you, but by feeling included in a circle of men who stood apart from the crowd. For boys like J.T., it was a strong, action-oriented, but sexually neutered place, relieving adolescents of anxieties that came uninvited after puberty had announced itself.

Aspiring to the priesthood offered the unsure young male a safe place in between boyhood and the uncertain demands, unsafe desires, and unpublished satisfactions of adulthood. Striving toward it seemed noble, secure, and prestigious at the same time, allowing us an escape from the dynamics at work in our families of origin that we could neither name nor fathom, but which seemed better to avoid. There was—we know now—a dark undercurrent of sexual insecurity at work in all this that could make the same naïve young man a victim of abusive behavior at the hands of the very men he had followed into what was supposed to be a safe refuge. But back then the attraction clothed in the somber garb of the priestly mystique offered a young man the chance to rise above the messiness of everyday existence. And what, pray tell, could be messier than the sexual dramas that men and women enacted every day?

That mystique, promising a way of escaping the mess long into adulthood, drew this Catholic boy on the cusp of adolescence in the late 1950s into its subculture. But I doubt I would have sought to join the priestly procession off the avenue and into the realm of the sacred so single-mindedly if I hadn't been surrounded by a lay Catholic culture that valued its priests and their separate lives so unreservedly.

For many previous decades, if not centuries, the sense that Catholic priests were a breed apart from other mortals provided powerful motivation for candidates to seek ordination. It also supplied the institutional church with enormous resources that had launched the great expansion of Catholicism in the New World because it was built on a culture of religious exceptionalism. By the 1950s, Roman Catholics had been well instructed by their leaders to self-select certain influences and pastimes and consciously ignore others in the society around them. We were expected to avoid certain movies, not read forbidden authors, and avoid frankly sexual displays, magazines, and discussions that even came close to flirting with that forbidden zone. All of these were "near occasions of sin," and if you wanted to avoid sin, you had better not even get near a near occasion.

For us, a religious way of life amounted to learning how to live amid family and friends in a closed social and religious system where crime and punishment were central. Faith and morals had a host of mathematical corollaries that made their demands concrete and even workaday: seven sacraments, ten commandments, six commandments of the church, nine First Fridays, five decades of the rosary, thirty days' indulgence. The list went on and on and kept us focused on being a good Catholic by performing numerically calculated deeds. The whole religious system enclosed us within rigid boundaries to keep us from offending God, and it set a host of priests and religious to guarding those boundaries. They themselves led separate lives, an inner core of the most faithful believers, to set an example to keep us from mixing with the goyim, or Gentiles, that is, Protestants and other unbelievers. In sum, avoiding the near occasions of sin meant staying within the religious clan and staying clear of unnecessary entanglements with the world outside or with the flesh and the devil who worked within our imperiled souls.

Catholicism as we practiced it wasn't subtle religion. It was filled with easy antinomies, and the choices it offered weren't known for their nuances. We were urged to consider saintly heroism. If we didn't, there was little doubt where we would end up—just part of what Saint Augustine had called, centuries before, the hell-bound lump (*massa damnata*) of humanity. Others had avoided this fate, and we could, too, if we avoided the "crowd" and followed the lead of our leaders, who chose a life in the inner sanctum of the church. This explicit propaganda for recruiting candidates for the priesthood wouldn't work for everyone, so other young people who had lived much closer to our time and been proclaimed saints much more recently, one as late as 1954, were offered as alternate role models—of sorts.

Not since Romeo and Juliet have two Italian youngsters gotten more notice for their life-choices than Dominic Savio and Maria Goretti. Their cults (or holy fan clubs) were Rome's antidotes to popular teenage culture as it grew in the postwar years. As grammar school was coming to a close, we new teenagers got a strong dose of these adolescent saints' stories because, in their indirect way, they were the closest thing we got to any form of sexual education—Catholic style. Dominic Savio had lived in the first part of the nineteenth century and became a student of the Salesians. Don Bosco, their founder, was an educational innovator, among the earliest social reformers concerned with the growing problems of the urban poor and, in particular, beggar boys (like those still found on the streets of Third World cities). Young Dominic took sick and died before his fifteenth birthday, but not before developing a reputation for precociously influencing his peers to put the temptations of the flesh behind them. After he died in 1857, his fame and his reputed motto—"Death rather than sin!"—were spread abroad by the Salesians, who, understandably, enjoyed taking credit for one of their own.

For her part, Maria Goretti was not even twelve when she was murdered by a twenty-year-old would-be rapist in 1902. Because she had fought off his sexual advances, she was heavily promoted as a model for youth. When Pope Pius XII canonized her in 1950, she was proclaimed a virgin and martyr who had given her life for her faith and her purity. Her cult never even mentioned the issue of violence against female children or women in general. No, Maria had validated Dominic Savio's motto and had *chosen* death rather than yield to lust, her own or her rapist's. One might demur and suggest that a young woman's panic and horror did not really represent a choice for martyrdom, but the opportunity for purity propaganda was too good to pass up. The message we got from her story was clear: Avoid sin in all its forms, but especially sex outside marriage. But nobody would venture to tell us what sex entailed, what we shouldn't do, or what we should do. It was enough to be warned and given models of young people who hadn't made it past fifteen. They may have been the earliest examples of the "scared straight" programs that take inner-city youth to prison and have them meet hardened felons who try to motivate them not to follow in their path! Did it occur to us that the teenage models offered to us looked suspiciously like the priests and nuns who were teaching us, just younger when they died? Probably not. But what was clear was that the norm for holiness being proffered young Catholics wore black. The best that girls could do was to follow the derivative vocation of the woman religious. The lot of boys was far more fortunate. We could aspire to the heights and throw in our lot with that portion of humanity that was uniquely God-like.

In the same year that Elvis Presley appeared on the *Ed Sullivan Show*, we were entering the eighth grade, full of curiosity about ourselves and our bodies. The famous TV host rated very high with us not only because he had hosted this new music phenomenon, but because his niece Beth was our classmate. What was more, we had shared the same first-grade teacher, Sister Agnes

Mercedes—who had originally come to the parish school *in 1900*! But at a time when most of us could have used some better sex talk than we were getting in the school playground, our religious instruction about what was going on with us bodily focused on Dominic Savio's motto and Maria Goretti's death. The whole approach had a way of shutting down natural curiosity.

Morality, the heart of our religion, was a matter of avoidance, not engagement. The style was modeled most tellingly by the Legion of Decency, the Catholic equivalent of the Protestants' temperance movement that sought to "guide" our access to popular entertainment. The A list was composed of films like *The Song of Bernadette*, which were Unobjectionable; the B list films were Objectionable in Whole or in Part; the C list contained films that were Condemned. Not unlike the Motion Picture Association of America's now junked X rating, the Condemned list often had the opposite effect of boosting a film's audience.

As a guide for parents, the Legion's list might have played a constructive role—had the anonymous censors bothered to provide explanations. But the Legion of Decency claimed much more for itself and sought to bind Catholics in conscience to follow its aesthetic judgments as moral law. Catholic leaders felt a great deal was at stake in this battle over the popular media. In the late 1950s, the premier U.S. prelate, our own Cardinal Spellman, went into the pulpit of Saint Patrick's Cathedral (he would mount those steps only seven times in the twenty-nine years he was archbishop) to issue a fire-and-brimstone condemnation of the movie *Baby Doll*.

The censorship issues caused me to have my own brush with judgment on a Saturday afternoon sometime before my visit to Father Brogan, when I confessed to another priest the dread deed that I had seen the movie *The Conqueror*. On the B list, it starred John Wayne in the role of Genghis Khan and featured a dance by a Susan Hayward wrapped in a red ribbon and nothing else. There was a lot of red ribbon, so it didn't reveal very much, but it was little enough to earn official Catholic opprobrium. I don't think I felt particularly guilty for seeing it—I was probably fishing for information, an explanation about the mystery of sex that was somehow encoded in the dance. But all my sensitive soul-baring got me was a good bawling out for my immoral ways. I remember trying to justify myself by explaining my interest in history. The priest wouldn't have any of it, so I left ingesting an early dose of shame about my burgeoning sexual curiosity that kept me mute about arousal and erection for years.

Our teachers promoted other avoidance strategies, the most creative of which brought together prayer and study. They challenged our eighth-grade exuberance by emphasizing academic competition in preparation for the upcoming New York State Regents exam, the brand-new cooperative exam to determine entrance into Catholic high school, and—for a select group of us—a New York State Civics contest (for which a select group of us memorized eight hundred short questions and answers). We faced each new challenge armed with a powerful strategy as well: a novena to Saint Philomena. Novenas, or nine successive sessions of prayer, vouched for the sincerity of the petitioner. After all, anyone could ask for something once, twice, or even five times. But only those who really cared would muster the energy and focus to repeat the same petition nine straight days (or weeks or months) running. Or so the thinking seemed to be. What was more, Saint Philomena, we were assured, would be a powerful intercessor for us—she was yet another teenager cut down in the flower of her youth, another virgin martyr whose prayers for us would not go unanswered. When we all passed the Regents exam in midyear, Sister took no credit. She gave it all to Saint Philomena—who, sadly, was later judged never to have existed and was dropped from the roster of saints by Pope Paul VI.

That spring, word got out that not all the boys and girls in the class were applying to Catholic high schools. Our parents had never paid any tuition for the parish grammar school, but

Catholic high schools operated differently. The fact that some families could not afford to send their children to a Catholic high school did not seem to enter into the equation. Instead, the question became a moral one. I have no idea whether the kids destined for public high school were taken aside and issued a stern warning that their souls were in jeopardy. But I know that happened in other schools to other eighth-graders who were opting out of the system. The parish authorities rarely treated these decisions individually, because going to public school contravened the group strategy about how to keep Catholic youth on the straight-and-narrow path to salvation. For some years yet, I would buy completely into the strategy of remaining within our enclosed Catholic world because it was an extension of the security that a tight family bond held out for me. I saw the world of the church and its institutions as an extension of my family, and even as a more expansive (and safer) place. It would be some years before I ventured outside the circle. In the meantime, I had a struggle to wage on the home front for even the limited autonomy I was seeking by wanting to be a priest.

In the 1950s, the very notion that families function as "systems" and according to certain dynamics, some of which are far less healthy than others, had not emerged into the light of day. When it came to any systematic thinking about marriage and family, the Christian Family Movement was making some inroads. CFM, as it was known, had begun to challenge an older, immigrant mentality that assigned rigid gender-based roles, with unequal obligations for husbands and wives and no questioning of the man's right, as husband and father, to physically discipline all the members of his family, his wife included. The founders of CFM, seeking to improve these behaviors and bring a measure of mutuality to marital relations, promoted an early version of the ecology of divided function in the relationship between husband and wife.

Using an organic metaphor loosely based on Saint Paul's image of the body being one but having many members, this strain of Catholic teaching named the husband the "head" (*caput*) and the wife the "heart" (*cor*) of the family. Dad made the decisions in his own, worldly, hardheaded way. Mom provided the affection and warmth and took the edge off her husband's strictly rational mode of operating. Or so went the theory.

My parents had never heard of CFM, but they would have consciously embraced its idealized family typology—except that my father's hardheaded rationality played second fiddle to his passionate commitment to his own authority, to corporal punishment, to the ability of the Yankees to beat the Dodgers, and to his undaunted belief that he should always win at pinochle. Hardworking to a fault, he felt inadequate when my mother returned to her profession as a nurse after my younger brother started school, yielding to the need for a second income only reluctantly. A fatherless teenager when the 1929 crash occurred, he confessed to me shortly before he died, sixty years later, "All I ever wanted to be able to do was to support my family." His simple desire had been formed early in his life but was also complicated by a family tragedy that remained hidden from us for years. My mother bore his authoritarian rages, tried to balance his mercurial states, went to bat for us, and more than once got in the way of his blows aimed in our direction. She played the helpmate role to the full and, slowly but determinedly, redressed the balance and moved into the driver's seat as age took its toll and he mellowed out.

But back then, no analysis of these roles, or of how my father's hardness and my mother's long-suffering nature were shaping my sister, my brother, or me, would have been allowed. The only dynamics at work were the obvious ones: Dad was powerful (hence, no one else could be); Mom cared for the household; we obeyed the rules, did our chores, and performed in school. Rebelliousness was met head-on and mutinous thoughts were quelled before they matured. The result was a very tight nuclear family where my father's word was law and my mother did not hesitate to take on even the formidable parish authorities when their decisions or actions transgressed our family norms or when one of her own was physically disciplined by a very cranky nun.

Although I watched my share of *Ozzie and Harriet, Father Knows Best,* and *Leave It to Beaver,* the idealized families that were trotted out there didn't resonate with me. Alice and Ralph Cramden of *The Honeymooners*—childless though they were—resonated more deeply with the volatile mix of tenderness and simmering anger that characterized life with Father. My early attraction to the other world of fathers, three blocks away—those with no obvious families but with a strong claim on my imagination—found its seeds here. It sprouted early, catalyzed by my subliminal reaction to an event that threatened the delicate equilibrium that held my family together. My memory of discrete facts is dim, but the neural tracks of those distant events and the images they left me with seared deep down. Returning from school to celebrate my seventh birthday, I found a motherless apartment. Who was there in her stead—a neighbor, my father? I can't recall. But she wasn't, and no one explained why. The one bedroom in the apartment that my siblings and I shared had a window overlooking the corner where the avenue that ran down from Saint Mary's intersected with our street. My mother would often wait at the window to watch us come and go from school. Maybe I looked up and expected to see her that day. I can't say. But in my growing confusion and sorrow, I conceived a mental image of me seeing my unknowing self from that window, coming home from school, bereft and oddly alone in the world. Over the next few days, I must have replayed the scene continually. Just as suddenly, after a week's time my mother returned home—from the hospital, where she had miscarried a child. To my recollection, little or nothing was said about her absence or her reappearance. Years later, when I posed the question "why?" my mother meekly excused the silence as an effort not to upset us.

Recovered memories haven't had the best press of late. Cognitive science seems to offer a nuanced picture of what happens when we remember: we literally re-member the past, new signals skittering down ancient neural pathways, assembling and reassembling the layered images that make up our fluctuating self. Yet in therapy thirty-five years after these events, I felt, suddenly and consciously, the paralyzing fear I had years earlier repressed. My mother had died and I would never see her again, and it haunted me for most of a week. Then somehow fate reversed itself. I remember nothing of the elation or the relief, only that she was home again. But long into adolescence I suffered recurring dreams that she had fallen from the fire escape and that I could not run fast enough to break her fall and save her. Or I imagined myself attending her funeral. In the tangle of emotions—which, even had I accessed them at seven, I could not have aired—I carved out a way to keep her. Not consciously, of course. I was hapless, not possessed! There, in the aftermath of all my unspoken turmoil, my plan to join the priesthood formed as a way to make her safe. Serving God and preserving my mother would go hand in hand. What could be better than that?! Assuming responsibility for her, and our family's well-being must have seemed an appropriate role for a very earnest and frightened boy.

If history is any guide, mine would not be the first vocation to the priesthood born in trauma. Years later, when I was consciously trying to sort through these dynamic elements in my psyche, I would discover that both my parents had suffered devastating traumas as children—losses that were never truly mourned and that they never spoke about when we were young. My dad at age twelve lost his father to suicide; my mother at nine was given to another family to be raised after her mother died: her miner father, perhaps too drunk to notice, did not want her. Both Mom and Dad, despite their differences, adopted the bravest of fronts, pretending that our lives *were* just like Ozzie and Harriet's. But not far below the surface, something in me knew differently.

Throughout my grammar-school years, we lived suburban lives—except that we weren't yet part of the car culture. We walked to school, church, the park, the doctor, little league, even taking trips to visit friends in my father's bread truck. Later we would ride our bikes in packs on excursions as far away as the county airport. My parents' main recreational activity was bowling, which my mother excelled at, contending for the women's high game and high triple at the local bowling alley. Shortly after I turned eleven, I began to keep a diary, noting the daily temperature, our activities, adventures, Sister's moods, how many times we were kept after school, and, invariably, my altar boy assignments. Homework was a chore my father enforced with gusto, and we all did well in school. We moved to a two-bedroom apartment, took vacations at Painted Pony Ranch in the Adirondacks, had family picnics at Pound Ridge Reservation and Sherwood Island in Connecticut (where we lured crabs to shore, netted them, took them back to my godparents' cold-water flat, and threw them into boiling water). On a few notable occasions, we even got to Yankee Stadium. But for me, the cycle of the worship life of the parish provided the constant backdrop to my out-of-school activities as I became an expert altar boy learning to negotiate the arcane inner world of the parish church's sacristy.

The sacristy was the ideal boy-priest's space. It served as vesting room, storage room, and preparation area for all the events that would occur on the altar. Though not large, it possessed its own lore, so learning its rules and rhythms became yet another indoor sport for me. Because priestly piety required that even vesting for Mass be a ritual act accompanied by prayer, the priest's chasuble, stole, maniple, alb, and amice had to be laid out just so. I learned this preritual ritual and others besides, getting good as well at the protocols for all sorts of devotions and sacred goings-on. Helping Charlie, the sacristan, in his holy housekeeping chores, such as digging out the spent votive candles and refilling them, became a convenient justification for hanging out there, an in-between world where I could encounter my parish priests and measure myself against the template they presented. Though they put forward a common image of uncommon humanity, they clearly did not come from any single mold or cut of the cloth. Their personalities were as distinct as the way they said Mass—one was mellifluous, one jerky and far away, one finished in record time, all different from Father Brogan. But none of them revealed much about himself personally. When not robed in the head-to-toe cassock, or in the vestments that went on top of it, they dressed in formal black suits and regulation black fedoras or the straw boater hats that were required from Memorial to Labor Day. Only once in a while did I get glimpses of the person behind the collar.

One morning while I was on duty, the pastor arrived for his assigned Mass. He bore the august nomen Monsignor Lafayette W. Yarwood and had known Maréchal Foch in France during his stint as a chaplain. So, anticipating his arrival in the sacristy always had the air of waiting for the general. Entering from the cloistered passageway to the rectory, he flipped off his floor-length black cloak, its black velvet collar showing itself darkly against the silver clasp and chain. As he did so, he turned and asked Charlie, who valetlike had taken the cloak to hang up, if he had seen the wrestling match the night before when Killer Kowalski had annihilated Gorgeous George. I had watched the same match! At thirteen, I was clearly fascinated with these pre-steroid muscular performers knocking one another around the ring, but I had no idea that something so goofily mundane could command the enthusiastic attention of our spiritual leader. Could the pastor really have been as taken in as I was by the show of strength and prowess they put on? I wondered that priestly holiness might not occupy the priests as fully as I had been led to believe.

But these glimpses of priests in real life were rare. So we looked forward to the annual day-long altar boy outing with Father Brogan each summer. This and our annual Christmas gift were the parish's way of saying thank you for the forty to fifty hours a week we collectively put in. Each summer, we awaited the announcement of the location, hoping it would be Playland Pool at Rye Beach, on the shores of Long Island Sound. Growing up in Port Chester, we were a bus ride away from the waveless beach and spent time there as part of summer camp. But the pool was more like a spa, with a resortlike setting, and an entrance fee that added something special to our being treated to the trip. Special, too, was the kind of time and attention we got, particularly from Father Brogan. In the pool, the mild-mannered priest, who even when he disciplined us refused to shame us, became a wrestling prodigy, taking on all comers, tossing kids into the water with abandon. He clearly enjoyed the free-for-all as much as we did. There were other moments like that with him, when he would be relaxed and available for us. Increasingly, I wanted to grow up and be like him, to present to the world the cool façade and sincere demeanor that his life as a priest broadcast to one and all.

Not surprisingly, he was the perfect complement to the aloof pastor and to my strict father. But neither he nor any of the other priests was the catalyst for me to apply to the preparatory seminary during the last year of grade school. I came to that decision with the active help of a remarkable woman whose intelligence and enthusiasm for learning and living a Christian life aimed me like an arrow at the priestly calling. She was the other half of *The Bells of St. Mary's* duo who shaped my early pursuit of ordination. When I think of Father Brogan and Sister Marita Anna Fox, all of my learned doubts about the clergy and the religious life fall away for a brief time. Both of them would eventually have sad chapters in their relationships with church authorities—for Father Brogan, when the parish team came apart after the old monsignor died, and for Sister Marita Anna, when convent life began unraveling. But during those last years of the classic pre–Vatican II parochial community, Sister's active promotion of what the priest exemplified was the icing on the cake of my prepubescent idealism. No picture of the priestly mystique that so beguiled me would be complete without a look at where she fits into the bigger picture, confirming for my young and impressionable mind that the priesthood and all it offered were worth pursuing.

Up to entering the eighth grade, my experience with the Sisters of Charity in my parish had been mixed. Sister Marcella and Sister Juliet, my fourth- and seventh-grade teachers, were harridans, right out of the script of plays like *Sister Mary Ignatius Explains It All for You* and other nun-bashing literature. The first, built like a tank, used a terrifying scowl under her Conestoga-style black bonnet, along with physical discipline, to terrify us into submission. The other made the stepmother in *Cinderella* look sweet. Tall and angular, she used the finger-poking kind of discipline, occasionally slapping us on the side of the head—which had set my mother on her—but mainly using psychological methods of tearing us down to keep us in tow. Years later I would learn how inadequately prepared for teaching children many of these women were by their novitiate experiences and religious training. Unlike monastic orders of men and women that had a long tradition of learning and spirituality, the *active* religious orders, which had grown by leaps and bounds during the nineteenth century and exploded with candidates throughout the Great Depression and into the postwar era, did not emphasize much by way of professional development or education. The process of becoming a nun was meant to wear away any individuality, quash creativity, and mold a young woman into a member of a sexless community where one sister resembled every other sister (which the nuns' habit accomplished externally). The motherhouse of each order served as the training center for new sisters, where each class of new recruits was subjected to something like a perfect Victorian ladies' finishing-school education. There was some teacher training involved, from what I gather, but when the parochial school system expanded rapidly throughout the 1950s, nuns with little more than a high school education were thrown into the classroom with as many as sixty(!) students. Their preparation consisted mostly in their being negatively socialized to obey their superiors, give orders to their students, practice their religious observances, and play the docile role of cog in the holy wheel that served the church's educational and institutional needs.

Not surprisingly, some of them broke under the strain. One young sister who came to our school in those years built a reputation, in a very short time, of shrieking regularly to control her second-graders. Then one day she was gone. Stories circulated about the ambulance arriving after dark at the convent to take her away, but the culture of silence prevailed and we never heard another word. If the rectory, or priests' house, was generally off-limits, the sisters' convent was sacrosanct territory. Nobody got beyond the visitors' parlor, right inside the front door, or beyond the kitchen, where deliveries were made.

Nuns' lives were even more hidden from us than the priests' and, to our knowledge, completely given over to God. In fact, as far as the general public was concerned, they had no individual lives. But the screen that shrouded their lives was pierced ever so slightly one Christmas, when it was habitual that families give gifts to all our teachers, even the nuns. One year my mother solved the puzzle of what to get our nun teachers by tapping an inside source of information. Living at the convent was a housekeeper, Margaret, a black woman who had been orphaned as a child and been taken in by the nuns. So she lived her whole life as their cook, maid, and laundress. Short and very rotund, with a laugh that shook the neighborhood, she was a fixture in the parish. Until it was replaced by a brick and concrete bunker in the early 1960s, the back porch of the Edwardian house that was the convent served as the lookout post for her all-seeing eyes. Margaret knew every child's name, reported what she saw, and gossiped ecumenically when she did the shopping at our local supermarket. Seeing her there, my mother asked her for a gift idea, as there seemed a limit to the number of fruitcakes and cheese assortments that any group of nuns could eat. Margaret made the scandalous suggestion that the sisters would love to get a gift of cosmetics like face powder, toilet water, and scented soaps. My mother bit and, when she received florid thank-you notes from the sisters, spread the word to other mothers: The nuns used toiletries! The veil had been pierced marginally, and it caused a certain amount of talk around town, but the sisters received a great deal more personal hygiene items the following Christmas.

Amazingly, some women survived the mental and emotional reconditioning that joining the convent required, even managing to thrive through their contacts with their students and a few sister friends in their order. Of course, active friendships or—even worse—pairing off in twos was forbidden. Any relationships that threatened the supremacy of the group would not be contemplated. Superiors would regularly make sure that one member of an affective pair was transferred to another convent at the earliest opportunity. Not that the phrase "lesbian relationship" would ever have entered into the conscious consideration of anyone involved. It was enough to allege an emotional tie for authority to act and break up a potential friendship. How was it, then, that my fifth- and sixth-grade teachers, Sister Carmelita and Sister Teresita, managed to be gracious, smart, good disciplinarians, and decent human beings? Well, Saint Paul wrote that though sin abounds, grace abounds even more. The proof of that paradox can be found in the lives and careers of women like these and other women whom I would come to meet over the years. But none had as profound an effect on me as Marita Anna.

In September 1957, coming off a bad experience in the seventh grade, I looked forward to having Sister Marita Anna because my sister, Gail, who was a year older, had been in Sister's class during the first year she taught at Saint Mary's. Gail shone in school and was the pride of the Sisters of Charity, earning full scholarships to two high schools that they ran in the diocese. After four years at the exclusive Elizabeth Seton Academy, she received a full scholarship to their College of Mount Saint Vincent. They probably had her pegged for joining the convent, but Gail had very different ideas for herself. Still, Marita Anna knew talent and brains when she saw them, and I entered the eighth grade basking in the reflected glory of my older sibling. How the subject arose of what I would do after grade school, I can't recall. But in short order, Sister had convinced me that, if I was serious about following the path I had laid out for myself, even the local Catholic high school was not good enough. I needed to head to the city and take the entrance exams both for the all-scholarship, Jesuit-run Regis High School and for Cathedral College, the high school seminary. Her mind was made up about the importance of my setting out on an educational adventure, as my sister had done before me. Convincing my parents that this homeboy needed some adventure would take some doing. Sister was up for it. She recruited the pastor, who called my father in for a talk— that was a shocker! Wearing down Dad's resistance was key, and the pastor's offer that the parish would pay my tuition at Cathedral went a long way to convince him. The decision about where I would go was made easier when I was rejected by Regis and accepted at Cathedral.

Without her enthusiasm and verve for learning and for loving God—she combined the two convincingly—my quest might have been all about status and would have lacked heart. While Father Brogan gave form to my idealized view of the priesthood, she gave it substance. Few priests whom I would meet during my thirty years among them could match her heart, her sincerity, or her gritty spirituality. Early on she had a major role in convincing me of the religious ideal of total personal devotion to divine service. When I doubted some years later, she came visiting to make sure I wasn't letting myself off the hook too quickly. For her, celibate virginity was instrumental in the best sense of the word. She saw her life in religion as complementing married love and family, not as a superior expression of commitment or calling. Twenty-five years after she taught me, having moved into an apartment with another sister who was her associate in a nonprofit educational venture she had founded, she was still as on fire with her mission as she was the day I walked into her eighth-grade classroom. The afternoon before she died, alone with her in her hospital room, I ventured to ask the kind of direct question that she was so good at, gently asking her if she felt ready to die. She glanced my way and summed up her desire for God in the simple statement "I love Him."

When word started getting around about my entering the minor seminary, extended family and friends responded with a certain amount of awe that I would make such a decision at thirteen. Collecting that kind of feedback can be a little heady for a teenager's narcissism—much like J.T. being caught up in Father Grogan's cloak. It certainly helped, as I'm sure it did with countless others, to buoy up my self-importance whenever it flagged. But my sister resisted, making it clear that she thought my decision precocious and rash. Over the years, she continued protesting that celibacy would not be good for my health. But her lone voice was not loud enough to overcome the overt approval on one side and the culture of silence in matters sexual on the other.

When I entered Cathedral Prep, I had been to Manhattan by train exactly once. My parents' plan for a practice run misfired, and I was advised that I should not travel all the way into Grand Central Terminal at 42nd Street and then return uptown. I could get off at 125th Street in Harlem, walk the three blocks west, and take the subway to school. So on Day 1, armed only with my father's verbal instructions ("Of course, I understand, Dad"), I started my career as a commuter. By the end of the day, I had gotten off at a wrong stop, gotten trapped in the wrong station (until I saw a person exit the turnstile), taken a wrong train, walked the width of Manhattan, and arrived home hours later than expected.

Once I figured out the transportation, the daily routine was easy enough. The 7:08 train got into Grand Central at 8:02, and with normal subway connections, I could get to Cathedral College, in its modest five-story building on the corner of West End Avenue and Eighty-seventh Street, by 8:25. As the two hundred of us arrived each day, we would tumble through the front doors and participate in a ritual that we were assured helped set us apart from your average, run-of-the-mill high school student. Above the mantel of the old stone fireplace located in the lobby on the main floor hung a portrait of the Madonna and Child. Beneath it was the prayer/motto *Vobis in Matrem*, "To you as a Mother." Students stopped before the image of Mary, knelt, and said one fervent Hail Mary before attacking the stairs and heading to their lockers. In front of the fireplace shrine sat a prie-dieu, or kneeler, large enough for three students at a time. But with ten to twenty kids piling through the door, a daily pious mob scene ensued, as wave after wave of adolescents hit their knees, dropped their bookbags, raced as decorously as possible through the prayer—Father Griffin, the dean of discipline, would regularly be watching—and climbed over the other momentary supplicants, rushing to join the melee upstairs before first period.

It was not long before I realized that I was one of the few students living in the suburbs and making the trip down to Manhattan. Brooklyn and Queens were a separate diocese, so most of my peers hailed from Manhattan and the Bronx. The trip from Staten Island was so formidable (physically and culturally) as to keep the number of students from there just as small as from Rockland and Westchester counties. Ask someone from anywhere in the city where he came from and he would respond, "Saint Brendan's" or "Holy Name" or "Mount Carmel"—his parish encompassed the neighborhood, his school, the microcosm he identified with. We were roughly representative of the white ethnic makeup of the church in the United States. The Irish predominated—Dunne, Heafy, Kelly, Lenihan, Meara, McCarthy, McGrath, Quinn, Turley (two of them: Thomas J. and Thomas P.), Sullivan, and so on. There was a respectable smattering of Italians, a few Poles and Germans, one Serbo-Croatian, and an Englishman named Bill Bishop, whose sidekick I became. Not being one for melding into the crowd, Bill made a point of wearing an orange tie on the day before St. Patrick's Day as a statement of nonidentity. Irate at the symbolic gesture, Father Griffin sent him to detention that afternoon (we called it "jug," and both Bill and I spent our share of after-school hours there). Working harder than Bill at fitting in, I purged the flat-sounding short *a* that we used at home in words like "camera" and "banana." For a while, I kept in touch with some friends from grammar school, making sure to attend the CYP high school dances, contrary to the explicit rules of Cathedral, which forbade such socializing. But little by little we lost touch as I worked at new friendships, migrating in the course of a few years between different groups of guys with distinctly different tastes.

Cathedral was a day school that provided four years of high school and two years of college (after which we would enter the enclosed world of the major seminary). The fact that we lived at home and commuted to school represented a barely acknowledged compromise with life in the United States. Though a continental ethos informed our self-styled "college," Cathedral contrasted with older European habits and the practice of most domestic religious-order seminaries. They recruited grammar-school-aged students to their minor seminaries or juniorates, where they lived as they would in a semimonastic community. Taking boys that young and socializing them, separate from their families, in an all-male world made those settings more of a hothouse for emotional distortion than day-school or prep seminaries ever would. Resident minor seminaries also commingled adolescent hormones and needy young priests in combustible amounts, producing some of the more notorious cases of priestly ephebophilia, the abuse of adolescent males by trusted religious mentors. None of these seminaries, to my knowledge, have survived to the present day, and their passing represents no loss to anyone.

In our sophomore year, a new student whose family had just emigrated from Italy joined our class. He had spent some years as a grammar school seminarian dressed up in a black cassock and living the conventual life back in the old country. The freedom that came with being a student in a prep seminary first daunted Michael and then became intoxicating. The Petrino family had moved into the shrinking Italian enclave in East Harlem, so that as the months went by, young Michael became more and more liberated and assimilated. By senior year, he was a greaser, complete with a "d.a." (duck's ass) haircut and black leather jacket. None of us were surprised when he did not stay with the class as we moved into the college division.

Despite whatever libidinal strain any of us experienced, the culture of the minor seminary kept any talk about sexual matters—let alone any sexual acting out—under wraps. We marveled that Michael the Greaser had stayed with us in the minor seminary for as long as he had. Generally, if a guy decided that he no longer fit in, that he wanted to socialize with girls or even in mixed company—no one would have imagined being sexually active at that stage of life—he would withdraw at the end of the semester. I remember a conversation with a very good-hearted classmate, Tom Heafy, who was about to take his leave, I believe in our junior year. Obviously feeling bad about separating from the group, he sheepishly explained to me that it just wasn't for him anymore. I guess I said that it was OK and that he shouldn't feel bad. When guys left and we stayed, it oddly confirmed the unique sense of "calling" that was supposed to underlie our being there in the first place. The rest of us seemed content not to have to deal with the everyday pressure of being massed with horny young men who were up-front about their exploding hormonal energy or of having to deal with girls and whatever they were about! I, for one, did not miss the unrelenting pressure to be cool, experienced, attractive to girls, or otherwise at ease with the ways of the world. The Saturday mornings I spent working for my father at his depot turned me off to the routinized way men socialized via sexual innuendo and vulgar putdowns. My seminary friends pretty much became my exclusive peer group, just as they were meant to be. The chemistry led to many years of estrangement from my younger brother, Richard, who had also become a commuter. At Fordham Prep, a Jesuit school in the Bronx, he met a much more robust mix of the Catholic male population.

At its best, our more insulated prep-seminary education helped us take ourselves seriously as students and gave us a firm grounding in the basic skills of language and the humanities. But the environment isolated us permanently from some of the most important developmental challenges adolescents face. It also denied us the normal rites of passage that help young men mark their individual progress by external, social measures. J.T. tells of his thwarted pride when, after landing a summer job as a lifeguard, the authorities at Cathedral found out and insisted that he be demoted to a "parkie" with responsibility for cleaning the grounds. Lifeguarding wouldn't do for a minor seminarian as it just might become a near occasion of bodily contact!

The problems that the prep seminary creates for its students manifest themselves mostly later in the life of its few graduates who are eventually ordained (an average of only 10 to 15 percent). It was not so much a single-sex environment as a no-sex environment, not anybody's sex, not even ours. In retrospect, it seems that students who spent time there and moved on enjoyed its benefits far more than those of us who "persevered" to ordination with a psychosexual foundation of wet clay. For just as amazing as the seminary's insistence that we bracket sexuality and leave it out of consideration was the extent to which we cooperated with the clergy's habit of silence. This might have been different with the small group of long-distance commuters who moved into the off-campus Ford House residence our second year at Cathedral. Evenings there may have been as boisterous as in most boys' dormitories. (Twenty years later, in a very different atmosphere, Daniel Donohue, now thirty-eight, has charged Monsignor Charles Kavanaugh with pursuing a sexually charged friendship with him while the priest was rector of Cathedral and resident at Ford House. Defenders of the priest have cited all his other good work and his not molesting any other young men to dispute the former seminarian's account of a priest's midlife blurring of the sexual boundaries between an attractive teenager and himself.) But at school, nobody talked about girls other than our sisters. The word "masturbation" was unspoken even though, by sophomore year, a really boring geometry class could provoke me to engage in a significant session of "pocket pool."

The closest we ever came to a sex talk took place that year when the retreat master, during the three days of talks and devotional exercises built into Thanksgiving week, spoke to us in serious terms about "keeping our vessels clean." He probably was using the metaphor generally of our bodies ("vessels of clay" in Saint Paul), but focused on my penis as I had secretly become, I guessed that he was cluing me in that I really shouldn't be playing with myself. But his admonitions excited no conversations or questions among us, and I never spoke about the matter to anyone. So began my long struggle with guilt associated with tumescence and release, the subtheme of much of my spiritual life for years to come. Although the sermon did not hit me like the famous one in James Joyce's *Portrait of the Artist as a Young Man*, I did take note and begin to worry. Within a year or so, I went to see the movie version of *L'il Abner* with Brian, a friend a year older and also on a vocational path. As the plot unfolded, it told of a miracle potion that the hero gives to a bunch of schleppy hillbillies, transforming them into muscular he-men but taking away their libido as its price. Afterward we joked about regretting that the potion didn't exist. More so than he, I think, I feared that my fate was the opposite: to be not very outwardly masculine but plagued with hormonal urges anyway.

In ways that I would not understand for years, the whole seminary culture existed on a foundation of prolonged latency. The underlying fear at work seems to have been that even talking about issues of sexuality openly could only stir up what was best left undisturbed, "latent," and unaroused. By bracketing sexuality out of personal development, the clerical mind-set wagered that, if young men held out long enough and developed the internal controls necessary to deny themselves sexual gratification, then ordination and "the grace of office" would suffice and they could stay chaste for life. Of course, chastity was twofold, as the catechism defined it, requiring total modesty "whether alone or with others." It turned out to be a distinction that did not help clarify the nature of sexual urges. For recent revelations have shown how wrongheaded the thinking was about isolating sexuality from a person's growth and how tragic the consequences of ignorance and silence about the pervasiveness of sexuality in personal inter-dynamics have been. Most all the cases that have come to light stem from years ago and involve abuser priests in their sixties and seventies. These men were trained in the "classic" seminaries of the Council of Trent's earlier reform, not the liberalized ones that made a brief appearance in the late 1960s and early 1970s. The seminary culture of silence and its insistence on conformity laid the groundwork for needy priests, many with histories of being abused, to engage in nonconsensual sex with minor students, to go undetected, and then to be protected by authorities who chose willful ignorance of sexual pathology as their best defense for not acting to prevent future abuse of the young.

In the seminary we were all expected to cooperate in sustaining a prolonged, but desexed, adolescent moratorium. "Sons of

the church" as we were, we took our lead from the fathers who
were in charge of educating and forming us, and most of them
were so far invested in the system that they had no stake in alter-
ing things even as the winds of change began to blow through the
universal church. With only some exceptions throughout the next
thirty years, priests in authority continued to resist change, and
to insist that the separatist male culture of the clergy could be
sustained as everything else in the church was uprooted and
replanted. But there were other factors that led us to become willing cooperators in our own filial bonding with the institutional
church.

Very few of the boys and young men I studied with, played
with, befriended, contended with, or came to know much about
in all these years had a close relationship with his father. In this
matter, I certainly was no exception. In the midcentury United
States, the masculine air we breathed didn't promote closeness or
warmth too readily. Many of our fathers were actively engaged in
parenting us, but this meant that they made demands, checked
our homework, administered punishment, assigned chores, corrected our pitching or fielding, got us our first jobs. In general,
they saw themselves chiefly involved in keeping their male children (at least) on the straight and narrow by perfecting habits of
negative reinforcement. They gave approval only sparingly, here
practicing the fine art of indirection—mainly by using Mom as
their mouthpiece to deliver anything like an explicit message of
assurance ("You know your father is very proud of you!" she
would insist). Most of the time, this silent father routine masked
Dad's panic and cluelessness about what to say and his fear of
looking or sounding foolish in front of his growing brood of children. Better to stay in the background, the dependable wage
earner, the quiet machine driving the family's prosperity forward.

Visiting the family of a friend and classmate, I mentally
recorded a scene that even then spoke to me about the place of
fathers in our lives. We had dropped into Kevin's family's apart-

ment late in the afternoon. A modified railroad flat, the likes of which I had seen only once before, it made the one-bedroom apartment I had shared with my parents and two siblings until I was nine very comfortable by comparison. Mrs. O'Hanlon was preparing supper, but we were not intending to stay because we had to get back for an event at school. As we talked, she informed us that "the father" would be home soon, and she busied herself with supper preparations. In short order the door opened and a workingman of medium build and balding brow entered. He took brief note of the company, nodded in our direction, greeted his son stiffly, and sat down at the kitchen table in front of the single place setting. No one else sat. His wife then began to serve him his dinner, which he ate in silence for the time we remained. Kevin's mother continued to share our conversation but was much more distracted by her serving duties. We took the cue, said good-bye, and headed back to school. The scene we had been part of drew no comment, but I privately wondered about how shut down Kevin's father seemed even as he clearly claimed center stage.

Another friend's father was a New York City policeman, but not of the Irish Catholic stock that produced so many cops, firemen, and priests. As a result, Bob's father had even fewer pat responses that would enable him to show any level of approval of his son's choice of a career and lifestyle. He was gruff, funny, enjoyed being shocking, drank too much and let it show, and did not seem to mind when his stinging jibes made his son squirm with discomfort. Not surprisingly, Bob turned to his mother as his natural ally and worked her sympathy for him full throttle. The father-son chemistry in that house seemed a worst-case scenario. It also mimicked my fears about my own father's reaction to me and most of the friends I brought home over the years. Not that the man lacked the social graces. He just did not know where my friends and I were coming from. Nor did most of them rate very high on the masculinity scale. Being more favored by our mothers, with whom we had bonded pretty early, many of us favored conversation over action or sports, didn't at all mind wearing gowns and flowing robes, and did not engage in sex talk or in dreams of conquests or boast of our prowess.

Rather than remaining in such a knotty Oedipal triangle—not that any of us would have even heard about this development dilemma—Catholic boys had an out, of sorts. They had at hand in the hyperextended family of the church a resource, an alternative fatherhood that sidestepped an overt conflict with their biological sire. It did not require dethroning him, and at the same time it reassured the mother of her irreplaceable role in their life. If our mothers had more to gain from the arrangement—and they were assured from the earliest of my seminary days that mothers of priests had special privileges—our fathers had at least the consolation of knowing their sons would be taken care of, would not face layoffs or unemployment, and would be held in some societal esteem. But underneath they often felt displaced by a rival for, if not the overt affection of their sons, then at least the respect that they thought they deserved.

Just over a month after I started in the minor seminary, Pius XII gave up the ghost after a papal reign of nineteen years. Some men who were in the major seminary at the time remember how disappointed they were when the austere and aloof pontiff, whom everyone their age took to be the model pope, was replaced by a roly-poly and seemingly jolly new incumbent. Damned unpapal it was! But by Christmas, the world press had picked up the scent of a news story when the new Bishop of Rome began acting in other than the regal and removed mode of his predecessor. In January, John XXIII issued his historic summoning of the Second Vatican Council. Right away, nothing changed. None of the seismic shifts in Rome initially registered on our Richter scales, nor did any of the faculty share with us any predictions that the world of the church would be shaken to its foundations in the next decade. As learned as some of them were, and as steeped in history, they could not imagine the set of changes that would engulf Catholicism in the matter of a few years. For it would have required a complete rethinking of the mystique of the priesthood upon which so much of the system rested. During one religion class early in my career, we were treated not to a lesson but to a meditation that illustrates how basic that mystique was. Father Mike Fleming, who functioned as both teacher and Spiritual Director, clearly did not feel like engaging in formal instruction that day—he rarely did. Instead, he had us close our eyes as he conjured up for us nothing less than the Beatific Vision of God, the eternal goal of communion that every believer sought. Using the image of a cosmic throne room, where all the saved were gathered in jubilant worship of the Three-Personed God, he described how Christ himself, seated "at the right hand of the Father," was himself surrounded by none other than his priests. Because it was each of our destinies to be an *alter Christus*, another Christ, we would—if we persevered—achieve such a cosmically exalted status. Not bad for the son of a breadman!

Though some of our religion classes were more substantive, none dealt with the New Testament narrative of the mission of Jesus of Nazareth. Instead, we were taught the genius of the Catholic system—and, mercifully, some of the important encyclicals, such as the recently issued *Mater et Magistra* of John XXIII. But this was presented cheek by jowl with a course in apologetics that schooled us in pat arguments about how the church's mandate flowed smoothly and uninterruptedly from Christ himself to the Apostles, chief among whom was Peter, whose direct, linear successor ran the church from Rome. I had the opportunity to try out the arguments one evening during a particularly contentious dinner at home. But I found out, to my chagrin, that my carefully marshaled arguments did not convince my father that the clerical authority structure should be able to tell him how to live his life.

Not uncommonly, we got to yelling at each other about what was at stake and who was right. I had come to take this dissonance between the fathers in my life for granted, and not surprisingly, the rift between us grew and took decades to close.

Much of this conflict was homegrown, though, because the priests teaching in the seminary did not seek to influence us, cultivate us, or personally model a life of dedicated service to us. Most of the faculty at Cathedral exhibited little by way of real solicitude for us. As minor seminarians, we had a long way to go to prove ourselves, and their presumption may have been that, since the majority of us would not endure to ordination, they had no serious obligation to get to know us or actively mentor us. During our last two years in the minor seminary, the college years, we were increasingly restless with the educational scope and style that felt nothing like an undergraduate experience. Classroom method and a number of professors, as well, were holdovers from high school. The daily routine remained unaccented—we were in a prep school for delayed adolescents rather than a college. As a group, though we socialized more in the city, we regressed socially because we tended to fixate on taking ourselves out of circulation when we went to the major seminary, Dunwoodie, for the six-year stint that would complete our preparation for ordination. Though the Vatican Council was already in its second session of meetings, it had little day-to-day effect at the Old World clerical bastion on West End Avenue.

On the verge of moving from a social and educational experience that had pretty much stalled at the end of high school, we awaited with great anticipation the start of our major seminary careers when we became college juniors. As a group, we may even have been aware that we hadn't made much progress recently. Isolated from other peers because we were shuttling back and forth from the hothouse world of Cathedral College, and defensively convinced that we had a right to feel different (and special) because of our choice of vocation, we didn't have much chance to fulfill the philosophical advice that our classical Greek textbook had quoted: "Know thyself." We didn't know what we needed to know about ourselves and our choice of a lifestyle, for which we might or might not be suited. Once we received word that we had been formally accepted by the seminary, all rational thinking about the next step receded before the details of getting ready to enter a world that had not changed significantly in almost four centuries.

Once we got there, we would become part of a seesaw struggle between the old priestly mystique and a new model of ministerial competence. Once locked inside the gated world of the major seminary, many of us sensed a creepiness about the clerical world that enfolded us. Responsive only to itself, it seemed too far removed from the path of aggiornamento that we saw the church as a whole taking. A battle had begun for the future of the Catholic church and we were in the vanguard. The promise of change beckoned, and a formerly closed world began to open up in front of us.

Two

The Order of Melchizedek

I F INDOOR PLUMBING and electricity made Saint
Joseph's Seminary, in 1964, seem like a twentieth-century
institution, the place nonetheless operated in a time warp. Like all
seminaries of its day—it had been built in the 1890s—Saint
Joseph's, which was nicknamed Dunwoodie for the section of
Yonkers it dominated, was built on a monumental scale. The
rooms had twelve-foot ceilings and the corridors were even
higher. We used to joke that the architecture was seventeenth-
century penal, modeled after the Chateau d'If. Taking up residence there, the forty-two of us would be joining more than two
hundred other students enrolled in the major seminary's six-year
course of studies (two of college and four of theology). But before
we could do so, we had to acquire a special clerical wardrobe and
a mind-set to match, that of the "long black line" of priests Saint
Joseph's had produced since the turn of the century. Unlike the
military, which issues uniforms on arrival, the seminary sent us a
mimeographed list of what we would need to have in order to
pass muster when we arrived. At the top of the list were three cassocks: one for Sunday and feast days, one for everyday (class-

room) use, and a worn-out one, perhaps from the altar boy closet
at home—to wear back and forth to the showers!

That spring and summer of 1964, my friends and I were preoccupied with assembling the basically black trousseau we needed
to take with us. We were given the names of several clerical tai-
lors who specialized in priestly couture—Gennarelli seemed to be
the favorite. At our fittings, we had to make decisions about style
as well as practicality. There was the fitted "Roman" style of cassock, with three pleats at the base of the back, giving it a bustle-
like effect, assuring that it flowed behind you when you walked.
There were the new neck-to-ankle zippered cassocks with their
faux front of thirty-two buttons. Their practical benefit was un-
doubted. It would be a lot easier to pull up one zipper while dash-
ing downstairs to be in chapel by 6:15 a.m. than to manage a
battery of small buttons. Big affairs required that we wear a
biretta, the four-cornered hat with three high ridges and a big
black pom-pom in the middle. The list told us to buy two: the
better biretta for High Mass on Sunday. The second was a col-
lapsible model good for traveling.

Four years after President Kennedy removed his top hat at his
inauguration and men began going bareheaded in America, we
were still required to wear hats in public. Whenever we were out
of the seminary on a "walk day" or when we were allowed to
roam farther or even to visit home on a "city holiday," we had to
have a black fedora, or homburg, or porkpie hat (straw boaters
were allowed in summer) atop our heads. Cardinal Spellman was
known to stop his limousine and correct a priest he spied out in
public without the required head covering. Elevating such sarto-
rial issues to religious requirements seemed passing strange, but
not so strange as the sight of a mob of us walking around the
Cross County Shopping Center, the country's first mall—not far
from Dunwoodie—in black suits and ties, hats all in place, looking like Hasidic youth minus the locks of hair.

Our uniform differed a great deal from military dress (with its supposed attraction to women and other two-legged creatures), but it, too, was meant to confer a corporate identity. Where it could be confusing for us stemmed from the uniform consisting of a long black dress that we were required to wear at all times except when off the grounds—even to and from the ball field, where it could be doffed temporarily while a game was being played. As I look back, the student body of the seminary divided up among those for whom wearing a cassock and all the additional accoutrements was a real cross, those who didn't seem to notice but did just about everything they were told readily, and others either comfortable enough with themselves so that it didn't matter what they wore or comfortable with the generally feminine style of life that the clergy often approximated.

How we wore our cassocks and surplices suggests some of what was going on beneath the surface. The first group generally looked uncomfortable most of the time, as if something was not fitting quite right. Out of embarrassment, they may not have paid any attention when they went to the clerical tailor, or bought a cassock off the rack hastily, or made do with hand-me-downs. But they always looked a little unkempt, ready to step out of the dress as fast as they could. The clearest hint about their discomfort would often appear around the neck because the starched band (plastic ones were just coming in) behind the tight Nehrujacket-type collar drove some guys to drink. A certain number of the uncomfortable were very athletic guys whose chests and shoulders were not easily accommodated by the average fit. They always seemed squeezed into their cassocks, and even when they slipped on the more ample white liturgical surplice over their tootight dress, they looked as if they were confined in an identity they didn't quite buy. Other guys simply seemed as if they had never finished getting dressed. Rebelling by their insouciant manner at the damned conformity of the whole arrangement, they rarely made it past the dreaded faculty votes that were necessary for a candidate to advance toward ordination.

At least as large a number wore the outmoded Roman uniform day in and day out (with sweat stains accumulating around the armpits) because it required only that they do what they seemed to do best: conform to the system's requirements. For them the seminary represented security, a place where fitting in required few demands on the imagination. The cassock covered everything, including a man's individuality—and it was meant to. A retired spiritual director was still quoted about the reason that the clergy wore cassocks: "Because in this way, all we are is hands and faces, hands and faces!" So in some ways, the costume was a perfect disguise for people with unformed egos, unmet needs, and no desire to let either be known. The seminary accommodated them graciously, demanding in return that they keep the Rule. (As the age-old saying we heard repeated went, "Keep the Rule and the Rule will keep you.") But some of their number, though they played along to get along as a matter of course, were affable and talented guys who often were tapped to fill leadership positions in the student body. Others populated the game rooms or clustered around the common ashtrays, smoking and chatting and waiting for the bell to tell them what to do next.

The third group was an uncharacteristic composite of what might be called Spartans and Athenians, or maybe even Romans and Greeks. Most of the Spartans were also athletes, but of the supple, fast-twitch-muscle variety, graced with an ease of movement that not even a floor-length cassock could hide. Several of these guys had quarterbacked at their high school, and others who came the year after would actually field a college-level basketball team. Larry, one of more articulate Spartans, had a saying for our dilemma: "This is a great place. First, they dress us up as little girls; then, they treat us as little boys."

Unlike these all-American Spartans, but often allied with them because of a shared interest in academics, were the Athenians, the group in which I would claim membership. We tended to be intellectually curious, tough on conformists, more comfortable with the slightly effete ways of the clerical establishment, but merciless with unimaginative faculty. Left to ourselves, we turned catty and got caught up in the ephemera of community living—seeing who was assigned next to whom on the monthly seating chart for refectory meals.

Upon reflection, there were a few factors that saved us from ourselves in those early years before the old system crumbled under its own weight: more than a few academically challenging professors, the promise of the Vatican Council that change was coming, and some singular personalities who helped change our expectations of what we should be doing when we finally got to disrobe and leave the cassocks in the closet. Until then, there was the Rule. The "classic" form of the diocesan seminary had emerged in the era when the French were struggling to implement the decrees of the Council of Trent and, simultaneously, were educating Irish candidates for the priesthood when Catholicism was illegal in Ireland. The Society of Saint Sulpice, an association formed to help inculcate discipline into the diocesan clergy, had established the oldest seminary in the United States, Saint Mary's in Baltimore, and spread from there. The Sulpicians had run Dunwoodie briefly before they were replaced for their "modernist" tendencies, embodied by the pioneering *New York Review*, one of the leading theological journals of its day. Before Father Duffy, the chaplain of New York's Fighting Sixty-ninth Regiment, became an icon of Catholic manhood, he was a seminary professor, booted out of Dunwoodie along with the rest of the suspected modernists. A new faculty was installed in the years before World War I, and in place of theological education, the authorities worked to secure the loyalty of student priests to a simpler task. The new attitude was expressed by a later rector, who would put it simply: "We raise our boys on baseball and Mary," meaning a program of physical activity and devotion to the Blessed Virgin that guaranteed good, obedient, celibate priests.

The schedule we kept in 1964 was substantially the same as it would have been in 1864. We could own windup alarm clocks, but you needed one only if you occupied the head room on one of the long, drafty corridors of the building. The occupant of each head room was called the "excitator," weirdly enough, and it was his job to rise early and, precisely at 5:45 a.m., to begin knocking loudly upon the twenty or so doors on the hall and hail the sleeper within with the greeting "*Benedicamus Domino*" ("Let us bless the Lord"), to which each of us was instructed to respond with the familiar altar boy line "*Deo gratias*" ("Thanks be to God"). Because the excitator's job was to make sure each of us had risen, he was not supposed to pass to the next door until he had confirmed that we had given thanks and were going to appear at morning prayers. The routine shifted a bit during Advent, Lent, and Easter, when the rote phrases changed to reflect the different seasons, multiplying the possibilities for scatological exchanges to start the day instead of multiple blessings. As innocent as the drill sounds, it was fraught with problems. The rules were enforced by a demerit system imposed (and policed) by the faculty, who resided one to a corridor like hall monitors. If a priest observed an infraction of the rules, he would merely say, "Drop a card," and the infractor would be obligated to write his name and rule infraction on an index card and drop it in a slot in a box mounted just outside the chapel. In the course of a day, a seminarian could be told to "drop a card" for sleeping in; missing prayers, meditation, or Mass; not being properly attired; skipping a meal; talking during the twelve to thirteen hours a day that silence was imposed; walking in an area restricted to the faculty; talking anywhere "above the first step" of the staircases that led to the living areas; being late for chapel, late for class, or late for meals; or missing any part of the clerical uniform. The Rule existed to enforce conformity to the letter, but an infraction could also be waived if a faculty member looked the other way or favored one infractor over another.

But beyond inculcating discipline, the Rule existed to condition us not to *need* to communicate or commune with others. We were being trained to become expert at spending time alone, in silence, and emotionally out of reach. Which is why the most serious infraction of the Rule was room visiting. I've spoken with men ten yeas older than I who assured me that they never visited another room in all the six years they were in the seminary and would not have dreamed of doing so. They understood that the discipline of being in solitary was part of the whole fabric of priestly training. That style of conformity, though, had already died the death by 1964. Rule or no Rule, we visited a lot, particularly in the "wing," an annex where the resident faculty member seemed not to notice or care what his neighbors were about.

Sitting at your desk at night, you would often hear the soft clunk of doors opening and closing as other guys moved around. There were whispers, followed by the sound of slippered feet heading down the hall to the johns, which served as conference rooms. When the johns were too crowded, there were the showers. Were these assignations? Not really. Sometimes a dozen of us would be there, just hanging out, chewing the fat, resistant to study, sleep, or more prayer than we had to attend daily. They were our refuge and an important aid both to sanity and to "normal" social life. One weekend, I debated subjectivism with Owen McCormick, a burly Bronx Irishman, nicknamed "the Sartre of Marion Avenue," during several sessions in the broad space between the urinals and the toilet stalls. It turned into something of a social event, with people chipping in and taking sides.

Licit socializing was restricted to two periods a day: "long rec" from after lunch until 3:30 p.m. and "short rec," the hour after supper before conferences and night prayer. Except for the coldest days, when everyone remained indoors, "long rec" provided the best opportunity for either organized or pickup sports. The most dedicated athletes would come to lunch with their rec clothes beneath their cassocks, tucking their sneakers in an out-of-the-way place or in their cassock pockets so as to get outside right after lunch and fit in a whole game before the bell rang. Handball was a passion for a hardy coterie; tennis courts gave even nonjocks a shot at competition. In addition to baseball, basketball, and football, soccer made an appearance until two guys shattered each other's legs and the game suffered a reversal in popularity. A small weight room had an equally small and casual following, the emphasis being more on outdoor activities. Rec was taken seriously—even required in some seminaries—because it was considered a remedy for concupiscence, like cold showers. Energy expended on the field or on the court was healthily spent and gave the men an outlet that, denied, might take on other less-desired forms. But these indirect ways of dealing with the student body's libidinal urges amounted to the sum total of how the issue of sexuality was handled. We knew both that our structured recreation, like the rules against room visiting, existed as a screen against sexual acting out, and that silence in these matters was golden. A few years later when some liberalization had taken place, rumors circulated among some of the clergy that there was a "wave of homosexuality" awash in Dunwoodie. We mocked them because, while we knew that there were guys who favored guys, we never took seriously the threat of homosexual sex taking place. Overtly repressive cultures, such as the seminary remained into the 1970s, had no accumulated body of sexual knowledge and, when the repression lifted, had few tools to help men negotiate celibacy in an open environment. Before that occurred, priests and students alike entertained only crude stereotypes about effeminacy and masculinity. Not surprisingly, they gave a negative edge to the atmosphere that could turn ugly given the wrong person or event as a catalyst.

Over the summer of 1965, a new faculty member was appointed who tilted the underlying sexual tension in the direction, briefly, of a mini-inquisition. Despite the damage he did, other arrivals eventually blunted the impact of the maleness crusade he launched. The net result was that the faculty avoided dealing in any real way with issues of effeminacy and sexual identity, pretending to act forthrightly about them, but actually fobbing them off by picking on a few scapegoats. This part of my tale illustrates how much the whole clerical system in the United States failed to confront the ambiguous sexual dynamics underlying a man's choice of celibacy. Since many of the bishops who have performed so dismally in the face of the abuse scandals were educated in similar settings, they were no more prepared for what Jason Berry first revealed in *Lead Us Not into Temptation: Catholic Priests and the Sexual Abuse of Children* than if they had to say Mass in Martian. Years of denial had conditioned bishops and their chancery yes-men to look no deeper than the surface when sexual abuse among the clergy began to surface. Their agenda has remained loyalty to the celibate corps. All other issues regarding sexuality fell victim to the silence and the secrecy that have kept the clerical system intact to the present.

Our academic encounter with philosophy had begun dismally. Going to class meant listening to lectures written years before and hearing the same questions and answers that had been laid out in the *Cursus Philosophiae*, our out-of-print textbook, which only a few students had acquired as hand-me-downs. To his credit, the new rector with whom we had entered Dunwoodie, Monsignor Ed Broderick, acted upon our complaints and enlisted the philosophy faculty from Fordham University to beef up the curriculum. The speed with which the rector moved encouraged our sense of the inevitability of change. In the fall of 1965, before the last session of the Vatican Council was to meet, the same Cardinal Spellman whom I had greeted as a flag-waving schoolboy paid one of his rare visits to Dunwoodie before traveling to Rome. It was an informal affair—or as informal as you can get with 275 men standing around in floor-length black gowns, the bishops and monsignors bedecked in their purple silk bellybands for the occasion. As we stood awaiting the great man's arrival, one wise guy went up to a member of the administration and remarked, "It seems the cardinal's late." The reply was firm and unironic, "The cardinal is never late. Everyone else is early." Spelly, as everybody called the cardinal—except his close aides, who referred to him by the code name Dudley—was one of the nominal presidents of the worldwide meeting of bishops, and he had taken some novel positions, opposing the use of English at Mass but voting in favor of priests using English in their daily recitation of the Divine Office. At any rate, he spoke very briefly and told us his goal was to return to Rome and vote yes on everything. The cheers of the student body in response seemed to surprise the faculty. It came from a well of repressed energy that drove our day-to-day struggle to bring life in Dunwoodie up to date. We were convinced that, if the church had declared itself *semper reformanda* ("always in need of reform"), then change was inevitable. Yet not all change would have a positive impact on the hothouse atmosphere of a seminary lurching from one era into an uncertain future.

The new faculty member whom I mentioned above, a Father Cuddihy, eventually got to teach in the area he was trained in, but he first arrived with another portfolio in hand. Rumor had it that the cardinal had actually gotten his name mixed up with that of another priest, whom he meant to appoint to the post of professor of dogma, and no one had corrected the error. Arriving just before the semester began, Cuddihy had a certain amount of catching up to do to teach a subject he hadn't trained in; nevertheless he allowed his attention to be grabbed by some of the personal politics and jock-versus-fem dynamics at work in the student body. Tall, imposing, and with striking good looks, he sought to come off as a breath of fresh air, loudly proclaiming that the two pillars that held up the central stairway outside the chapel were named "Hypocrisy" and "Bullshit." To aid him in his campaign, he recruited a group of pious, athletic guys whom he cultivated and through whom word went out that the faculty was concerned about some students' place on the index of appropriate maleness. Most of us just thought he was strange. Gathered in his sitting room one evening, a small group of us whom he had summoned to "get to know us" were practicing how to say little as we parried his questions about what we thought about how the "men," in general, were doing. I couldn't help but notice how he moved around the room so nervously, constantly adjusting his genitals beneath his cassock. I didn't know very much about unconscious motivation at the time, but it wasn't a comfortable conversation at all, and we were glad to get out quick when it was over.

One Sunday it was Cuddihy's turn to lead the High Mass, at which I was assigned as one of the superfluous torchbearers. At the central action of the Mass, still in its medieval Latin, as we knelt, flambeaus alight, on the marble tile, he came to the words of consecration (*Hoc est enim corpus meum*). So overcome was he at the words and at the power he was exercising that he stuttered, broke out into a sweat, paused, tried again, and strained to push himself through the phrase. The same drama repeated itself at the words over the chalice. A momentary solemn ritual became a ten-minute psychodrama. Extreme examples like this of men burdened by the weight of the priesthood's mystique were not common. But watching the mystique so unhinge a priest helped the more thoughtful of us get past some of our own simplistic notions of priestly power at work in the sacraments. We came to disdain the implicit bargain being proposed by the clerical establishment, which offered us sacramental power in exchange for our individuality or, to be blunt, our sexual potency. But it seemed there were enough others who were perfectly content to secure their eternal significance by making such a deal with the mitered Mephistopheles who would ordain them.

Another missile in the arsenal of the masculinity crusade involved us for a year or two in hosting weekend retreats for cadets from West Point, an hour away up the Hudson River. Commingling army cadets with church cadets would fortify both, or so the thinking went. Cardinal Spellman was the Military Vicar and one of the current war's most loyal supporters, and so the word went out that, under no circumstances, was the issue of Vietnam or the morality of American intervention there to be discussed. So there was about as much room for dissent on the war as there was on celibacy. Biting yet another bullet, we soldiered on.

In the same year, the masculinity crusade and its allied whispering campaign took out its first victim. After two years in the major seminary, we became candidates for tonsure, or ritual shaving of the head, the first of seven steps into the clerical state and its sacred self-understanding. Nobody at the seminary actually got shaved in 1966; we just had a lock of hair clipped off. Only monks still observed the original ritual. But before we got to kneel before the administering bishop and officially become a cleric, each of us had to be approved by a vote of the faculty and confirmed by the candidate's receiving the "call" of the rector, acting in the name of the bishop. Aside from the number of cards an individual might have dropped and perhaps failing grades, there were no standards other than the faculty's casual observation, rumors passed along by their sources, and their personal preferences for some students and not others—methods that were all approved instruments of the Holy Spirit. When the voting was done, I had survived a move to expel me but was "cut," or had my reception of tonsure deferred—along with some guys who had been caught missing daily Mass. My record was clean. I had never dropped a card or been accused of breaking a rule. My questioning attitude was enough.

As I left the rector's office and headed out to the courtyard, my friend Rick intercepted me. Assured that I had not been expelled, he broke down and told me that, with no warning whatsoever, he had been told he would have to leave the seminary. His offense? Rick walked in a way that was adjudged too feminine. His eight years of exemplary marks, his sacristan's job at Cathedral, his affability and dedication amounted to nothing. (All right, he did organize a group of us to sneak down to the rec room and watch the Academy Awards after hours one year!) But he swished and his laugh was a little too shrill. It was enough. At the time, Rick was no more aware that he was gay (as it turned out he was) than we knew that an obscure Polish bishop would one day be pope. Nor did they tell him this was the problem. He just didn't fit the robust image of the priesthood a majority of the faculty agreed was in vogue that year. Another guy escaped the ax because he'd been warned that his voice was a problem and so had walked around affecting a basso profundo for a few weeks before the vote. He returned the following year with his original whiney mode of speaking intact.

Other types of masculinity—the marrying kind—were not so welcome and were handled with an equivalent lack of candor. The following September, as my class began theology study, Father John Cannon, a musician and liturgist, arrived fresh from studies in Rome. He was approachable, affable, and eager in the ways of reform. But he was also secretly in love. He had met a stewardess on a New York–Rome flight, and suddenly only months into his new job, he left to marry her. One night, he literally disappeared from the building, never to be seen of or heard from again. Because he had been popular, guys were shaken up, so at the rector's conference (a regular Sunday night event), Ed Broderick tearfully faced us to explain. He professed ignorance of any details, convincing us that he, too, was in the dark. Later we were to find out that John had written a letter explaining his decision to the seminary community, a letter far too frank to make it through the veil of lies being used to protect us. A consummate performer, our leader was practicing the clerical arts of prevarication that would help get him promoted to be Bishop of Albany a few years later.

But before he moved upriver, we had already begun to benefit from an arrival from the same direction. Into our enclosed society, only slowly responding to the Vatican Council's mandate to update, Stan Pawelski arrived at our prestigious hilltop in Yonkers as just another student from the hinterland. If some Albanians, as they were known, came upon the scene like country boys come to the big city, standing out for their wide-eyed naïveté, it was not the case with this man. Fourth in a family of eleven surviving children, he had returned to college at twenty-five to seek ordination. So his years and his experience as public employee, actor, and tank crewman in the N.Y. National Guard already set him apart. Fluent in Polish and in unaccented American plain speaking, he arrived unpretentious but clear-eyed. He spent the next six years unraveling the seamless garment of clerical hauteur for which Dunwoodie was so famous. To us New Yorkers, Stan was a peer, yet not quite a peer; older, wiser, yet still very much one of us.

His major weapon was his ability to disarm people. Graced with a physical self-presence, he was solidly built with workman's hands and engaging eyes. He had no trouble being comfortable with brash jocks or with brittle academics. Few could resist the bear hugs that he could administer or the broad, toothy grin that would break out beneath his prominent nose when he engaged them directly. He always called himself ugly, but the way he carried himself encouraged people to take in his whole person, not any part of him. In the strange mix of personalities that the seminary had garnered from the male Catholic population, he did not so much stand out as weave himself into the fabric of the community—he certainly helped it feel like one on occasion. The full impact of his personality was not felt for a few years, as even he had to tread lightly when living in an institution where some people possess all the authority and there's no accountability for their actions. As capable as he was of winning over the wary guardians of clerical propriety, they could still counterattack in secret and issue their baseless judgments with impunity. After his second year, his evaluation from the faculty contained the observation that he had a foreign accent that he needed to work on!

Unlike so many of us, though, he brought a certain authority to his quest for ordination because he had resisted it for some years. Like Saint Augustine (whose "O Lord, give me chastity, but not yet" lasted a lot longer), Pawelski had been around the block. Few of us, and few of the faculty either, had been there. Raised in a family that had had to struggle with poverty at the door, he became his mother's helper in raising his younger siblings when his father was permanently hospitalized, and he had worked for some years before going back to school. Only once did I ever observe him wield his experience as a club, and even then it came in a moment of defensive weakness. The scene was a grassy mound behind the main building. It was a hot day and, still in head-to-toe black dresses, a group of us were sitting on the grass with our collars off passing some time between classes. In joking fashion, one of the short-lived basketball team stars, named Don, made an unflattering comment about Stan's seniority. To which Stan shot back, "Well, at least I won't die wondering!" I don't think he meant it to have such an impact. Yet a few weeks later Don packed his things and went off into the world to satisfy his curiosity.

In another setting, Stan's easygoing maleness, as nurturing as it was firm, might have been a small thing, but at Dunwoodie, where everything was at stake if you wore a surplice too long, or quoted the wrong author, or spoke out of turn, his presence was a tonic. If you walked the "loop" around the property with him, the male patrol would probably leave you alone. Because he was as close in age to some of the new faculty members who continued to arrive each year as he was to us, he acted as a bridge, able to connect on a personal level with them and connect them to us in a way that challenged the faculty's former aloofness.

Those of us looking for signs that the momentum for change could sustain itself also received some encouragement from Father Jim Connolly, who had quietly arrived to join the faculty the previous year. He was a priest of the archdiocese who had researched and written a theological work—no small credential when most others still taught from outdated manuals. His *Voices of France* had surveyed the theological and cultural scene that had laid the basis for the Vatican Council's renewal of church life, and his research had provided him with a perspective on change that other priests lacked or preferred to ignore. Father Jim, as we called him to his face (a novelty at the time), spoke with a deep, throaty, cigarette-scarred voice and used spicy—no, salty—speech that brought with it a hint of his own deep-down struggles. Now, every professor has personal quirks that get blown out of proportion in a classroom. What bubbled up out of Jim was a sacramental mixture that spoke about how historical happenstance shaped the church and how these accidents occasioned grace, often in spite of themselves. He incarnated one of the rock-bottom principles of Christianity, framed by Saint Paul: We hold a divine treasure in the earthenware jars of human experience. Grace, the unlooked-for encounter with deep acceptance, or an undeserved release from a doomed sense of self, comes through its seeming contrary. This holy paradox altered my sense of the very chemistry of the spiritual life, a deep mystery never elucidated for us in the hours of spiritual exercises or forced meditations we had to sit through. Grace and nature do not repel each other like oil and water nor oppose each other on principle. They engage in a delicate dance that allows spirit to enter, inhabit, and suffuse flesh. The love of Christ for his bride, the church, is an earthly—even earthy—not only a heavenly, affair.

The unofficial classroom in which some of these paradoxes came to life occurred during our off-hours, whenever Father Jim and Stan Pawelski were in the same room. These unofficial soirees made some of the hours still meant for monastic solitude far more bearable. Amid a torrent of gossip and normal bullshitting, ideas would be hatched, mulled over, and fleshed out. Insights into ministry and worship would be shared and stored for future use. Jim had a way with words as well, and he knew the power of words in the life of faith, the force of poetry in any grounded religious sensibility. He taught a brand-new course entitled "The Theology of Preaching." According to the Code of Canon Law that we were having spoon-fed to us in another course, preaching consisted in instructing the faithful in the Ten Commandments, the articles of the catechism, the Six Commandments of the church, and the statements of the *magisterium*. Although the Vatican Council's documents had recently set out the far more ancient notion that preaching sought to make God in Christ present in this time and place, how this might happen had not been detailed at all. In tackling the history and theory of how a preacher facilitates such a Presence, this rough, bright man gave us tools that made our solitude into fruitful hours of study. Instead of refuting Protestant theologians, he used them as sources to help us understand how to be a "servant of the Word" and not just someone who ranted about moral truths. Learning how to translate the idiom of the Bible into the idiom of our own present would take time, discipline, a sense of humor, and a fresh commitment every time we preached. Armed with the vision he offered us, we could convert our time spent alone into a creative outlet for ourselves and our long-suffering communities. Into the 1970s, Jim longed to be recognized as a theological educator, campaigning to become seminary rector, but to no avail. Disappointed, he became increasingly embittered when his vision of the role he had wanted to play in the church soured. Sadly, his own earthen vessel gave out on him in his sixties. When he fell asleep in the Lord prematurely, I'm not certain that many remembered how seminal his presence had been in the years in which the study of theology was being liberated and made available for thirsty minds.

After a year of graduate theological study, I got the faculty's negative judgment of me reversed, was tonsured, and received the first of the "minor orders." Things were back on track, but then the Summer of Love came along and derailed my ordination express. I had a job running a day camp as part of the federally funded Summer in the City program in the South Bronx, which gave me some distance from the daily scrutiny and the "everything's on the line" atmosphere of the seminary. With a chance to breathe a little more deeply, underlying questions made their way to the surface. Baby-sitting for my nephew one afternoon, I fell into a conversation with my sister when she arrived to pick up her son. Again she challenged my timetable. "Why not take a leave of absence, date, get to know yourself, and then make your decision?" she suggested. Packing up little David, she headed out and left me slumped in a chair in the gathering darkness of the evening. As I sat there, a voice deep down said to me, "You know what you are going to do." It took a few hours for me to admit it, but "time-out" had been called.

Within the week, I had seen the rector and gotten a formal leave of absence—a key concession when the alternative was being reclassified for the draft and called up for Vietnam. A few weeks later, I got a job teaching high school English. That fall, I dated several women, with one of whom I definitely had some chemistry going. But I stayed in touch with my cronies, including Rick, who had already been teaching for a year and had been refused readmission to the seminary the previous spring. When some guys put together a ski trip over New Year's, both Rick and I accepted an invitation, rented some antiquated equipment, and found ourselves with a mixed crowd of seminarians sharing an A-frame in subzero Vermont. Stan Pawelski was the common denominator and very much the animator of the group when we came back from the slopes. None of us could foresee the events of the next twelve months: the Tet offensive, President Johnson's withdrawal from the election, the assassinations of Martin Luther

King, Jr., and Robert F. Kennedy, inner cities and campuses erupt-
ing, the Catonsville Nine draft protest, the papal encyclical *Humanae Vitae*, the Chicago police riot, the election of Nixon, the
deaths on the same day in December of Thomas Merton and
Karl Barth. But in the four nights of eating, drinking, and talking
we had together, we hashed and rehashed every world-historical
topic that touched us or affected the church in the United States.
By the end of that time together, neither Rick nor I could shake
an appetite for the camaraderie we had shared again, thanks to
the frigid conditions outside and the warmth that Stan radiated at
the center of a group of young male idealists. The cause of the
Vatican Council seemed alive and real again. If the cost of joining the ranks of those who could make church renewal happen
meant spending three or four years under scrutiny at Dunwoodie,
then we might just have to pay it.

In the following weeks, I broke up with my sometime girlfriend. It had been hard for me to negotiate the intimacy I had
begun to share with Diane. Her intense feelings about me made
claims that I just didn't feel that I could match. In another time
and place, I would have met the learning curve over time, but the
days in Vermont had reignited a strong desire for doing ministry,
for preaching, for interpreting human experience in the light of
the Gospel story. Access to the opportunity to work in the church
and to live for others came at a high cost, but in the highly
charged atmosphere of the late 1960s, sacrifice seemed noble,
and refusing it, cowardice. Intimacy had its appeal, but I wasn't
yet prepared to be naked in any fashion, so the intensity we guys
had shared made merely personal contentment along with sexual
fulfillment seem second best. Was there a certain homoerotic
charge in the atmosphere in Vermont? More than likely. But no
more than men on the job, on the police force, or in sports fire up
in one another to perform at their peak. Celibates just lacked fall-
back relationships, partners to pick us up and fill out our lives—
or so I thought. For us, the urgency of events made the time seem

short to do some vital work, and we were willing to gamble on being able to sustain that same kind of intensity for the foreseeable future.

Readmitted to Dunwoodie because of the changing makeup of the faculty who had approved me for orders, I found a changed institution. Several more young, vigorous, and intellectually high-caliber professors had joined the faculty, more concerned with our acquiring competence than keeping an outmoded Rule. Its constrictions of daily life began to loosen and then fell away almost completely. A new arrangement, linking us up with priests in parishes, allowed many of us to come and go, teaching and doing pastoral work. The momentum that had begun with the Council began to bear fruit, and at first even Paul VI's letter prohibiting "artificial" birth control didn't stop it. Aside from having the text assigned to read and its essential points outlined, we neither analyzed, nor discussed, nor dealt with the worldwide fallout. In other dioceses, such as Washington, D.C., priests were fired for their public opposition to the prohibition. In Cardinal Krol's Philadelphia, most of an entire class of seminarians was discharged after participating in clandestine services in the bowels of the seminary. In New York, we were far more discreet. The whole institutional apparatus pretended that we were in lockstep with the new archbishop Terence Cooke's fawning telegram to Paul VI, signed, "Your obedient Son." Privately, we decried its betrayal of the reestablished doctrine of the collegial authority of the bishops along with that of the pope and were convinced it could be sidestepped by recourse to individual conscience. But push never came to shove: no one demanded that any of us sign on the dotted line or even asked us what we thought about the pastoral problems the letter's negative position was causing.

The tacit decision of thousands of bishops and priests to live with the anomaly that the church's teaching on marriage and birth control was out of sync with the life that the faithful lived sowed some very destructive seeds. In the letter's aftermath, even many priests would decide (as the laity had begun to do) that the church's teaching was no real guide for their sexual lives. Many would resign and seek their happiness elsewhere. But others proceeded to make their own adaptations of official teaching about licit and illicit sexual relationships. Here the clergy's old habit of silence in matters sexual colluded with an underlying current of dissent to create an opportunity for some priests to begin to make their own rules. Had even half the energy that church leaders have spent on keeping the birth control decision in place been available for opening up the profound depths of human sexual life and developing church teaching on human sexuality in the light of newly developed knowledge about it, the Catholic church might not be looking as flat-footed as it has recently, as wave after wave of news about clerical sexual abuse has washed up in the media and soaked into the public consciousness.

I had a preview of some of what was to come—though I was hardly prescient about it—the year before we were due to be ordained deacons, the last step before the goal of priestly ordination. Home for a few days, I dropped by to see one of the priests I had known when teaching high school two years before. He lived at the cottage on the grounds of another school in the locality. Instead of finding him there, I came upon another priest from the same faculty, whom I presumed to be visiting. But I sensed something amiss, as he was even more wired and high-strung than I remembered him. The last time Bob McBride and I had talked was the day I had informed him I was returning to the seminary—and was treated to a barrage of his disgust with my decision. He wanted to know why I was throwing my life away when I was enjoying teaching so much. I had heard him whine previously that the priesthood for which he had been ordained no longer existed, so I understood his dissatisfaction with my decision to stem from his own loss of bearings. He was not a happy person, but this day more was afoot, and before I knew it he was telling me his tale of woe.

As a teacher, he had a reputation for being demanding and acerbic, so he was usually assigned junior and senior classes, which he sought to whip into intellectual shape before they went off to college. His reputation seemed well-deserved. The classes were small and informal, but in this case the informality had allowed him to hook up with one of the student athletes, with whom he had begun to spend personal time. As the priest dragged away on cigarette after cigarette, he spelled out his "poor me" tale of how all he and the barrel-chested youth had done was lie on the bed together to watch a movie and, before either of them knew anything, someone was sucking off the other—I never got the details totally straight, nor did I really want to. He saw the student as the aggressor, not holding himself responsible for the sex play that had occurred. But the worst part of his tale came next. The student had gone back to school and boasted of the encounter to a friend, who had told his father, who had gone to the bishop about it. The town was full of whispering, scandal had erupted, and Father McBride was to be removed from the school in disgrace.

By this time, Father Donovan had returned, and I took the opportunity to gather up my confusion and shock and take my leave. I bracketed the event as a tragic aberration; I had certainly never heard of anything like it up to that point in my life and presumed I wouldn't hear more. At the time, I didn't share the incident with anyone at Dunwoodie—no one knew either the priest or the student back there, where we all remained relatively innocent of the depredations of the clergy. (Neither did I ever hear from the priest again, nor about how he was doing—until fifteen years later, when I read the news of his being bludgeoned to death by a black youth on a street in a neighborhood where he had little call to be driving. News coverage never hinted that the priest had initiated contact, nor did it indicate whether the adolescent was prostituting. Was it possible that a sexual encounter may have been covered up to protect the priest's reputation and that a kid had been sent to prison without an adequate defense?)

As spring approached, we readied ourselves to survive another faculty vote approving us, this time, for major orders. But first, there was the peculiar rite of stepping over the line into official celibacy at subdiaconate. Though we abbreviated the whole event under the code word "sub," it had long-term consequences. For, notwithstanding all the press reports and rhetoric that speak of the "vow of celibacy," we knew that there was not, and never had been, such a vow in the life of diocesan, or secular, clergy. Monks and other members of religious orders—male and female—take vows, solemnized promises that bind them together as members of a community of poverty, chastity, and obedience. The vows are the bond they have in common, made to elected leaders of the community who receive them in the name of the community of brothers or sisters in Christ. The vows, in other words, were meant to define and to support community life. But when the Jesuits added a fourth vow, of obedience to the pope, they shifted the understanding of vows to a more suppliant-to-superior framework. The shift also strongly suggested that the society members were individually dispensable, like foot soldiers to be deployed by the religious superior (known as "the general") wherever battle was to be waged against the infidel. In the same era, diocesan seminaries were organized to instill better discipline into diocesan clergy, one of the chief signs of which was celibacy, a commitment not to marry or bear children of one's own. By extension it came to mean (in some cultures but clearly not all) no sexual relations, no concubinage. Period.

But because the discipline of celibacy among secular clergy could hardly prosper in a vacuum, celibacy was touted as if it were indeed a vow, a building block of a priest's spiritual life—basically the same as "perfect chastity"—by which a priest seeks to be satisfied with "God alone" (the motto of Cistercian monks).

Difficult to sustain on purely economic or disciplinary grounds, celibacy has been ringed round with a sacred aura that it did not have in the Bible or in the earliest generations of Christianity. Peter, the first Apostle of Jesus, was certainly married, and if Paul the Apostle, who knew he himself was the exception to the rule, can be believed, Peter traveled with his wife as did Jesus' own brothers (see 1 Corinthians 9:5). The hybrid spirituality that developed to support mandatory celibacy for diocesan priests came to resemble a blend of Neoplatonic horror of the flesh, Celtic heroic self-denial, monastic dedication to prayer, and quasi-military zeal. As a hybrid, it proved hardy in some climates but wilted easily in others.

Even as theological students, we may not have known all the sordid details of how celibacy became mandatory for the Latin rite clergy, but we knew that the issue was contested and that it deserved to be treated as a "disputed question." Knowing that we knew this, some of the faculty proposed to have a series of talks, discussions, and even a debate on mandatory celibacy in order to help us make an informed decision at subdiaconate. During that ceremony, we would not make a promise—let alone, take a vow—but would be asked to step forward as a public sign that we accepted the condition or discipline of celibacy, and it was thought that we should do so with our heads on straight about it.

The notion that the very substance of the priestly vocation (as some of the faculty saw it) would be opened to question in a public discussion was enough to send celibacy's defenders into a frenzy. But the series took place in any case. The formal debate for and against mandatory celibacy was conducted by two older priests *from outside the diocese*, the presumption being they might be freer to speak, perhaps. The priest defending the imposition of celibacy, Father Adamo, had difficulty adjusting to the debate format and preferred to commend celibacy to us in warm and friendly terms. The priest opposing mandatory celibacy, Monsignor Hastings, a very cultured gentleman with a mild demeanor, surprised everyone with his withering attack on the waste of love that celibacy entailed. Kindly Father Adamo moved to reassure us that, of course, Monsignor Hastings was "a good celibate." The monsignor shot back, "Reluctantly so!" and received an ovation.

The next day we had a moral theology class with Monsignor Ronny McGynne, a most perfervid defender of the discipline, who had vehemently opposed the public discussion. Working himself into a lather about what he perceived as a slight to the priesthood, he commented, "I just wanted to ask Monsignor, 'When did you become a reluctant celibate?' " as if the answer would have told us when the priest had betrayed the essence of his ordination. We were used to Monsignor McGynne's outbursts and to maintaining a certain composure when he went off. We were attuned as well to his frequent Freudian slips: he once explained that the spiritual and legal bond of marriage, though existing independent of sexual relations, was given "a certain firmness" by a couple's having intercourse! One of his most famous *mal mots* occurred one day when two men with the name Richard were both in class and raised their hand when he asked a question. He burst out with "Hey! I've got two Dicks and don't know what to do with them!" Another day, he was delivering a stem-winder about the sagging state of nuns' morale. He seemed to be pushed to the edge by news of the resignations of religious women from convents that had then begun. Reaching his climax—which we had to listen to with straight faces—he exclaimed, "I want you to go out there and *buck up* those nuns!" Stan's response was to dub the clueless professor "Numbnuts," and it stuck. Stan always hated it when I would make this claim, but he single-handedly expanded our theological vocabulary by incorporating everyday speech into it. Scatology helped us neutralize the tension we often felt between what people in the seminary were saying and what we thought might really be the case.

Another of our professors once sought to justify celibacy as the moral equivalent of dying for the faith. In contrast to "red martyrdom," it was called "white martyrdom" because no blood was spilled in carrying it out (no, we cracked, semen was!). Unhappy with such facile justifications, we hoped for some emotional rationale for accepting the discipline. At the time, some argued secretly that we had a safety valve: we could step across the line with a mental reservation because we expected the rule of celibacy to be dropped in the future. Though we might hope this was to be the case, it also seemed too facile. So when a panel of laypeople made their presentations, one of the most persuasive arguments—it swayed me—came from Sidney Callahan, a convert, mother, psychology professor, and author who averred that, in the present atmosphere of political and social strife, unmarried witnesses to the gospel of justice were needed. The impact of the Berrigan brothers, members of the Catonsville Nine, loomed large (though one of them, Phil, would shortly leave the Josephite order and marry without becoming any less committed to civil disobedience and consequent jail time). Twenty years later, I reminded Sidney of the talk she had given and told her of its influence on us. She had no memory of delivering it, but at the time, she was persuasive.

When the day for "sub" arrived, I remember sitting in my room before the service, dressed in my good cassock, and wondering what it meant to proceed. When the time came to assemble and vest in an amice and alb for the first time, I knew I did not know how this lifetime commitment would turn out, but I was determined to give it my best shot. Without a sense that I was in this with my friends and peers, I never would have proceeded. But together with these guys, I was ready to cast the die and make the required commitment in order to serve. My commitment to God took shape through the company I kept, a link that is undersold in the official rationale for celibacy. That evening, we were initiated into the discipline at a most unusual ceremony. Perhaps it was an omen of bumpier days to come, but in the heady atmosphere of affirmation we felt that evening, a little episcopal oddity went down easily. The bishop who came to summon us to take the fatal step had himself been ordained to his office only the day before. One of a number of Cardinal Spellman's secretaries—known for their raconteurial skills and good singing voices—to ascend to the hierarchy, he displayed all the wit and charm that had made him such a success carrying the late cardinal's bags. Maybe he was saying more than he knew, but in the place of a dry sermon citing the great honor and responsibility we were assuming, he surprised everyone in attendance—faculty, priests, and families—-by issuing a warning to us about the perils of "dangerous friendships" in the priesthood. He gave no specific clues about whom or what he meant; he may have been alerted to the friendships that had grown up between the seminary students and young nuns who had been assigned to study Spanish in Puerto Rico the previous summer. A couple of romances and some marriages had already been spawned there, and he may have been trying to alert us to the unique vulnerability that existed when men and women found themselves all of a sudden not in single-sex closed societies, but out in the world. Ironically, many of the friendships between my ordination colleagues and their nun friends have proved anything but "dangerous," perduring for over three decades and providing the priests and the nuns involved with both a chaste and a vital companionship in their otherwise solitary work and life. So in the flush of our own convictions that risking friendship made sense, even for those of us about to be ordained deacons, we took the bishop's advice with a grain of salt. It was also another hint that we were entering a world in which the leadership often mouthed a message that it didn't exactly live out. Some time later, word came that the bishop was apprehended outside the boundaries of the archdiocese for driving under the influence—accompanied by a female companion.

May 1970 brought with it ordination to the diaconate. In the months before this penultimate step up and out of seminary bondage, a scheme came together, engendered as much by the faculty's desire to see us off as by our desire to move into ministry forthwith. As deacons, we would spend an internship of five full days a week in pastoral assignments, returning just two days a week for final course work at the Big House. So, shortly after the school year ended, our headstrong crowd moved into parish assignments, occupying the lowest rung on the ladder. The experience of being neither fish nor fowl, neither priests nor laity, in a parochial setting did not always work in our favor, but most of us coped pretty well with what the ministry threw at us, and we came back for more. We certainly had firsthand experience of what we had read in the Columbia Survey that had just appeared, the first study of priestly life ever done in the archdiocese. In the light of the Vatican Council's openness to the modern world, social science enjoyed a brief honeymoon with church authorities, who sought to determine scientifically what believers thought rather than merely to assert what everybody was supposed to think. The survey of the priests of the archdiocese revealed that a wide gap existed between different groups of priests—determined roughly by age and clerical habit—with regard to basic expectations. At issue were fundamental images of the church as a society, how it ran, how authority should operate, and so on, questions that split priests into three distinct groups: traditionals, moderates, and progressives. I don't remember there being many in the middle group: rectories were divided between men whose experience predated even the whisper of aggiornamento and those who had bought into it fully. The interpreters of the survey predicted that, as time went on, rectory living would become more and more difficult because priests under the same roof would share fewer and fewer basic premises about how to carry on the daily mission of the church. Many could not fully buy into the Council's renewal because it threatened too many of their hard-won perquisites. But the Columbia Survey was not asked to measure their resistance or the forms it would take.

We could have saved them the cost of the project. Commuting as we were between the seminary—where we enjoyed weekly reunions and the chance to share war stories and breathe common air—and rectories scattered up and down the Hudson, we developed our own perspective on what life might be like as full-time priests in the rectory. And we intuited that it just might be the ruin of us. So, as priesthood ordination approached, we put together a white paper on ministry and living conditions. It was an exercise we were used to, because we had waged a constant struggle to reform seminary life through creating a barrage of proposals, most of which went unanswered. The most extensive of these efforts had actually been reported on the front page of the *New York Times* in March 1969, and almost got a few of us issuers thrown out on our ears. But we survived to write again and, with less than two months to go before ordination, formally asked Cardinal Cooke's advisers to appoint us in teams of two (as Jesus had sent the first missionaries). Our reasoning was that collegial ministry required some form of community, and we knew rectories to be hotbeds of resisters, each priest doing what was required, neither socializing with nor coordinating his efforts with others in ministry, but carrying on like a sacramental Lindbergh soloing across the Atlantic. We were seeking safety in teams of two, but the men in the chancery perceived us as conspiring to gang up on unsuspecting pastors and questioning one of the essential building blocks of the priestly mystique: that every priest by virtue of his office performed equally well. As a priest, his actions were the church's actions and were sufficient to the task of sanctifying souls. We had challenged that notion, convinced of the social dimension involved in all that priests did, and the cardinal's advisers would not have it. They were determined that the clerical shape of the priesthood needed no adjustments. It had worked fine for them—hadn't they risen to the heights under its benevolent premises?—and a group of upstarts wasn't about to challenge a hundred years' worth of installing diocesan priestly prerogatives!

Their big concession came in the form of an actual reply, instead of just ignoring us. The negative response regretfully cited reasons of pastoral necessity and a shortage of priests—resignations from the priesthood had reduced the New York presbyterate by several hundred by 1971. But the fuller answer came personally in a visit from His Eminence the Cardinal for an unprecedented tête-à-tête between himself, alone, and us, his deacon candidates for the priesthood. Basically, he tried to lay down the rules and assert that he was in charge. But, trained as a social worker, he just wasn't cut from the previous cardinal's autocratic cloth. His strongest statement, on that occasion, went something like "You know, some people think I'm soft like jelly. Well, I'm not jelly!" So we filed the white paper with the class archivist, got off a final shot by refusing to don cassocks for our group ordination picture, rose early on the morning of ordination for a group swim in the buff, and then lay prostrate (but clothed) on the floor of Saint Patrick's Cathedral before receiving the laying on of hands. Hence, we were priests "forever according to the order of Melchizedek." The adventure we had embarked on so long ago had finally launched us into the church at large with our newly minted credentials of ordination and our commitment to renew church life.

In the classic system that, by the early 1970s, was defunct, newly ordained priests had been classified as "junior clergy" for five years and had to return each year to the seminary for an exam. In addition, all priests were expected to sign up for one of the five-day retreats run at the seminary over the summer. Both practices had a regressive effect on priests, who were made to relive portions of their extended adolescent moratorium for years. For our part, convinced that we had been confined there long enough, my contemporaries and I sought to renew our spirit in other settings. Then, while we weren't looking, many of the forms of clericalism that we had actively rejected began to sneak back into the daily life of the country's seminaries. But with a difference. The old repressive atmosphere that banished sexual thoughts, not to mention actions, from every place but the confessional had given way. In its place, a tacit tolerance of sexual acting out took up residence. Clearly, most of it was homoerotic and, from what I have gathered, intramural. It stayed within the walls but involved men on both sides of the ordination divide. In the early 1980s, word reached me that a former student of mine who had entered the seminary and was approaching ordination had a boyfriend with whom he regularly slept. Looking for an opportunity to meet with him, I confronted him with the rumors, which he more or less confirmed. I reasoned with him that integrity represented the moral coin of the ministry and that living a lie would only corrode his own sense of self and devalue the best work he did. He listened, was ordained, and continues to serve to the best of my knowledge. What good I might have done, I cannot say.

Surprisingly, none of this sexual acting out was undertaken by "Young Turks" intent on dismantling the old clerical system that denied the role of sexuality in the life of well-adjusted men and women. Rather, many of the actors were men in authority, who bought into the system, no matter the private compromises they made. The most notorious accusation that has come to light from this sector is that of the seminary rector Anthony O'Connell, later to resign as Bishop of Palm Beach, whose way of comforting a teenage seminarian who had been abused sexually by two faculty members was evidently to undress him and take him to bed. In cases like this, the sexual acting out seems to represent the clumsy groping of older men, emotionally and sexually fixated in adolescence, who took advantage of confused and ignorant boys.

But recent revelations have indicated that there were even darker machinations at work in much of the secret sexual life of priests. What has not gotten much attention, though, is the extent to which seminaries have been the original seedbed (the meaning of *seminarium*) of the problem, first by promoting a repressive culture where innuendo thrived and frankness was absent, then by going secretly soft on the issue, if not being explicitly permissive.

Another Columbia graduate I knew well joined the seminary and, at an orientation session, met a deacon preparing for ordination. They hit it off, and afterward, Todd, the younger man —handsome, athletic, and still a little naïve about his attractiveness—received an invitation to the deacon's ordination and first Mass. He was also invited to stay overnight at the man's family's house between the two events because he was from out of town. Alas, there was no separate bedroom for him, so he candidly accepted that he would share a large double bed with his new newly minted priest friend. But he spent an uncomfortable night after the priest rolled over to him and gave him a good-night kiss on the lips. As soon as the new day's festivities ended, he checked out real quick. Faced with this kind of acting out, as well as other overripe emotional reactions from priests in charge of his placements, he wisely withdrew and is now the married father of four.

Bed sharing, which might or might not lead to arousal and genital activity, seems to have become the halfway house of clerical desire. Another young man I knew on campus received more than one invitation from a friend who had entered a religious order to snuggle with him and was assured that intimate touching of the type that his brothers engaged in did not violate the order's vow of chastity. What seems to be at work in such thinking is a version of the casuistry, common in the 1950s, in which priests in confession would advise teenage boys (mostly) on how far they could go in the backseat without violating God's law. One now prominent churchman, as a young bishop, would invite groups of student priests to his country place. When they arrived, he would assign each to a guest bed but would invariably run one short. The last guy, the bishop's pick of the pack, would be told, "Well, I guess you get to sleep with your bishop," to the nervous laughter of the group. I have no idea how all the chosen young men responded, but some for sure saw the choice as a sign of ecclesiastical favor that they willingly accepted. A few years after hearing this report secondhand from one of the chosen ones, I also heard a rumor that the same bishop had been summoned to the apostolic nuncio in Washington, D.C., and given a dressing down. If, in fact, he received any such admonition, it didn't adversely affect his career; he has been steadily promoted, first to archbishop, and then to what has become a regular red-hat see in the United States—and, as such, is one of the Catholic cardinals now sanctimoniously crowing about the church's need to protect its children. News accounts of Father Paul Shanley's bed sharing with adolescents for whom he felt a special "ministry" are frighteningly similar to the then bishop's method of showing his personal approbation to selected seminarians.

In June 1971, these sick deeds and painful revelations were all in the future. As newly ordained priests, we sought to balance our learned skepticism with an affirmation that priesthood could live up to our expectations of it. Almost none of us still looked at it through the tinted spectacles that we had inherited from the immigrant church our parents and grandparents had brought with them. We had already seen and heard far too much of how the clergy acted to ignore the anomalies present in the "great fraternity" to which we were welcomed the day we received our first priesthood assignments and prepared ourselves to move permanently into our first real rectories. We did not want a priesthood that lived on the strength of the mystique that had built up around it. We wanted to be part of a profession that was respected for the fruits of its labors, for how well we preached, counseled, advocated, taught, and built up the Body of Christ on earth. So we determined to gird up our loins and go out to tilt at windmills, to try to change not only society's expectations of the Catholic church but the church's own expectations of its ordained ministers. Little did we really know about how deeply embedded was the clerical culture which would continue to insist that God Himself obeyed the words of the priest at the consecration of the Mass! Old saws about the priesthood, it seems, don't die or fade away; they generate asexually among needy celibates hungry for respect.

Three

Gents

PART OF THE APPEAL of Agatha Christie's *Murder at the Vicarage* stems from the contrast she drew between the deed and its locus. By juxtaposing a terrible crime with the pastoral setting of a priest's house in Saint Mary Mead, she set the tone for a whole series of whodunits featuring Miss Jane Marple. In them, the unlikely always vies with the expected to provide the deceptively intuitive lady with clues that enable her to solve the crime.

Only an author as adept as Christie was when she portrayed the distorted actions of proper English folk could do justice to the clash between the mystique and the reality in the average American rectory or priest's residence. Perhaps the writer who comes closest to catching the foibles of the clergy in this setting is J. F. Powers, in his stories and in the novels *Morte D'Urban* and *Wheat That Springeth Green*. But those are merely good fiction; the truth, if told, is far stranger.

At least from the time of Saint Augustine, Bishop of Hippo (d. A.D. 425), the challenge to find the right formula for the clergy's living arrangements has taxed the best minds of the church. His solution was to make his clergy become monks, to sell their individual property, and to live as cenobites, sharing a common table and a common life devoted to ministry. The arrangement assumed the exclusion of women, except in the role of servants, a formula that has lasted to the present day. In spring 2002, a report that the Cardinal Archbishop of Chicago was considering selling the mansion where he and his top advisers lived mentioned that the three housekeeper nuns lived in the old servant's quarters over the carriage house on the grounds. Although Augustine would have approved of the segregation of the women, I doubt he would have approved of the lifestyle at the mansion, given all the problems he had getting his clergy to conform to his ideal of simple living. And while his solution might have worked in the cities of the late Roman Empire and in the fortified towns that survived the empire's collapse, it had little chance in less defended places. Over the following five hundred years, in the scattered villages that grew up around castles and keeps, the village *parochus*, appointed and supported by the local suzerain, generally lived with his housekeeper wife and family, sustaining the sacramental life of the local community (and often being succeeded by his son) much as Eastern Orthodox clergy do to this day. Only in the twelfth century, when new monastic communities (especially the Cluniac Benedictines and the Cistercians) became ascendant, did the situation change. In the name of reform, the monks elected to the papacy in that era first struggled to keep it from the rapacious Roman families that had controlled it for centuries. When they succeeded, Gregory VII, the reforming Hildebrand, successfully demonized all nonmonastic styles of life for priests, putting in motion a radical change in the life of the church that played out for the next hundred years. Clerical marriage was outlawed by Lateran IV (1215), the wives of priests were arrested and removed, and celibacy was imposed on all clergy, no matter their living arrangements. At least, that was the theory.

Rectories emerge from the mists of time as houses belonging to the priest in charge of a cathedral or large church. Before them, semimonastic chapters of clergy (known as canons) lived in the cathedral close and took responsibility for the cathedral compound together. Outside English-speaking countries, diocesan rectories of the size and extent that Catholics in the United States have known as the standard arrangement have rarely existed. Rectories here slowly developed into a strange hybrid of pastor's house, religious enclosure, business office, counseling center, meeting space, and even youth center and choir practice room. They also became in their heyday the residence for all the assistant priests, who, no matter how long they resided there, were the pastor's guests. If, in fact, the pastor's relatives—maybe even his mother—were also guests, they often had precedence over the assistant clergy, who were, in a sense, just visiting.

Even so, rectory living, as we have known it, became the norm in the United States only after the great immigrant waves of the nineteenth century created the megaparishes that became typical in North America's large cities. In other countries, when more than one priest inhabit a dwelling together, the living arrangements tend to be modest and more on the scale of the way middle-class laity live, except in places like the barrios or favelas in Latin America. But even there, with the death of the base-community movement, the local clergy have become discontent with life among the poor and have started insisting on separate dwellings more appropriate to their status.

Still it is doubtful that these residences will ever get to the point reached in the United States after World War II, where parishes grew to become like Our Lady of Mount Carmel in Astoria, Queens. In the early 1960s there were seven resident priests, nineteen hundred children in the parish school, a reputed twenty-five thousand parishioners, more than a dozen nuns teaching in the school, and fifteen Masses on Sunday occurring in three different locations. Few rectories of this size and scope have been fodder for Catholic fiction, but the possibilities are enormous. Instead, the lone parish priest, as in Georges Bernanos's *Diary of a*

Country Priest or the recent *Last Report of the Miracles at Little Horse* by Louise Erdrich, have seemed far more ripe for fictionalizing.

The average rectory in a diocesan parish in the postwar era may have looked no different from the Franciscan friary in the next parish. But it would have felt nothing like a house of friars. Religious orders, though they have staffed parishes much as diocesan clergy do, believe that they are brothers living together, and the heads of religious orders are *elected* by their peers. They hold office for a set period of time and have to be reelected to stay in office. A diocesan rectory, by contrast, has headquartered a fief, the parish itself, given as a *benefice* to the pastor and the pastor alone. Like its Anglican equivalent, which was historically called a *living*, a benefice was bestowed as a kindness by a feudal lord. Its holder, in turn, performed a service for which he had the wherewithal to "do well," that is, not starve.

In the "classic" pre–Vatican II shape of American Catholicism, pastors had the authority of mini-lords-of-the-manor. A few were benevolent. Having themselves suffered at the hands of tyrannical pastors or other church authorities, these few refused to replicate the abuse. Instead, they promoted some measure of camaraderie that sought to buoy up rather than weigh down the men in residence. The chances of this occurring increased enormously if the pastor belonged to that rare group of priests known to be actual gentlemen. The qualities that dubbed these pastors the real thing even to their curates, or assistant priests, might not have won them awards for warmth and fuzziness, but these men had weathered "the burden of the day and its heat" while managing to hold on to the basic rules of charity and civility. They understood such rules to flow from the ideal of the priestly mystique which joined them to the great company of the apostles. Rectories headed by gentleman pastors were the closest anybody got to this ideal living situation. Nor should anyone underestimate the difficulty of the task in an all-male environment deprived of the leavening agent of women and their superior social skills. Gentlemen's rectories were a little like a men's club, where established rules guaranteed a high level of politesse and mannered personal exchanges. Today we recognize that these social codes of behavior usually presumed the absence of women, so the behavior itself has come to be seen as sexist and outmoded. But having lived in almost a dozen different groupings of ordained men, I would argue that rules of etiquette in all-male settings are imposed precisely because of the absence of women in them. Left to themselves, men revert to adolescent rituals and can't be trusted to maintain high standards of civil behavior for very long. So gentlemen's rectories were really never the norm; they were the exception to the rule. They did not of themselves create a community of those men residing in them, but they provided the conditions for a measure of social communion at the common table. Often the only place where priests gathered ("common rooms" for socializing, which are fixtures in religious communities, were virtually unknown in diocesan rectories), the dining-room table either melded or fragmented the group.

If the man presiding at the head of the table was not an actual gentleman, then he probably came from the ranks of the clergy who, some steps down the ladder, had adopted the collective nickname "Gents." A title appropriated by many of the clergy of a certain era for themselves, and a conscious parody of the real thing, "Gents" was coded speech meant only for other members of the in-group, cleverly formalizing aspects of the clerical culture that had long been operative. As Gents, men who became priests indulged their delight in their unwarranted social status even as they lived together in rectories like boys in a patriarchal household. Though their cop and fireman brothers were respected, they weren't quite as well placed as Gents. As a result, Gents soaked up the social deference they received, as they knew it was far in excess of any they would collect if not for their wearing of the black. In a dining room of Gents, young priests were socialized in the ways of the clerical life, according to informal rules that stressed deference to status and a profound inequality between priests of different age and rank. Often beneath a bad reproduction of Leonardo's *Last Supper*, at a neo-Renaissance wood-carved table at which only priests were allowed (a convenient way to exclude women from ever being invited), they learned the ways and lore of the Gents. Pity the newly ordained or the foreign-born priest who did not fit in. In short order, he would have to become used to a diet of veiled ridicule or to take his meals elsewhere.

Gents insisted on being treated reverently in public, but privately they reveled in irreverence and their secret sign was the knowing smirk. Gents were big racing fans, aficionados of cigars, steak, and scotch, who rummaged around for invitations to the premier golf links in the surrounding suburbs and expected free tickets to ball games. A famous group of them celebrated their status in a most particular way on Holy Thursday, bogusly touted as the anniversary of the priesthood's founding. Late at night, after the liturgical celebrations, while their devout parishioners maintained an all-night vigil at the repository shrine to recognize the special gift of the Eucharistic Presence, they would gather for an all-night card game because Good Friday was the one morning of the year they did not have to get up for Mass. Most Gents were willing to pay their dues and come up through the system, with its tightly structured indignities, because they knew that, if they waited patiently, they would eventually be able to dish out the same as they had received when they came into their own. Socialized to be acutely sensitive to status, they prized the pecking order that they had successfully negotiated and lorded it over younger priests like master sergeants over grunts. Having finally been recognized and promoted, they set out to enjoy the fruits of their long labors. Without knowing it, they were taking a page from the Renaissance pope who declared, after his election, "God has seen fit to bestow on us the papacy, and we intend to enjoy it!"

Certain pastors were notorious for upholding the norms peculiar to the rituals that socialized men as Gents. If a newly ordained priest was assigned to one of their parishes, he knew that his priesthood, his faith, and his sanity would be tested from the get-go. The front door was locked at a prescribed hour and assistant priests did not have a key. Nor did they possess one to the lock on the refrigerator in the rectory kitchen. Monsignor the pastor's assistant clergy exercised a constricted and meaninglessly subservient ministry, which scarred more than a few of them and prompted at least one whom I knew to decide within the first year of ordination that he had better things to do with his life than be demeaned daily. Among the constraints was the "duty system" that required a round-the-clock presence of priests in the rectory so that they could attend to tasks like hearing confessions on demand, responding to emergencies (particularly if the parish covered a local hospital), taking intentions for future Masses, and endlessly writing out Mass cards. While this task may have seemed purely "clerical" or secretarial, it was reserved for priests because it lay at the heart of the clergy's system of remuneration. Because the pay of the average priest was so poor (it was still twenty-five dollars a week plus room and board in 1970), donations from the faithful that accompanied their request for Mass to be offered for the departed soul of a loved one made up at least half the average priest's income. But in money, as in every aspect of daily ministry, the pastor exercised seigneurial privilege, and the assistants acted the role of serf—at least publicly.

Priests did have some other sources of income: the offerings for All Souls' Day Masses and tips for performing the sacraments (the remains of the "stole fees" that even today in the Third World determine whether the priest will celebrate sacraments for the faithful), but these extra and potentially rich emoluments lay completely within the discretion of the pastor to dispense or withhold. In these matters his rules were law and there was no avenue for appeal. In some dioceses, pastors continued to receive as a personal perk the entire Christmas and Easter collections, which could more than triple a man's annual income. Having survived for twenty-five years and more on the morsels his own pastors had doled out, the newly ensconced pastor reveled in his new-found power of the purse. Often, however, he found that, though he had been successfully socialized in the role of boss, he really had no training for the administrative burden of the job.

Many pastors found themselves in the unenviable situation of having had nothing to say about finances for decades, then being thrust into managing million-dollar plants with enormous budgets. No diocesan training in financial management existed; no oversight of the books was required. Collections, which provided most of the parish income, could be plundered with relative ease by unscrupulous volunteers or by the pastor himself. More than one gained competence in skimming collections for either a pet project or a personal nest egg. My first pastor after ordination was personally a parsimonious man who refused a salary, but he squirreled collection money into a secret account to provide subsidies to the parish school. It was not going to close for lack of funds on his watch! He enlisted the help of the chief collection counter for his creative accounting, only to be personally crushed when the parish accountant caught the collector-in-chief with his own hand in the till right after the pastor's.

Perhaps the authorities expected to lose a certain amount to pilfering, for reporting it to them raised nary a ripple of notice. One day, I had an opportunity to tell the vicar-general of the archdiocese about the administrator of the parish where I was residing. This administrator, a Gent's Gent, and a particularly entrepreneurial one, had already been removed as pastor of a larger parish. He regularly wrote parish checks to a woman friend living on Long Island. Then a donor's thousand-dollar check for the organ renovation fund came back endorsed into the administrator's personal account, an endorsement adding to the evidence of financial impropriety. The V.G.'s entire response—"Joe always seemed like such a nice guy"—left me with the impression that I was doing something wrong in making the report and violating the code of the Gents. Within the year, the rapacious priest had moved to an even smaller parish, the management strategy being to reduce the size of the potential pot so he could steal less. In another parish that I temporarily administered, I never got the opportunity to submit the parish budget, which by then was required by the chancery office. The pastor, out on sick leave, realized that I would have to report the five hundred dollars a month that he took off the top of the collection, which he used to pay for his condo a few towns away, and had me removed—no questions asked—for spending too much of the parish's reserved funds on needed repairs.

Even when a pastor was not larcenous, he was often duped into becoming the unwitting accomplice to fraudulent charitable schemes. The recent case of the kindly Monsignor Thomas Gradilone of Queens is a case in point. Unlike the great majority of these cases of clerical malfeasance, this one made the papers, which documented how far out a man could carry his "discretion and authority as church pastor" and still not be liable to prosecution, according to the Queens district attorney, Richard A. Brown. Reports did differ on whether the money missing from the parish collection basket amounted to $2 million or $3.7 million dispensed to "needy people" over the monsignor's nineteen years. Of the total amount, $600,000 was said to have gone to three men, one of whom reportedly stayed at the pastor's beach house regularly. Though the days of the tyrants had already passed, no one questioned or even knew about the pastor's discretionary expenditures, so closed off from public scrutiny were the actions of the parish pastor. Bishops have kept it that way because they exercise the same unmonitored use of diocesan funds.

Before the 1960s began to reshape expectations of how authoritarian a pastor could be, rectories modeled the unresponsive chain-of-command social structure to a T. While nominally beholden to those above him in the chancery and the bishop's residence, a pastor needed merely to pay his bills and keep his numbers up. Some were not above currying favor by sending generous checks to the chancery, and many looked forward to the reward of the title monsignor, recognition from the pope himself, for doing so or for engaging in the ambitious building plans that covered the landscape where Catholics were thick on the ground with ecclesiastical white elephants. Today's empty religious houses, oversized schools, and convents, as well as under-occupied rectories, all stand as memorials to the "edifice complex" that mesmerized so many in authority in those years.

By and large, pastors disguised their lack of accountability behind the modest façade that most rectories presented to the world. Few of the clergy had grown up in lavishly decorated homes, so plainness came naturally. Life at the seminary, in turn, promoted drabness, which then became generalized as rectories grew and new ones were built. The seminary Rule had specified that no art or decoration could be hung on the walls of a student's room other than the single eight-by-ten-inch reproduction of a Giotto or Fra Angelico provided by the seminary. The massive hallways were bare, broken only by the occasional alcove sheltering yet another statue of a patron saint. One visiting psychology professor dubbed the effect of the environment "sensory deprivation." Nor did the curriculum contain any instruction in liturgical art or architecture or the appreciation of either. Despite a sixteen-hundred-year tradition of beauty behind them, few diocesan priests in the U.S. church knew or cared much about aesthetics. The same earnest but uninformed pastors who administered parish churches, schools, convents, rectories, youth centers, and their staffs by the seat of their pants also made decisions about church design and the artistic enhancement of the parish's worship space, based purely on their personal taste or financial whim. Most Gents felt they could leave art and architecture in the bailiwick of Benedictines and their fellow travelers in the liturgical movement, which was eyed with suspicion by most members of the hierarchy.

Their unquestioned authority allowed many pastors in the heyday of parish plant building to indulge their desire to leave themselves a memorial not even disguised as catering to parish needs. When the pastor of Saint Mary's, where I grew up, passed away in 1961, having himself built an addition to the school and a new convent, he was replaced by a man who was eager to move on up from the Bronx to a parish in close proximity to the Westchester Country Club. Arriving in an automobile the likes of which no one had seen a priest drive, "Cadillac Jack" Corrigan had clearly decided it was time that he come into his own and live the life of a real country Gent. (Most Gents had begun to abandon the inner city, making for the suburbs in pursuit of their white flock.) Corrigan determined that the rectory could not accommodate his needs and, in short order, announced plans to extend the rectory into its modest backyard. The addition would have three floors, to accommodate an underground garage for his capacious auto; a dining room above the garage to seat twenty; and on top of that a five-room suite for himself. The skylit sitting room was lined in teakwood, a bit of opulence unknown to suburbanites at the time. But even the size of the one-man house paled next to its execution in a Swedish Modern glazed black brick—which sat amid a cluster of standard red-brick and terracotta structures. If the pastor had burned a bucket of dollar bills on the front lawn, I don't think he would have caused more comment in our mostly working-class village.

Gents like Cadillac Jack had to please only one man, the cardinal archbishop, to keep their jobs and maintain their CEO-sized lifestyles. Clerical belief in the final judgment, where the "thoughts of all hearts would be laid bare," seemed to exist in inverse proportion to any notion of accountability here below. The monsignor's peremptory style did more than deplete the parish coffers. It took a toll on at least two of the parish priests, whose fate mirrored the lives of so many of their colleagues as the 1960s unfolded. Under the old pastor, for whom propriety and piety were closely linked, the parish's three assistant priests would meet nightly in his room for a cocktail before descending together for dinner, as was common in the men's club-style rectory. Each had his assigned responsibilities, and while they did not seem personally close, they had lived and worked together cordially for at least a decade.

But in the new regime, the interior landscape of the rectory took a dark turn as church renewal entered the picture, on one side, and the pastor's palatial residence rose, on the other. The hero of my youth, Father Brogan—now a middle-aged man with twenty years of experience—became the object of Cadillac Jack's special ire. Treated either as the errant son or as an ex-favorite and subjected to the pastor's daily indignities, he descended into a pit of ulcerous but silent rage. Conditioned by a system that thrived on personal passivity, Ed Brogan moved from the milk bottle to soothe his ulcer to the wetter scourge of the impotent cleric. He began drinking to assuage his emotional and physical pain, and he let it show. By this time, I had left the parish for Dunwoodie, and I did as most people at home did: we impotently watched the drama unfold and turned our backs on the obvious injustice at work. When he was finally transferred out of the parish, Father Brogan had been dubbed "the problem" and basically moved on. The last time we spoke was on the occasion of my celebrating Mass at Saint Mary's the day after I was ordained a priest. He had graciously returned to be a concelebrant, and as it happened, he did not have to meet up with his persecutor. Due to a new policy—since abandoned—of requiring pastors to retire at seventy-five, Cadillac Jack had been ousted. At my first Mass celebration, the new pastor had demanded that a collection be taken up, though the event was scheduled separately from the parish Sunday Masses. After it was taken up, he left the altar and was not seen again that day.

The first parish where I served after ordination was set in the heart of New York's Greenwich Village, occupying a church building constructed by New York Catholics in the modish Greek Revival style of the time (1833). (To this day, Saint Joseph's, Waverly Place, has assumed a role as a beacon parish of the Vatican Council's reform of worship and life.) Given the right pastor, a young priest thinks that he can do almost anything. And for a year the tide flowed only in one direction. Things went screwy after that. But not because of any confrontations I had with the Gent establishment. They would come later. The newly appointed pastor—a former professor whom I regarded very highly—along with myself and another new assistant, Bob Lott, five years my senior and a workaholic, all strove together to refocus the parish's orientation toward the neighborhood and its vibrant cultural life, opening the church and rectory to social concerns and inviting a host of parishioners and visitors to the previously off-limits rectory table. The pastor loved to entertain, and sumptuous dinners as prepared by Assunta, the new cook from the neighboring Italian parish, became regular social events. A pastorally minded intellectual, he had once named a friend's dog Hincmar, after the medieval theologian Hincmar of Rheims. "He was a reasonable proponent of papal primacy and a staunch defender of clerical celibacy" was the way he explained his choice. But as his tenure lengthened, somehow the intellectual aspects of the job and the thrum of pastoral life no longer held his attention the way they once had. In short order he was pairing off with women he had invited to dinner, settling at last upon one whom he moved into the rectory after an apartment fire dislocated her. He withdrew his support for some of the new programs that Bob, an incomparable crusader, had put into place. Confrontation followed, and when the local episcopal vicar became aware of the strife and announced a formal visitation, he resigned after twenty-nine years as a priest, moved out the next day, and was married in a few weeks' time.

The day after hearing from this man who had been my mentor that he was chucking the priesthood to marry, I was still in shock. Just before I left the rectory the next day to say the noon Mass, he called me to his room and, amid his packed belongings and books, knelt before me and asked for my blessing. Managing to get through Mass (it was the Feast of the Beheading of John the Baptist), I walked out to the porch of the church afterward just as he was finishing loading his car. He waved and sped away. Sitting on the fire escape outside the sacristy ten minutes later, I broke down in tears, because I knew that the issues that had driven this consummately devoted priest to leave the celibate ministry would haunt me for years to come. One week to the day later, I was summoned to the chancery and asked to accept the position as Catholic Chaplain at Columbia University and Barnard College. The deal sweetener was that the diocese would underwrite my doctoral studies, something previously withheld. I remember calling home and telling my mother of the offer. Her response made a lot of sense: "Will you be your own boss there?" she asked. I thought about it and replied, "Yes, I think so." "Take it," she said, and I did.

During the two years that I was assigned to Saint Joseph's in the Village, some aspects of priests' lives came into my purview that might have been lifted from the pages of bad fiction. Some of these men I ran into unintentionally, like the seriously mean, tough drunk I was asked to look in on one night in the E.R. at Saint Vincent's Hospital. Clued in by a resident that he was "one of yours," I tried to extend some brotherly concern to the priest, only to be treated to vituperative wrath: What did some young shit know about what he was going through? Others I met in the rectory when they arrived unannounced and confessed anonymously. The first time this happened, I found myself sitting face-to-face in the office with a mild-mannered, balding priest from the Jersey suburbs who told me of his habit of coming into the city on his days off to wander around Times Square (these were the days when Forty-second Street hosted almost nothing but porno movie houses) or to come down to the Village to assuage his loneliness. Figuring him to be bored, I gave him a penance that required him to read the Gospel of Mark meditatively, to keep him occupied for an afternoon. His face registered more than a little surprise.

Others who opened up to me were more tortured by their desires, especially those who came from very culturally Catholic countries to the south and now found themselves in a far less repressive environment. One man bitterly told of his seminary spiritual director, who gave these instructions to help men in holy orders remain chaste: "If you are tempted by a woman, think of her as your mother or sister to stem your concupiscence. If that doesn't work, imagine yourself lusting after the Blessed Mother. That should stop you!" Sadly, it hadn't, and he remained seriously conflicted. Another man, struggling with his homosexual urges, had spent time as a student in Rome and assured me that the Vatican was full of people like himself. His tales of the highest-level curial coupling seemed a little overheated, but the dilemma in which he was caught, between a promised chastity and hopes for sexual fulfillment, rang terribly true. Slowly, I began to learn about the unexpectedly broad spectrum along which the clergy stretched their adherence to celibacy.

For a year after my reassignment to the campus, I remained in residence in the Village, but a new pastor, the demands of my new job, and course work in biblical studies militated against my staying. Moving to a residence housing almost forty priests, most of whom taught at Cardinal Hayes High School, which was on the floors below, gave me neutral space in which to retreat and do academic work. But it also gave me much more contact with a cross section of the clergy I had previously been able to avoid. With so many priests collected in one place, you could count on finding a fair number of Gents in residence, regularly looking for an opportunity to break up the monotony of their daily routine. In congregate settings, avoidance would go only so far because Gents often sought opportunities to be cock of the walk. A few months after I moved in, two of the Gent brethren who had been reassigned returned to the school for the traditional farewell dinner thrown in their honor. I arrived back from my campus job after the dinner hour and so missed the speeches and, that night, passed on the conviviality. Instead of joining in, I chatted with a friend who lived at the end of a wing of rooms farthest from the never-ending party, then went to my own room.

But the Gents never liked it when everyone wasn't having the same fun that they were having. Opting out obviously threatened the good feeling the group sustained with alcohol past eleven o'clock on a school night. So, like frat members on the prowl for victims, the main celebrants started wandering the halls, banging on doors, trying to rouse guys who had left the party too early for the needy egos of the honorees. Ready for bed and weary of the noise, but an outsider who was a guest and was suspect (the school principal had already told me) for wanting "to change things," I hung back for as long as I could. When the carousing went on and no one checked the celebrating drunks out in the corridor, I finally opened my door and confronted Big Mike, who was closest to my room. He seemed a little cowed, but not so his street-tough companion. Father Jim Gorman was not going to let some young snot who hadn't paid his dues in a high school classroom of horny Catholic boys reprimand his buddy. Even as the bigger man turned away, Gorman came hurtling down the hallway cursing at me for disrespect as I braced myself to throw the first punch of my adult life. Like guardian angels, two men who had been commiserating across the hall emerged. One was the dean of discipline, who spent most of his days containing the teenage boys of the school. Quiescent up till now, he stepped between me and the irate party animal just as my friend, Charles, moved me firmly out of the hallway and back into my room. No one ever spoke of the event again.

Gents indulged in other rites of camaraderie, vacationing outside diocesan boundaries to ensure some protective anonymity. Attired in loud Hawaiian shirts or Caribbean-style guayaberas, the Gent's version of mufti, they often gave themselves away with their black socks and black shoes sticking out from their holiday attire. But they went dancing anyway and, like sailors on liberty, often drank too much and flirted liberally. One time, after carousing the night away in the Hamptons, a couple of clerical swells dropped off their dates for the evening (normally they kept their sexual activity to the level of groping, faithful to rules they had learned in adolescence). As they got back in their car after some good-night snuggling, one of the women—a nurse from the city also enjoying a few days at the shore—turned to her date for the evening and surprised him by cooing, "Good night, Monsignor Barry."

Being unmasked like that after a night's harmless socializing only confirmed Jack Barry's place in the lore of the Gents. A talented and personable man, he had enjoyed a career in the diocesan administration, graced as he was with Irish wit and the ability to charm both lay donors and members of the higher clergy. He clearly had set his sights high, which made some of his adolescent acting out unusual, but he seemed invigorated by the riskiness of the behavior. As the years passed and his career dead-ended, his wit took on an edge of simmering anger. When he recounted his exploits, as he enjoyed doing, he would become animated, particularly in the hearing of younger priests whom he could shock with his vulgar accounts. The force of his personality emanated from the underside of his charm, his delight in bullying guys from whom he thought he smelled the scent of disapproval. I felt it up close, one evening, when he dropped in on a group of my peers as we gathered to visit a friend at the rectory where he was residing. Entering, he scanned the circle of faces and measured how best to mark his territory before departing. As he regaled us with some details of a recent night out, he offered this perverted tidbit of male bravado, striking a dancer's pose and moving his hands to illustrate: "Wouldn't it be great if women had a third teat? You know, one on their back, so you could work it while you're dancing with them!" Amid the nervous laughter, I spoke up, taking exception to an idea as disgusting as it was misogynistic. His just-below-the-surface rage flamed forth right at me. I had challenged the lion in his lair and I would not come off unscathed. He belittled me as a "fem" who didn't participate in the rituals of maleness. All I ever did was "piss up a rope," he declared. I guess I had come to expect a Gent like him to do a little cock waving when around other members of the tribe. After he left, I picked up some sympathy, but most of the group expected little more from him and seemed content not to have fallen prey to his foul mouth. Again, the incident became wrapped in a shroud of silence from that night on. For, even among my close peers, any candid discussion of these behaviors got buried beneath the evasion and silence that many priests had brought with them from boyhood. Like children of alcoholics or the victims of child abuse, silence about the most neuralgic issues affecting us remained the rule. I used to joke that the unwritten rule aped the saying "*De mortuuis nil nisi bonum*" ("Speak naught but good of the dead"). Nor of priests! Sadly the two groups mirrored each other in more ways than one.

Gents, in particular, thrived on this habit of self-protective secrecy, which has deep roots in both ancient taboos and modern dysfunction. It insists on privacy above all, under cover of a bogus sacred quality that supposedly attaches itself to priests because they deal with holy things. But like all sacred cows, the notion of an essential or ontologically distinct character attaching to any person (or an object or a place) easily becomes a substitute for the real thing—an idol. The reality of a man's ordination lies in its confirming the gift given him in baptism and in its issuing a

further calling: to commit himself to greater personal and ministerial accountability, not less. But in an effort to be exempt from
the painful growth and change that comes from a dynamic vocation—the life of "intolerable purifications" that Thomas Merton
struggled after and wrote about so movingly—Gents place loyalty
to the corps over honesty, candor, or integrity. In our present situation, when priests shielding priests has produced such tragedy
and fostered actual criminality, the complex of attitudes and actions that this distorted idea of loyalty sets up in the lives of
priests deserves much better than an ism. But "clericalism" will
have to do. The system of thought and action that exempts clergy
from the common lot of accountability and makes loyalty to the
fraternity a supernal virtue, clericalism gave rise to the code of
the Gents. But it is really more basic than vulgar acting out and
deserves to be looked at in its more official manifestations.

The system may nowhere be codified, but it operates almost
instinctively, like the jaws of a steel trap. At a meeting sometime
in the early 1970s between Cardinal Cooke, his lieutenants, and a
committee of the Priests' Senate—one of those ambitious but ultimately futile efforts at enacting Vatican II's doctrine of collegiality—I heard that trap snap shut. At issue was a yearly assembly of
the clergy that I was involved in planning. We had chosen the
topic "Ministry and Morale" for, less than ten years after the Vatican Council, we felt the momentum flagging and the challenge
of renewal falling victim to institutional stasis. A steady stream of
priests continued to resign from the ministry, most of them to
marry. Those of us relatively new to the ministry, and others who
had been energized by early efforts to democratize spirituality
and leadership, were anxious to call a spade a spade and confront
the problems facing the whole institution. But the cardinal was
not anxious to do so, and we were meeting to hammer out our
differences.

Meetings with this cardinal were always a bit of a trip. Their
normal style took indirection and periphrasis to new heights,

though in retrospect I see that they probably reached the height of Catholic participatory democracy. His Eminence always played facilitator—his social-worky style coming out—but he was a past master at massaging the discussion, hearing what he wanted to hear and disregarding the rest. We senators were not exactly playing along, and as tempers heated and the boss was plainly getting annoyed, one of the chief's men chimed in: "But surely you fathers see that if you press your agenda and bring these matters before the assembly, you will appear disloyal to the cardinal. Surely, no one here would think of public disloyalty, would you, Father Bob? What about you, Father Ray?" He glanced reassuringly toward the head of the table and passed control of the meeting back to the boss. The argument had come to a close, the cardinal wrapped up the agenda, and the committee left with its tail between its legs again.

Loyalty to the reverend chief assumes assent to his policies and actions, as well as closing any gap between them and the person of the leader. The personality cult that results, whether at the Kremlin, the Vatican, or the local chancery, makes all would-be collaborators play the role of mere dependents. The clerical brand of loyalty binds a priest not to the office of bishop or even to the church but to the individual holding the office. This loyalty, in turn, displaces religious commitment to the community of believers, as personal loyalty glues the clerical corps together. Instead of fostering faith among the people, the clerical system seeks to command further loyalty to the corps above all. The whole system presumes closed ranks and closed mouths.

The average priest will buy into this model of his life and work because there are benefits for him as well. Words and actions said or done under cover of the priesthood earn not just credibility but a certain unimpeachability—that is, until the recent past. In previous years, respect for the office spilled over and created a protective force field around the holders of the office that makes the infamous "blue wall of silence" look like Swiss cheese. The two codes have been justified by similar us-against-them thinking. The police have felt that they deserve the special protection extended when brothers watch one another's backs because of the clear and present danger they see themselves in when doing their jobs. In similar fashion, priests have not felt accountable to the laity (or even less to the public at large) because they see their lives as difficult exceptions to the common rule. But cops bond personally and emotionally with other cops. Priests bond with an ultimately faceless ideal. Discouraged from forming close personal relationships with other men in the seminary, priests (even the most convivial of the Gents) often find friendship daunting. There is an additional strain that comes between priests as each develops certain client-type arrangements that vie with peer relationships. Because a celibate priest must be a loner by definition, he is always prone to become a mini-sun at the center of his own system of orbiting satellites. Like Father Cyprian in Mary Gordon's novel *The Company of Women*, who collected a circle of needy women about him, a priest compensates for the loss of personal intimacy by radiating his needs outward. As surely as the sun's light is reflected off the moon, people willing to be a satellite gather and confirm the special role that Father plays for them.

Like stars of media, sports, and entertainment—where serial marriages and broken friendships abound—men at the center of a circle where they receive undue attention have a problem when they're offstage. They become so conditioned to performing that they can't turn off the public smile, tone down the rhetoric, or play a supporting role for anyone else. There were times when I'd be eating breakfast among the dozens of priests I was residing with at the high school when I could not help but get the impression that I was listening to simultaneous monologues by stand-up comedians competing for an audience. One old monsignor would be lamenting not his approaching death, but his social situation afterward ("The goddamn thing about purgatory is that you're going to be stuck there with people you don't like!"), while one of the resident history professors would be reading the *Times* and, apropos of I don't know what in 1975, he'd denounce Franklin Delano Roosevelt. Out from behind a lectern or lacking a pulpit, the typical priest's life of crowded solitude makes growing in relationship with a genuine peer particularly difficult. Gents, in particular, tend to duck the challenge, responding to any demands for intimacy with braggadocio and pack loyalty. They circle the wagons and hunker down among their own, more convinced than ever that "they" just don't understand how much crap "we" take. But they offer no genuine emotional support to one another, only a semblance of it.

But, of course, not every priest is a Gent or seeks to be one. Still, unless a man has strong convictions to inoculate him against the culture of the Gents, it acts as the default mode for the New York priesthood and will suck him into it. Resisters could be found in several camps: the gentlemen priests I have already mentioned, for whom a certain social and religious breeding counteracted any attraction to the Gents' macho bluster, and a more numerous group, who combined learning with pastoral strategy in a way that helped them to avoid the shenanigans of the clerical society boys. Some of these were academics, whose years at graduate institutes, like Catholic University or the Roman universities, broadened their intellectual and social boundaries. But most were the men, drawn from the 1940s onward into what was loosely termed the "Spanish apostolate." My own story pulled me into campus work, but many of the men I admired most in the priesthood mounted their collective defense against the values of the Gents by making, early on, what became known as "the fundamental option for the poor."

Almost every one of them came from the clergy's ranks of

Irish-Americans, by far the most numerous subgroup of priests, but also the group seemingly most sensitive to exclusion of an immigrant group. (Not that they had always been so. Perhaps a new generation had decided, "We're not going to do to the Hispanics what we did to the Italians!") In the period after World War II, when Cardinal Spellman was recruiting priests from Italy to serve their compatriots in New York, he also launched a proactive initiative to minister to the waves of new immigrants from Latin America. He established an institute at the Catholic University of Puerto Rico in Ponce, eventually run by the charismatic Father Ivan Ilych, and began sending newly ordained priests there to undertake a course of study that would mark most of them for life. Forty and fifty years later, some New York priests are still serving in the same parishes among the poor that they went to when they came back from "P.R."

In its classic form, the institute was a rebirthing experience. Priests (and later seminarians) went there, were doused in Spanish-American language and culture by the likes of the Jesuit sociologist Father Joe Fitzpatrick, and came back *puertoriceño*, or later a Dominican from the Republic. Reputed to be one of the most brilliant and intense priests, Father Ilych would meet with each student alone for lunch to get to know him and personally help in his transformation. Most days, at the end of the seven or eight hours of intense language instruction in Spanish, he led a holy hour in the chapel to fill out the learning experience with an ascetic component. While the program did immunize the great majority of its participants from getting caught up in the worst of the clerical subculture, it could not completely isolate them from all of the influences of the inner city back home. One of its most successful graduates, Monsignor Bob Fox, a fabled activist in charge of the Summer in the City program that targeted minority youth and brought needed government money to poor areas, upped and left to marry during the years of the Great Defection (the late 1960s). But many of those men who went this alternative route in ministry have continued to fight the good fight down to the present.

In the last thirty years, the living situations in which Gents thrived have been severely reduced by the grim actuarial statistics of the aging priesthood. Many rectories today host only one or two occupants, a reduction that exacerbates the tendency priests already have to self-isolate. The best priest, in such a lonely setting, develops ticks and habits that stem not from his nature, but from a starvation environment. All the challenges faced by a man who is not personally accountable on a daily basis to any other living person grow grimmer by the year. Even when we were still in the seminary, stories filtered back about a number of priests recently moved into rectories who cracked under the strain. One man was so traumatized by the daily task of facing a crowd of people and communicating with them—once the altars had been turned to face the congregation—that he lapsed into catatonia. Other men responded to their discomfort with life in a house of noncommunicative men by taking advantage of the more general openness of rectories by the late 1960s. They actively socialized with the parish population of teenage boys. Nothing could have seemed more natural or more comfortable to them. The rectory provided boys and young men, often at odds with their families, a place to hang out; it gave the priest a role to play in the parish (as well as company and a hedge against loneliness), won him admiration for spending time with teenagers, and gave him the kind of narcissistic feedback that he got from no one else. Few knew at the time that some priests were playing with fire and, in a minority of cases, were pursuing an explicitly narcissistic sexual agenda that used and discarded young men.

But in most cases, priests who attracted adolescents and young

men into their social orbit and hosted them in groups in their
rooms or other social spaces in rectories had no predatory
agenda. No one can deny any longer that the predators existed
and that, under cover of creating an opportunity for male adolescents to socialize, men like Ed Pipala, allowed by the chancery to
take his sickness with him from one pastoral setting to another,
manipulated young men's burgeoning sexuality to meet his own
stunted and deprived sexual desires. But the most ruinous aspect
of the fraud that he and others have perpetrated lies in their pretending to do what generations of other priests had done so well:
to make a place for boys to fit in, to provide adolescents with an
adult male who cared about and could nurture them, and help
them move on from this temporary peer support group into a
wider world of friendship and love. If they lack this kind of interaction with their peers, guided by adults who help create some
kind of neutral ground—not unlike that which therapists are supposed to create—adolescent males themselves often become
predatory, seeking out weaker males to bully or women to molest.
In adolescent male groupings (not merely a teenage category), biology can become social destiny, with everyone the worse off for
it. Part of the tragedy that the Catholic church is enduring in the
early years of the twenty-first century stems from how the sins of
the relatively few (but far more than we ever imagined) have
tainted the record of generations of priests and others, like both
the French and the Irish Christian Brothers or the Salesians, in
civilizing and socializing young men. Helping teenage boys not to
feel like outsiders, giving them a safe space to be themselves over
against an adult world they do not yet understand, gives them a
shot, according to Erik Erikson, at consolidating an individual
identity in concert with society rather than against it. Focusing
their latent idealism through physical discipline or academic rigor,
helping them test their strength (even by wrestling with them), not
judging them by their acne or their accent, and being appropri-

ately affectionate—all these activities that older men in the
church have done for centuries are now threatened, but not just
by the depredations of the molesting minority.

In at least some cases that have also become notorious of late,
the activity of the priests involved clearly stemmed from their
own arrested sexual development. In this matter, there are obvious analogies between priests engaged in sexual acting out with
adolescents and Gents who reenacted their unfinished adolescence by fooling around with women. And both are akin to the
experience of so many alcohol and drug abusers (clerical and lay)
whose emotional maturity is said to have stalled at the approxi-
mate time they started getting wasted. Priests who were not
"successful" adolescents, or who brought into adulthood their un-
fulfilled emotional agendas from earlier in life—not unlike Boy
Scout leaders who bring their own traumatized youth to their job
of toughening up the next generation—often had a boundary
problem when hanging around pubescent boys. They didn't
know where their needs ended and where their young charges'
curiosity would get the better of them both. Society's presumption that the adult in this situation is always the more responsible
person makes sense. But needy adults, especially those raised on a
diet of silence, denial, and deprivation, don't make good moral
subjects, even when they remain legally liable for their irresponsi-
ble behavior. Their guilt has a social dimension that church authority would like to be able to avoid, claiming, for instance (with
the IRS), that priests are indepenent contractors, not employees
of a diocese!

For whatever the individual pathologies may be that James
Porter acted out in his multiple acts of child molestation (genuine
pedophilia) or that Paul Shanley, and others like him, brought to
bear in their sexual abuse of male adolescents, they shared something dreadful with their leadership and with many other priests:
a clericalism designed to insulate them from the consequences of
the underside of their spiritual desires. These priests represent a

small minority (no more than 3 percent by recent counts), but their pathology is telling and representative of the priesthood, for it combines clerical exceptionalism with a sense of deprivation in equal parts. Their bishops, who shuffled them around, preserving their status as priests at the cost of making more young people victims of priestly sexual abuse—these men shared the same pathology, expressing it only to a different degree.

Allow me to explain, if I can. From early in their seminary education (the word "formation" always sent shivers up my spine), candidates for the priesthood were encouraged to see themselves "not like the rest of men," because of their ability to eschew the "normal" sacramental route to sanctity, namely, marriage and child rearing. Lacking a religious vow to life in community, the secular priesthood forged a necessary link between celibacy and ordination, thereby creating a deep tension in a priest's self-understanding. He possessed a unique power, but he gained it only by promising to deprive himself for a lifetime. Though the call to ministry was understood as a gift from God, even a sign that he was one of God's chosen, the church had attached strings to the call. Only those willing to be tied by those strings could answer the call. Leading authorities always assured us that God would not allow us to be tempted beyond our capacity, but it was clearly *not* God who was demanding celibacy of us—no matter what the bishops claimed. What's more, by laying down a privation as the stepping-stone to the glories of the priesthood, they set up a group ideal that was sure to feel as empty as a baptismal font on Good Friday when the individual priest spent five years, then ten, then decades without intimacy with a partner. One by-product of the exchange has been a lot of spilled semen in the rectories of America—and that by priests who are considered faithful; a greater one is a range of sexual acting out, from the severely pathological to the normal but hidden coupling that a subset of priests have always engaged in.

A priest's resentment of celibacy usually does not emerge full-blown until some years after he is ordained. Then, not surprisingly, a sexual awakening, though delayed or repressed for years, can emerge at least as energetically as, if not more than, it erupts in a horny teenager. If a priest's self-discovery is coupled with strong sexual attraction—often akin to a first crush—he will find ways both to entertain and to justify his desires. For the ideal that he has of himself as a self-giving, generous, other-directed person dedicated to serving God does not shrivel up and die when he feels overwhelmed by recrudescent sexual desire. His newfound feelings do not cancel his conviction that he is one of the chosen. They usually get woven into his grandiose notion of his calling. The resulting attitude has been described to me by a therapist friend as an eruption of virtually infantile omnipotence, a willingness to defy any parental authority, internalized or actual, that might disapprove. A priest in the throes of lustful self-discovery will say things like "If *their* God doesn't forgive me, I know that *mine* will!" Welded into the priesthood by the explicit ideology of perpetuity ("You are a priest forever according to the order of Melchizedek"), and unable to imagine life outside the all-encompassing world of the clergy, a priest can act out in a variety of ways. Some begin to behave flirtatiously—with teenagers, with available women, or with other priests. I was twenty-seven years old the first time I was propositioned by a priest ten or fifteen years my senior. We both had had too much to eat and drink at dinner after a Senate meeting. But I was clearheaded enough to know that he was looking for sex and, though finding it difficult to believe what was happening, told him I wasn't interested. Before that evening's shock, I had been flattered by the attention of a clever and very charming older colleague, but as a result of his seductive maneuvering, I chose never to be in his company again. Other priests bypass the subtle efforts that he engaged in, visiting the seminary gym and trawling in the steam room, for a friend. They take up much riskier behaviors like prowling gay bars to find Mr. Right, at least for the night.

I first learned about this subculture when I made the mistake of seeking out a priest friend to get a read on how he was dealing with celibacy. As I approached forty, I had sought counseling and had been urged to talk to my peers and find out how others in my position were handling it. So I turned to Rocky, as I'll call him. Over an otherwise pleasant lunch, Rocky told me that he had decided there was no reason to fight his feelings at all. He had sex with random partners whom he would meet at bars, on trips, wherever. It was too great, he said, to waste energy on avoiding. I was startled. Seeing this, he sought to reassure me that, far from throwing off his equilibrium, being sexually active in the gay club scene made him a much happier person and a more productive member of the cardinal's staff.

What allowed Monsignor Rocky to lead his double life was clericalism's rule of silence: as long as you don't make a mess and can be discreet, then you remain a "priest in good standing." So it was when my longtime friend Rick, who had waged a successful campaign to reenter the seminary and be ordained, went to the cardinal ten years later and asked for time off to determine whether his newly emergent gay identity and his being a priest were compatible. As he later told me, Cardinal Cooke made no demands that he resign, and assured him that exploring the one did not have to mean compromising the other. Today, he, too, remains a "priest in good standing," but we grew apart over the issue and lost touch. From his perspective, the only mistake he made was initially violating what my therapist friend has called "the Canon Law of the hierarchy: 'Don't ask, don't tell' " in matters of sexual activity. In general, frankness creates a disturbance in the Force Mystique. It's unnecessary, for as long as your needs (and, regretfully, sinful deeds) don't interfere with your duties, God will forgive them. The fraternity of Christ's alter egos will not turn its back on its own, no matter who it is that they're banging, because priesthood once conferred isn't just a job for which you can be declared ineligible. In the common view of the hierarchy (which opinion still has a strong lobby in Rome), ordination alters a man's very being; hence, the health of the clergy's group ideal depends less on the integrity of any of its members than on maintaining the priesthood's special status in a world filled with corruption and moral compromise. The recent press accounts of the priest in Queens, New York, who spent parish school funds for his live-in boy lover seem to confirm the pattern. Reported regularly by the laywoman principal, he was neither removed nor disciplined for several years. When finally made to move, he took up residence in another parish while the civil, not the religious, authorities looked into the matter.

It seems that guys of a certain type, for whom the priesthood is too encompassing to leave but too constraining to live within, act out their conflict by engaging in riskier and riskier behavior. I can't help but believe that the risk taking helps some priests deal with the inner dissonance they feel between the ideal they once espoused and the anger and confusion they now feel over its demands. Not surprisingly, some of the resentment has turned inward and led directly to some men bringing on their own destruction.

Take the rise and fall of Bishop Emerson Moore as one of the starkest examples in recent memory. What I relate here is nothing more than what was common knowledge among the clergy in New York in the last five years of his life. Loyal to the memory of a kind man and to the old saw of not scandalizing the faithful, would-be tellers have maintained silence. Because bishops are twice-anointed after baptism, they wield for Catholics double the mystique of the priest. So silence about episcopal indiscretions guards the ideal at least twofold. But telling his story will certainly cause no more sensation than the news bulletins we have become familiar with in the last year or so. Perhaps it will remove another brick in the wall separating the clergy from the people in matters of accountability. A congenial, handsome black man, Emmy Moore went through the seminary at a time when very few men of color made that journey. He was ordained in 1964, earlier in the same year that my class entered Dunwoodie, at the halfway point of Vatican II. As the 1960s unfolded and the civil rights movement drew bonneted Sisters of Charity, among others, into the streets of Harlem and Selma, Alabama, the relatively small number of black Catholic priests became more visible and symbolically significant. In April 1968, the newly appointed Archbishop (not yet Cardinal) Cooke marched prominently just behind the mule-drawn wagon that bore the slain Martin Luther King, Jr., to his burial, just two months before he would preside over Robert F. Kennedy's funeral in his own cathedral. It was only a matter of time until one of the few black priests in New York would be made an auxiliary, or assistant, bishop to the cardinal.

When that time came, one priest whom most people pegged for the job had resigned the ministry and left to marry, and a second had proved such a thorn in the institution's side that he wouldn't be considered. Years more passed until finally, in 1983, Emerson got the call from Rome and was ordained a bishop at the comparatively young age of forty-four. Statuesque in his full bishop's regalia, he was appointed pastor of Harlem's principal parish, Saint Charles Borromeo, and named Episcopal Vicar (or the cardinal's personal representative) to Harlem. By all accounts, as one of the three or so black bishops in the country, Emmy had a future in the hierarchy, a thought that gave many people hope because he was accessible, democratically inclined, and not at all princely in his manner. For some years, he carried on his duties admirably, during which time his social-worker boss died and was succeeded by Archbishop John J. O'Connor. But somewhere along the way, riven by either self-doubt or sexual torment, Emmy became an addict. Stories circulated about young men of dubious pedigree coming and going from the rectory. His behavior grew erratic, and he occasionally missed celebrating confirmation at a parish that was expecting him. For years, nothing changed and no action was taken. Then he was caught siphoning a donation of some ten thousand dollars or so (said to be from George Steinbrenner of the New York Yankees) from the parish coffers. Removed from Saint Charles and assigned to the priests' residence at Cardinal Spellman High School, he seemed to be living a relatively unmonitored life, ducking rehab, left on a very long leash by his new boss even when family members pleaded with the new cardinal to do something. One morning, the story goes, Emmy walked into the residence's dining room and asked an elderly priest if he could borrow his car to go to a funeral. Finding it hard to turn down a bishop, the older man gave him the keys but insisted that he needed it back by supper. The hour came and went. No bishop. No car. The mystery only deepened the next morning when Emmy walked into the dining room again and informed the priest, with regrets for not telling him sooner, that the car had been stolen. The tale provoked some outrage, as most priests who heard it guessed he had hocked it for drugs, but the clergy's eleventh commandment, "Thou shalt not be accountable," was operating in high gear.

Soon after, Bishop Moore, drawn and feeble, developed wasting syndrome, and word got out that he had AIDS. A friend who greeted him at a church event bear-hugged him and found almost nothing left of him. Shortly afterward, Emerson slipped away to a hospice far from his family and friends, where he died, his occupation listed as "a laborer," of an AIDS-related illness in 1995. Media silence around his unhappy end may have been prompted by sympathy and by a scandal surrounding the country's highest-ranking black prelate, Archbishop Eugene Marino of Atlanta, a year or so earlier. He was caught misusing funds to maintain his mistress, with whom he had publicly vacationed and traveled, and was forced to resign. No one in the archdiocese, for over a year, had managed to confront His Excellency or go public with the scandal. Only his financial mismanagement finally called a halt to his fling, not any ability of the clerical system to police itself. Disgraced, the archbishop apologized and retired to a monastery and has not been heard from again. After this fiasco, to make a lot out of the story of Bishop Moore might have seemed gratuitous.

All these tales of the clergy's sexual activity—from the friskiness of the Gents, to actively gay clergy cruising and the sexual abuse of underage youth, combined with alcohol and drug abuse—do highlight moral lapses on the part of individuals. But taken together with the hierarchy's willingness to cover it all up, often at great monetary expense to their people, they show how an institution with no accountability structure for its top leadership turns corrupt. Recently, I attended a meeting in my own parish which drew over two hundred parishioners, angry that their pastor, who had been summarily removed because of previous allegations, had in fact been assigned to our parish when the previous pastor had functioned for years under a cloud of allegations of impropriety. Though Cardinal Egan had been invited to attend to listen to the people's anger and frustration, his office pleaded a scheduling conflict. Auxiliary Bishop James McCarthy, who came in his place, put on a bravura performance, highly recommending the fill-in priest who had been assigned—he had done the same for the now-removed priest!—and instructing the faithful present on things that couldn't be expected to change ("There are some things that have been revealed," he said to one woman who urged that we try some female leadership for a change). He also sought to win sympathy from the crowd when he recounted how difficult it was to counsel a woman who came to him about an affair with a priest, asking about how she should handle her complaint. He stayed that night until midnight, talking with the most concerned and distraught parishioners.

Then, within the space of two months, Bishop Jim himself resigned as pastor of his parish and as an auxiliary bishop, admitting to serial affairs when he was still a parish priest. Another bag-carrying secretary to the cardinal (this time, John J. O'Connor, who did not live long enough to see his protégé disgraced), Jim was a Gent of impeccable credentials who had been vetted and approved by the Vatican's bishop-making machine. Without all the unrelenting publicity regarding the clergy's sexual misconduct in the previous six months, he probably would never have been outed and would have continued to play the role of concerned member of the hierarchy. But though the bishops at their Dallas meeting in June 2002 did little to police their errant members, he never made it to the meeting. Cardinal Egan was not about to bypass this opportunity to discipline a protégé of his predecessor's—there was no love lost between them. He ordered Bishop Jim to resign and go for psychological testing.

To this day, most of the diminishing number of Catholic diocesan priests in this country go about their business dutifully and as imaginatively as they can, given the constraints of dwindling finances and their own depleted reserves of energy. They are ipso facto not corrupt or guilty. They are trapped in a system where, no matter their years or their experience, their personal holiness or their preaching ability, they have virtually nothing to say about the shape of Catholic leadership. Their own ministry and counseling evolve. Through struggling with their own sexuality, learning from their mistakes, and listening to believers around them, they follow the general law of religious development: "To live is to change." But that law, formulated a century and a half ago by John Henry Newman, has run smack into a religious ideology of changelessness. As a result, priests who minister fifty years are expected to act the same way, preach the same things, spout the same ready solutions to complicated moral problems, and relate the Good News as if it were yesterday's edition of the Old News. The men who run the church see this as "fidelity," not a failure to grow.

For their part, as priests get older they accommodate themselves to the discouraging reality of clerical life. As one bishop after another is imposed from above and proceeds to make decisions about them, their flocks, and their lives and then moves on to his next job up the hierarchical line, they become resigned and often just plain tired. These careerist hierarchs have but one loyalty—to the fathers above them, whose favor they have attracted in the past and wish to maintain above all. They all mouth a commitment to bringing the reality into line with the ideal of selfless service, but they act principally to protect the mystique that itself exists to gloss over the far more ambiguous reality. Chaining priestly ministry to celibacy cuts most men off from their own interiority far more than it unleashes their generosity. It creates the Gent mentality as surely as the rigidity in the Soviet Communist system created the boorish habits of the comrades who, when the winds shifted, robbed their countries blind.

Rectories, too, have become traps, where today the empty rooms match the hollow hopes of the remaining residents. As living situations, they promote the solitary habits that isolate many men from their own energy sources and reinforce their own social dysfunction. In such environments, lonely men turn to a variety of self-soothing mechanisms, the chief of which is probably the solo alcohol consumption that debilitates so many. Drinking alone is a coping strategy that helps a priest face endless repetitive tasks, feigning dutifulness, but fooling no one other than perhaps himself. Other men become pet caretakers, dogs being their chief surrogate companions, as they are for a lot of single people. It helps when you come home to be able to talk to another living being that retains loyalty and puts your need for comfort on a par with its own needs for food and affection. Dogs will, in fact, return the affection, share your bed, and even minister to your wounds, licking where it aches and asking no questions. In these solitary kingdoms, other lonely men become collectors of every imaginable object, piling papers and trash as if to insulate themselves from the world whose demands seem so overwhelming.

To combat these propensities, many dioceses have created mentoring programs for younger clergy or have combined men-

toring with clerical affinity groups to help break down the isolation that besets so many. Early after ordination, a number of us
formed such a group on our own, meeting monthly, making annual retreats, getting together socially for dinner, and so on. This
certainly eased the wrong kind of solitude, but it also locked us
into a strange half-world of pseudointimacy. We talked, we shared,
we laughed and told some of the same stories, over and over and
over . . . But we didn't reveal ourselves beyond a certain point.
References to sexual ideation had nowhere to go. We spent years
in one another's occasional company and barely got to know one
another, so fixed were the constraints built into our expectations of our brother priests. As the years went by, I was fortunate
enough to have found another source of self-knowledge and met
some genuine companions in spiritual struggle in a place where I
was not looking for them. Paradoxically, it was at Columbia University, the "big factory of a campus" where Thomas Merton
experienced illuminating grace via human friendship, that a different template for how nature and grace interact emerged in my
life and thinking. Being a priest there for fifteen years allowed me
to shape a ministry that wove together many threads of experience in ways that I could not have imagined by myself. But the
ministry there shaped me as well and confirmed my convictions
about the vitality of our sacramental heritage and the way the
priesthood, as now configured, was stifling its enormous potential
for good.

Four

On the Heights

*I*N HIS CLASSIC AUTOBIOGRAPHY, *The Seven Storey Mountain*, Thomas Merton described the university where I had accepted an assignment in September 1973 as Catholic chaplain as "Poor Columbia!" It had been "founded by devout Protestants as a college predominantly religious" but had gone astray, by which Merton meant it had adopted a very secular philosophy. Nevertheless, for the next thirty-four years, Columbia continued to support a chaplain, assisted by a Protestant, a Jewish, and a Catholic "counselor," all of whom worked in Earl Hall. But after the clergy had supported the most activist students during the pitched battles that were fought on campus in 1968, the trustees resolved to tolerate the presence of religious counselors only if they were invited by student groups, whose imprimatur was required for them to receive office space or use the chapel. After 1969, it seemed as if the separate religious chaplaincies might eventually wither away.

When I arrived at Columbia, most of the students active in those 1968 protests had moved on, but the wider community of alumni, faculty, and administrators, as well as local adherents and opponents in the fracases fought over U.S. involvement in

Vietnam and over a white-oriented institution's infringement on a minority neighborhood, remained seriously traumatized by the violence that had occurred. Good feeling toward the university had loosened and old loyalties had frayed. For its part, the Catholic chaplaincy had recently functioned as a halfway house for priests transitioning out of the ministry to marry. At a time when the role of religion on campus went up for grabs, the Catholic chaplaincy seemed to hit the skids just when Columbia had a president and a provost who were Roman Catholics for the first time in its 220-year history. Monsignor James Rea, Cardinal Spellman's replacement for a priest who had dared to write something positive about Sigmund Freud, had arrived in the mid-1950s to practice Newman Club apologetics and had stayed on as an interim director of the now secularized chaplaincy. But the job had taken its toll. In the baptismal records kept at the local parish, his handwriting was bold and florid, at first. Thirteen years later, it was reduced to a hardly legible scrawl, and he faded from the scene without leaving much of a mark. In the next four years, three different priests, up-and-comers all, came and went, resigning from the priesthood to pursue other careers. So when I was summoned to the old chancery office on Madison Avenue and then accepted the Columbia chaplain's job, it seemed as if I might be entering the campus through a revolving door that would put me right back out on Broadway—in mufti.

In May that year, I had received a master's degree at Union Theological Seminary, one long block up Broadway from my new office. Having an advanced degree helped me feel somewhat qualified for a campus position. And I had worked part-time during my deacon internship at Vassar College, so I had been around undergraduates not so long before. My two years in the Village had given me experience in building up a community around good liturgy and preaching, and I came to the job at Columbia armed with that pastoral strategy above all. My background then, coupled with an enormous amount of ignorance about the local political scene and about much else—I was twenty-eight at the time—stood me in relatively good stead when I took up the job a few weeks after classes had already started in September. Not welcomed by the pastor of the nearby parish, who was feeling put-upon by serial chaplains, I remained at Waverly Place for a year before I moved to the Cardinal Hayes residence.

Nationally, Catholic chaplaincies on secular campuses were struggling. The Newman Apostolate (recognized by the U.S. bishops in 1962 as the national organization for college and university chaplains) had not survived to the end of the decade, beset by too many upheavals on campuses and in the church as well. A replacement group was just starting up, so I took the opportunity the following January to attend its national meeting in Boca Raton, Florida, to see what I could learn from my new colleagues. I found out that campuses come in all shapes and sizes, as do the men and women who work in ministry on them. While there were some notable exceptions, the dominant tenor of the meeting spelled big-time confusion over roles, over mission, and over what constituted worship. Although not officially part of the program, Mass was to be celebrated just before we took our leave. It was the Feast of the Epiphany, or Little Christmas, and so enough people felt that they should mark the day before traveling home. Against my better judgment, I stayed for the thrown-together liturgy, which was led by a last-minute volunteer—Father Rusty, who wore shorts and flip-flops with a fishnet T-shirt that showed his athletic pectorals right through it. Blessed with not a shred of self-consciousness, he ad-libbed a homily in which he expressed admiration for King Herod, who, though not a good guy, had acted the way he did (murdering the innocents) "from his gut." "And I like that," he affirmed. Revolted, I fled back to Columbia to figure things out from the resources at hand.

My diocesan orientation to the job had amounted to a half-hour conversation with a mid-level official, whose clearest directive was that I should wear clerical garb at all times, so there was little help coming from that direction. To most other priests I knew, campuses seemed alien territory, and university students untamable and unlovable. But I brought to my new task two central convictions: that the Catholic church had itself been reborn by the experience of the Vatican Council; and that sustaining the church's rebirth "for the life of the world" had summoned me to the priesthood. Before young Catholics could meaningfully act on a religious identity that associated the "joys and hopes, the griefs and anxieties" of the church with those of the human race (as the opening of the Council's final document had declared), they needed to have their personal identities enlarged by an experience in common. They needed a faith community, not just an office to drop into when they were depressed and felt like eating some cookies. But how was I to swim against the campus tide that had abandoned any investment in adult religious leadership for purely grassroots student activism? The challenges I faced in seeking to carve out my role as campus minister at times pushed me to my limits. It also showed me some of the shadow side of the personality I had brought to ministry. Fortunately, I did not have to face those challenges alone.

Help arrived from an unexpected but congenial quarter in the person of my next-door neighbor at Earl Hall, Rabbi Charles Sheer. A man of Orthodox sympathies and practice, he really wasn't looking for a Catholic friend. Our separate offices branched off a common reception area that also functioned as a mini-lounge for students, so we could hardly avoid each other coming and going throughout the day. This made it easy for me to observe his basic community-building work, which I decided I wanted to emulate. When I made a courtesy call to introduce myself, I found him almost perplexed that I should bother. Was I going to stay that long? he may have been asking himself. But I had reasons to personalize our contact. My graduate studies had taken me deep into the Hebrew idiom and Jewish identity questions, out of which so much of the New Testament had sprung; I wanted to express the same respect for Judaism and its traditions that the Vatican Council had done; and he looked as if he knew what he was doing. We had a cordial meeting, but I couldn't blame him for thinking me a little meshuggah!

That October, the Yom Kippur War broke out. Rabbi Sheer cautiously asked me to speak at a rally expressing support for Israel, attacked by its neighbors on the holiest day of the Jewish year. Even then, friends of Israel were beginning to have reservations about the pace and implications of Israel's West Bank settlement policy, and I was warned by one of my professors about the risks of saying much of anything. When I did speak, buoyed up by some of my students, who had maintained a round-the-clock vigil for peace at Saint Paul's Chapel on campus, I cited all that the Western, historically Christian, powers had done to lay the groundwork for conflict. Refusing to take a smug stand that placed the blame at any one party's door, I tried to be sympathetic to Israel but not partisan. It was a good start, and over the next several years, before both our offices expanded and faced each other across the hall, Jewish and Roman Catholic students dared to cross a few lines as well. In an effort to raise money for famine victims in the Sahel, they staged a tug-of-war in the middle of campus, attracting both TV coverage and condemnation from a right-wing Jewish group. The Flame, as they called themselves, took the position that any social interaction, even a competitive game, blurred Jewish separateness and promoted assimilation and intermarriage. On campus, tempests in teapots were the order of the day and fodder for one of the most ambitious (and occasionally over-the-top) campus publications, the *Columbia Daily Spectator.*

Over the years Chuck and I attempted to model genuine interfaith cooperation, but neither of us rushed to embrace the spiritual free-for-alls common on other campuses. Both reserved about our liturgical traditions, we committed ourselves to studying together first, organizing several rounds of on-campus, and then metro-area, faculty study groups on the Books of Jonah and Ruth and on the Akedah, or Binding of Isaac, tradition. And I joined his Chumash class, studying the texts of the Torah set in the middle of the page surrounded by the authoritative rabbinical commentaries. Combining this study with my own doctoral work, carried on simultaneously, I came to appreciate how Judaism and Christianity had developed as competing midrashim, or interpretations, of the original body of revelation in the Torah, the Prophets, and the Writings. In an effort to flesh out our disputed heritage, we taught several noncredit courses in "Issues in Jewish and Christian Mis/Understanding," transgressing yet another normal boundary, and risking a certain spiritual cross-fertilization in the process.

But Rabbi Sheer's greatest contribution to my own development came from the way he modeled life as a religious family man, as a leader who was also husband and father. So, even more than my Protestant colleagues, "my rabbi" modeled for me the married religious leader, devoted as much to his broad-ranging religious and ethnic constituency, as he was to his family, with time and concern to spare for the goyim in his extended flock. The experience of being his colleague, of visiting with his family for Shabbas dinner or during Succoth, and of sitting Shiva with him when his wife, Gloria, died of leukemia, helped convince me that many of the arguments advanced by Catholic leaders about the rigors of the priest's life and the consequent need for celibacy look silly when compared with the religious commitment of the observant Orthodox Jewish husband. Celibacy as a lifestyle amounts to a luxury, in contrast with keeping the halakoth, the rabbinical interpretations of the Torah. Now in his thirty-fourth year in the Jewish chaplaincy, with a new center for Jewish life under his belt, Chuck continues the work in which I was proudly his colleague for my years on campus.

His leading the way also helped give the Catholic community

a toehold as early as my first year on campus. Chuck had spear-headed an effort to open a Jewish communal house in one of the university's undeveloped buildings, and when that was successful, he added a second. At the time, the university was desperate to provide more housing for both undergraduate and graduate students, and the year before my arrival, plans had been drawn up to convert two adjoining brownstones to create a Catholic version of the Jewish Beit Ephraim. But to do so would require capital, and unlike the rabbi, whose funding came from a Jewish alumni network, we had minimal program funding from the diocese and nothing else.

It helps, though, when money is lacking, to have a history.

Some of the best-regarded chapters in the history of Catholics at Columbia belonged to Father George Barry Ford (1885–1978), whose ghost-written autobiography, *A Degree of Difference*, I had read while still in the Village. My hunch was that, even though he had left his position on campus almost thirty years earlier, he was remembered fondly by alumni who might be of help. Writing to him and proposing that we meet paid off. Just shy of ninety, he was still spry and a natty dresser, moving in social circles where he was pretty sure to be the only Catholic priest present. He invited me to lunch at the Century Club and proved to be every bit as engaging a raconteur as his book had promised. He graciously accepted my offer to open a residence named in his honor and allowed me and the students working on the project to fund-raise for it. Tangling with the university bureaucracy, finding the funds, and beginning the renovation took us into late August. We were still dealing with plaster dust and paint, trucking in furnishings, and outfitting a kitchen when we admitted the first of the twenty-seven students who took up residence. I was now a landlord with all the attendant pleasures that thankless job entails.

Still, a facility like Ford Hall allowed us to run some programs in a student venue around issues that few would have come to hear about or discuss at the campus religious center. Dr. Herbert Hendin, an admirer of Father Ford's, had recently published a book, *The Age of Sensation*, that was causing a minor buzz with its daring conclusions about students' sex lives. He had treated numerous students caught up in the protests of the late 1960s for a range of emotional problems, then did interviews with an equivalent number of nonpatient students over the next few years as a comparison group and had published the results. Invited to Ford Hall for an evening's conversation, he wowed the students with his clinical finding that many of them got sexually involved for unconscious reasons that differed greatly from their conscious, sexually liberating agendas: some young men and women made love precisely to cause emotional hurt and turmoil to their partners. It was great to sit back and listen to another professional willing to indicate to my constituents how complicated sexual matters were, so that I was not the only one playing the heavy, pointing out the ambiguities present in some of the seemingly innocent carryings on.

Such as the ambiguities attendant upon the rash of streaking, "the thing in spring" that broke out on campuses all over the country in the mid-1970s. Streaking occurred sporadically, usually on the first warm nights in April before finals were imminent. Undoubtedly fueled by drink to help them get up the nerve, cells of students—mostly guys, but some girls—would either plan their streak from Point A to Point B, making some provision for seconds to have spare clothes for them, or follow a circular route and retrieve the clothes they had left behind—if no one had removed them. The ritual seemed to create the fiction that students had gotten beyond their inhibitions about sex. The first year, one young man, who hadn't participated, defended streaking to me as a harmless spectator sport. Later that night, a naked female student got jumped during her cavort and had to struggle to prevent being raped, an event that revealed the darker side of all the mayhem. The next day, the young man returned to admit that he now saw things differently.

Being an official spokesperson for chastity was never very gratifying or easy, but it came with the territory and with the collar. That role attracted a certain number of people to me who needed to feel safe when they dealt with issues of the heart and of the genitals. Thus, along with my efforts to get students to associate around their inherited identity as Catholics, much of my work corresponded with my official title: *Counselor* to Catholic Students. There seemed to be lots of students in need of counseling. In the aftermath of the "troubles" of 1968, Columbia College, at least, had made a conscious effort to expand its applicant pool by recruiting both Catholic and Jewish students from less-well-established economic groups. The college's strategy was based on the presumption that these students were less likely to "want to burn the place down," as the director of admissions told the assembled chaplains one day. So there was soon an influx of students from the parochial schools, who found themselves in a bigger and more diverse environment than they had ever negotiated. As one freshman from Ohio expressed it to me, "I can't believe it! My roommates talk about who their sisters are sleeping with!" Though the undergraduate schools offered psychological services and the university employed psychiatrists as part of its health services, Catholic young people often harbored a defensive distrust of mental health professionals. With the Catholic office fully functional again, students showed up in droves. A Jesuit priest who worked with me for two years helped to build the case-load, but he moved on and I was hard-pressed to sustain it by myself during the following year. In fact, the more I took on long-term clients (including some nonstudents who came to Mass on campus), the more I got pulled into a therapeutic milieu I did not always negotiate that well.

As I had started discovering in my parish in the Village, being an accepting, empathetic listener—while an important counseling strategy—bore a certain risk of overinvolvement for a priest who was basically training on the job. One-on-one counseling makes priests a pretty big target for needy counselees with a yen either for love from unavailable men or for attention from a father figure. In turn, it exposes both priest and student to unconscious dynamics where anger and desire meet, dynamics that the counselor must deal with ascetically—refusing to meet his own needs. That's Freud, not the priest speaking. It would be years before I adequately understood the rules of transference and countertransference, which Ernest Becker's *The Denial of Death* identifies as potentially so spiritually and politically liberating once they are ingested. Had more of us priests been schooled in how human relations are dogged by the universal fascination with persons who hold or symbolize power, fewer of us over the years might have crossed the line, acted out sexually, or yielded to the temptation to behave abusively. But that insight is not easily enacted in a profession still presumed to wield a unique form of power—the spiritual kind. Until the last decade or so, the church as an institution, and its vocation recruiters in particular, has had little to gain from reining in the narcissism of its clergy and their own fascination with the power entrusted to them. For generations, a certain spiritual narcissism has functioned as the clergy's single most effective recruiting tool.

I can't say that I regret the years I spent counseling. I believe I served people well and learned a good deal about myself in the process—and about what I didn't want to do full-time. Slowly I got better at dealing with the women who became attracted to me. Without being very conscious of it, I'd come to rely on clerical black and the collar in particular to mask the masculine vanity I harbored. The daily sameness of the garb made it easy to fulfill the gospel mandate not to worry about what to wear, but it also acted as a cover for a certain kind of self-involvement that didn't advertise itself. *Tout noir* had not yet become a chic fashion statement, so we priests donned it to be bland instead. When I didn't sport the collar, people who would normally greet me seemed not to notice who I was, a reaction that contributed to my personal sense of male invisibility—the downside of wearing the uniform. For the most part, though, clericals were a neutering defense that worked—up to a point and not with everyone.

The first time that defense clearly hadn't worked was back at Saint Joseph's. Sometime before my assignment to the campus, a middle-aged woman came to the rectory seeking practical assistance. Though she came from money, she was divorced and was about to lose her apartment. I arranged for her to store her furnishings, met with her several times, then with her and her well-heeled daughter in the suburbs, taking phone calls from her constantly. Before I realized it, Linda had become a "client" in the wrong sense of the term. I missed many of the signs of the growing charge of dependency and emotional connection that were building up—she was old enough to be my mother. After accepting the campus assignment, I took a call from her in which she told me of her disappointment in me; I had not delivered on my promises of aid. With some relief, I told her that I had been reassigned and would not be so available in my new job. Back at me through the phone came a blistering, vituperative outburst listing all of my shortcomings. Her final shot: "By the way, if you're going to work with students, you'd better lose some weight. You're too fat!"

She was right. Assunta's pasta-a-day regimen had helped me add twenty pounds to my medium-height frame in the two years since ordination. So a few months later, still smarting below the surface, I took up a dentistry student's challenge and began running. Except for the coldest mornings, we would jog a few times around Washington Square Park, as I ate more carefully ("Rabbit food," said Assunta) and lost more weight than I had put on.

After my experience with Linda, I probably should have been more wary when, the next summer, fate took me to the Catskills to perform the wedding of a couple who had prepared for marriage with me on campus. Louise was a bridesmaid whom I met at the rehearsal dinner. Too tall and a Texas Baptist, she hovered around me both the night before and after the wedding ceremony, and I made the mistake of dancing with her at the reception. (Though most priests will tell you that attending wedding receptions is a penance that will win them time off from purgatory, I was still young and foolish.) Within a week or two, Louise had become a fixture back on campus at Sunday Mass, looming in the front row, volunteering for refreshments, joining the fledgling graduate school group I had formed. One Sunday I was partially vested, greeting the students as they arrived—we rang a Liberty-sized bell on the chapel porch to summon them— and I had just finished pealing it by the hawser that hung from it. Up the walk came Louise in white flats and her go-to-meeting dress, rushing toward me affectionately. Deftly I moved behind the small offertory table in the aisle and kept it between us as she circled to get close to me. Another Sunday, when I wasn't present, she was told that my father had been hospitalized, and she made a hysterical exit from the chapel. Then she joined my confirmation class, having realized that her fondest wish was to become a Catholic. But she made a wrong move, enrolling for a graduate course at New York University. It gave me the perfect excuse to invent a jurisdictional ruling, banishing her to NYU's Newman Club and getting a priest friend there to take on her instruction. She really did get confirmed, as I remember it, and became a stalwart volunteer at our sister campus ministry.

If I had been in the market for a one-night stand, weddings would definitely have been the place to pick up a partner. Many of the couples who came to campus to be married were young professionals who had clearly detached from church for a while. They saw the campus chapel as a convenient way to get married "in the church" and, perhaps, assuage their Catholic parents' concerns about their souls, so I used my meetings with these couples to do some evangelizing as well as premarital counseling. But there were also Columbia alumni coming from out of town, with whom the pre-Cana counseling relationship was as brief as it was often intense. These couples could be pretty high-powered and interesting, and socializing with them and their guests at the reception could also be pretty intense, especially since so many of the couples and their friends were my age. One couple had both been Peace Corps volunteers, among whose wedding guests was a TV news correspondent. I had no television so I was not familiar with her, but she was engaging and we struck up a conversation at the reception. When it came time for her to go, she asked whether I wanted to come over to her place for a drink. When her friends reacted with shock, I grew a bit peeved, and partly to show them up, I coolly accepted. Playing with a little fire probably came easier in the aftermath of a wedding. For a priest, pronouncing the final blessing over a newly married couple and sending them down the aisle arm-in-arm to the boom of the organ and the tears and smiles of friends and family can be one of the loneliest moments in ministry. It definitely hit me that way. Seen by no one, I would do my solo exit down the side stairs, having done my job as chief witness for the church—Christ's bridesmaid, I guess—ever in attendance and never getting an opportunity to step up to the plate. So that evening, I guess I risked a little coziness for once and accompanied the correspondent to her apartment. We conversed some more over a drink, and that was that.

I never allowed myself to be picked up again, but the low-level electrical charge was confirming for me because, for a change, the emotional traffic flowed in both directions. She was not a client or a parishioner, and she wasn't a nun either. And that's a whole 'nuther story, which I don't think has ever been well-told. For a man to fall in love with someone he calls "Sister" may sound terribly Freudian or bent, but it's really not. A priest or a male religious easily has far more in common with a woman religious than mere sexual attraction. They have a shared faith and background and, more than likely, have a sensitivity to symbols, to sacraments, and how the divine is manifest in the ordinary. It is not surprising, then, that so many priests and nuns acted upon the impulse, particularly in the decade after the Vatican Council, when so many repressive restraints were lifted, and left to marry each other. I came close to getting involved with religious more than once—they were great women—but we managed never to compromise our commitments. When one of them left the convent, I was more than once tempted to seek out her company but kept pushing myself away instead. But the time I fell most deeply in love with a nun I had met while working with her as a priest, I remained ignorant of it for some time.

Sister Mary Frederick, a Sister of Mercy, may have done more than any other individual to hold her parish in the South Bronx together during the worst of the economic rot that infected that area of New York City. She radiated strength even as her cancer reduced her in the prime of her life of service. Freddy—as all the sisters called her—was a smart, attractive brunette about ten years older than myself, with a noticeably wry sense of humor and a ready laugh. Trim in her modified blue-and-white habit, she was the superior of her convent and principal of Sacred Heart Parish's school in Highbridge. During a partial sabbatical I took in 1977 to work on my Ph.D. dissertation, I began leading the sisters in the liturgy once a week. Freddy and I were never alone with each other or did anything but enjoy each other's company as part of a community gathering, sharing the kind of humorous moments that sustained these women who lived and worked every day in the bleak house of the struggling urban poor. Her order linked her cancer's remission to the cause of their founder Mother Catherine McCauley's sainthood, and for a brief while, both seemed to be moving ahead. But the cancer reoccurred with a vengeance and took her the day after Ascension Thursday. Asked to preach at her funeral, I struggled mightily to maintain my composure, ending the homily by saying more than I knew, as I invoked the Bridegroom's words from the Song of Songs:

> *Arise, my love, my beautiful one, and come!*
> *For see, the winter is past, the rains are over and gone . . .*
> *Let me see you, let me hear your voice,*
> *For your voice is sweet and you are lovely.*
> *Arise, my love, my beautiful one, and come!*

Somehow I managed to get through it, and after her funeral, I did not return to the convent for a solid year. When I did, it was to offer the Eucharist with the sisters for Frederick's anniversary. Minus the adrenalin pump and the public spectacle, the feelings of grief I had repressed overwhelmed me. I could not get through the homily, breaking under the weight of a loss I had denied even having.

As shepherds, priests spend a lot of time and energy tending to the emotional and sexual boundaries of their flock and, if they are honest, tending to their own as well. Working with so many bright and ambitious students, who often possessed a misplaced confidence in how well they knew themselves, I ended up patrolling the boundary lines a good deal. (The 1970s added to the boundarylessness of students, because the general culture of the sexual revolution had declared them to be adults, leaving them often in the lurch when dealing with needy older men and women.) Norm was such a student. A member of the five-student Catholic Student Organization that had "elected" me its adviser, winning me a key to my office and a valued ID, he wore a bright, infectious smile and his dark curly hair tousled carelessly. A student in mining engineering, he was earnest, candid, fun to be around, and not sufficiently guarded about his personal space.

Sometime into his dorm life, he and his roommate became partners and lovers, but the catalyst for his coming out seems to have been his involvement with a Jesuit priest with access to the campus, who seems to have played sexual initiator for more than just Norm. By the time Norm graduated, he was a figure in the bathhouse scene and continued to wear his boyish sexual availability on his sleeve. In the end, he was also one of the first victims of AIDS, dying before his fortieth birthday. Was he a victim of abuse? At the time the question never even would have been raised.

At times, the aura of safety, civility, and intellectuality that campuses exude becomes the honey in the trap. One famous humanities professor, witty, literate, and eccentric in the most entertainingly academic way, was known to bestow very generous grades on male athletes who took his core course. The price was putting up with his flirtatious attention, which most guys seemed to think a harmless bargain. But other more serious faculty predators also roamed the halls. Pete took up with one who flattered him, took an interest in him unlike that of any other previous adult, had him over for drinks, and seduced him. Back in class, he didn't know where he stood. The professor's interest soon wavered, and Pete was tossed aside. Unmoored, he dropped the course too late, failed, left school, and confessed his shaming to no one. Ten years later, he sought me out after I had left the campus. I put him in touch with a dean back at Columbia, to whom I gave the barest details to ensure some attention to what might have been considered a fault on his part, in order to regularize his academic record. He finally earned his degree a year later and started putting a professional life together.

But predatory behavior within the confines of the campus also ran both ways. Tommy may not even have been a student, but he joined my counseling practice somewhere along the way and would come to see me occasionally with dramatic tales of his sexual encounters. At a time when so many priests, who for years

engaged in secret and pathetic sexual fondling, have been publicly outed, it may be difficult to make a case for their vulnerability. But some priests also get trapped in webs where the sexual
threads remain hidden for a while. Tommy was good at that and
represented a type who carried out his agenda up close and personal. A softly handsome boy-man, he exuded neediness, combining an adolescent's fresh sexuality with the world-weariness of
a professional. It all came to a head one session when he popped
the question, wouldn't I like him to "do me" right there in the office. He knew I would like it. He had done a bishop at Saint John
the Divine recently, and the holy man had enjoyed it. Wouldn't I
like it, too? Part of the reason my armor held that day was my
aversion to being added to his victims' list rather than any horror
at a sexual encounter. So I assured him that my not wanting him
to "do me" was evidence that there was more to him than his sexual availability, and I was not going to read from the script he carried around with him. I ended the session ("No, I won't be giving
you a hug"), and he left my life, to my immense relief.

The longer I was on campus, the more I sought to network
with the mental health professionals and, if necessary, school authorities when students seemed really in trouble. I would make referrals when there were clearly issues beyond my competence, as
with the Catholic young man with a guilty conscience about masturbating who did not remove the dried semen of his ejaculations
for days after masturbating, or the frat member whose roommate
had accidentally hanged himself from their bunk bed trying for a
sexual high. The professionals reciprocated, sending me patients
whose problems seemed more religious than they were emotional.
One was Hank, a football player, who seemed consumed by religious anxiety. As I sat at my desk in the late-afternoon fall light,
suddenly the room darkened. When I looked up, Hank's beefy
frame filled the doorway. We began a counseling relationship of
several years' duration, during which I think he became healthier.
It took a lot.

Hank's Catholic upbringing had loaded him down with an enormous scrupulosity and active guilt, which he attached to just about everything he felt once he became pubescent. To motivate himself about even everyday responsibilities, he would pray to the Blessed Mother, making a vow or promise to her that he would accomplish his duties. It seemed to help getting his homework done through high school, but dealing with sexual urges this way only compounded his problem. Failing regularly (it really does seem the Blessed Virgin has better things to do than come to the aid of every horny adolescent), he then was guilty both of the act itself and of breaking a solemn vow as well. His formula for virtue spelled disaster, and I made several attempts at weaning him from the practice. Exasperated by his stubbornness, I then explicitly forbade him to make any more vows: "You're a layperson. Only monks and nuns can make vows." Fighting moral scrupulosity with legal scrupulosity seemed to get his attention, so I pressed my direct approach, figuring that, as a football player, he might listen to the firm directions of a coach. But the next time he came in and wanted to go to confession, I girded myself, and sure enough, he 'fessed up to making a vow—I can't quite remember what for—so I leaned over from my office chair, hauled off, and landed a punch. It glanced off his massive shoulder.

"What did I tell you about vows?" I asked sternly.

"You punched me!" he exclaimed. "A priest punched me in confession!"

I shot back, "And I'll do it again if you keep it up."

In the months afterward, we worked on his coming to terms with his sexuality, learning to tame rather than deny his libido, and to see young women as other than either immaculate virgins or voracious vixens. I think our counseling helped him to move on and escape some of the misunderstandings that seem to plague conscientious Catholic kids well into their adult years. I remember how hard a time I had convincing a very dutiful graduate student who had confessed to me she was sleeping with her boyfriend that she did not have to add using "artificial" birth control to her list of sins. When she seemed surprised, I explained, pastorally applying the papal teaching in *Humanae Vitae*, that the ban on "artificial" birth control affected married couples, not the unmarried. It spelled out "the will of the Author of life" for "the constitutive design of marriage," not for every random act of sexual love. In fact, I told her, she had an obligation to practice birth control if she was making love outside a marital covenant. I didn't go as far as my friend Denny, a pastor who inserted a module on birth control into his eighth-grade confirmation curriculum. But I understood why he felt his inner-city adolescents needed some practical religious instruction in matters of sex.

More than just young students evidenced confusion relating sexuality and religious meaning. In fact, the question of where one realm leaves off and the other begins has taxed a lot of professionals as well. In one case I knew too much about, the confusion had a tragic outcome. A student whom I had first known as a sophomore started coming to see me a year or so later. Dale had played hockey through high school but had not really grown into the body he had conditioned for slamming other guys against the boards. He commuted to school, staying at home and not separating at all from his very controlling parents. Coming to campus one weekend, he ended up at a party and ingested some angel dust (at least) and had some overwhelming hallucinations. In short order I referred him to the campus psychiatric service, but I continued to see him as a backup counselor. Again, as a priest I thought I represented someone familiar and safe, someone in whom he could confide his sexual feelings, which he regularly spoke about, repeatedly speaking about his frustration with his old girlfriend, who wouldn't put out for him and on whom he seemed to have a real fixation.

Since his psychiatrist and I were involved in regular meetings between the religious counselors and the mental health professionals, the psychiatrist chose to use Dale's story as the subject of a case conference. Twenty minutes into the presentation I found myself reacting negatively to the doctor's treating the images of crosses and daggers in Dale's fantasies as if they had some religious significance. I understood that he was trying to be respectful, but he was bending over backward and ignoring their blatantly psychotic content. Soon, I interrupted him: "Excuse me, Doctor, but you need to understand that when Dale is speaking religion, he's really thinking sex. It's the only safe way he has to approach the topic." He seemed startled, then relieved, and we were able to start talking about Dale's psychic issues for the rest of the time. Shortly afterward, Dale was hospitalized near home because he had threatened a neighbor he perceived to be trying to harm him, rushing to his apartment door wielding a kitchen knife. When I visited him, I met with the therapist as well and gave him some background I thought helpful, receiving his word that I would be included in the discussions of the team that would be treating Dale. No call ever came before the student, now on leave from school, was discharged and sent home.

After his discharge, I maintained contact with Dale and responded to an invitation from his parents to visit their home. He was friendless and pretty hapless, and I probably overvalued how therapeutic our contact was. But he was getting no treatment, and seeing him in that setting only confirmed for me his real need of it. His father, a bull of a man, couldn't tolerate weakness in his son; his mother had become her illness, controlling both husband and son through her obvious debilitation. My only trick was knowing how to be ego-supportive, so I got Dale talking when we were alone—again, I was going to try and coach him about hanging in there. But his response was to show me the pornography collection his father had assembled for him to help relieve his stress. Then, when he got on the explicit topic of sex, he tearfully revealed how he had been sodomized as a high school student by a trusted parish priest. As disturbed as I was by his telling me about it, I never got enough information from him to act upon the outrage. Had I done so, it might have brought some issues to the fore and prevented the tragedy that eventually took place. Here was a young man, unable to grasp any whole sense to all his parts, fixated on sex as the missing link. While his parents' illness had everything to do with his own emotional disarray, the bastard priest, who had ridden him like a stud in heat, had contributed to the damage I was trying to contain with mere friendship. But if I was seriously out of my league, so were the other professionals involved.

Over the next several months, Dale would come into the city to see his doctor and stop by to see me. One day, I received a frantic phone call that I might be in danger. The doctor had told Dale that he could not reenroll at Columbia until he had stabilized, and he had burst from the office in a rage. He arrived, meek as a beaten dog, giving me the chance to try to assuage his disappointment and to give him some hope beyond the darkness that had descended on him. When next the doctor asked me to help persuade Dale to be hospitalized, I got him to agree to the idea. But when I called the doctor back, he said that the university's allotment of psych beds was full. Maybe next week we'll try again. After that, there was little that could stave off doom. For some days, Dale stewed at home, then on impulse drove to a sporting-goods store, where he bought a hunting knife. He tucked it in his book bag and was on his way somewhere (my own guess was home to murder his parents), but the car ran out of gas. Two helpful police officers gave him a ride to an office building where he had briefly held a job. There the unwitting cops dropped him off, where he found a former boss alone in his office and stabbed him to death. Before the man died, he identified his attacker to the police, and so, by the time his father called me, Dale had been arrested and charged with murder.

The sickness involved in this saga did not belong to Dale alone. Every system meant to rescue victims from their own psychosis had failed him—and would continue to do so. His lawyers got Dale off on an insanity plea, after which he spent a few years in psychiatric facilities, in one of which he actually got some treatment. But by then enough Haldol and Thorazine had reduced him to a shell of his former self, and he returned to live with his parents. Through much of my ten-year involvement with Dale, I flattered myself that I was carrying out a pastoral mission for a young man who, except for my contact with him, would somehow become a lost soul. Now it seems to me that, like so many priests working with troubled young men, I was more than a little narcissistically involved, thinking that my personal concern could somehow make up for the damage that his parents and the anonymous priest had done and so contribute to Dale's possible rescue. Slow to learn both my own limits and the limitations on the ability of grace to effect change when nature, nurture, and abuse conspire to do such damage, I eventually told Dale, after he had moved far away, that long telephone conversations with me were only hindering him from getting the help he needed.

Anyone involved in ministry who takes the calling seriously will be dealt lessons similar to mine about personal boundaries, making slow progress in correcting my overinvolvement. But because engaged congregations act like dragnets, coming up with some whopping big fish, it remains a challenge for those in ministry to try to meet a religious inquirer's needs when they are also impossibly psychologically complex. I had already had a bad experience with preparing a woman for baptism, in which I got caught up in the dynamics of her parents' rejection of her—something my baptizing her only worsened. As a result, she concluded that I had done the baptism poorly. It hadn't "taken," so she went off and had a female Episcopal priest redo it! Some pastoral relief arrived when the Second Vatican Council's new Rite of Christian Initiation for Adults (RCIA) was published. It called for a small community-within-the-community to share the responsibility of initiating adults into the church. Immensely fruitful as a pastoral strategy, the rite served our community, which met in one of the jewels of church architecture in New York City, Saint Paul's Chapel, well indeed, bringing into the church generous and committed believers.

Despite this change, some would-be converts were put off by the rite's provision that candidates publicly declare their status as a catechumen, or learner, in the middle of a community. They would go find a priest to act as their individual baptismal coach. It wasn't hard to find one to help them sneak in the backdoor, as many priests still haven't bought into the RCIA model of conversion. But for others candidates for baptism, the attention and approbation they received by becoming a public figure in a group who made a fuss over them turned out to be intoxicating, almost a substitute for any real growth in knowledge or self-understanding. So it may have been inevitable that, RCIA and all, candidates for baptism, as often as not, wanted the opportunity to be near a priest, spend time alone with him, and be involved with him personally. The problem seems to occur most of the time with men or women who weren't sure that any other man would ever take the kind of interest in them that a priest would take in a candidate for baptism or confirmation. My hairiest encounter with such a person can serve to illustrate the kind of ambiguous territory priests have to negotiate in the field of dreams called ministry. Working hard enough at it, I did get a chance to "build it" (a community), and they came. But the effort was often dogged by obstacles that came in many sizes and shapes.

Just before the fall semester one year, I spent a day or so painting my office suite with Joe, a graduate student and staff member. Taking advantage of the office's being closed, we were dressed in T-shirt and shorts and were probably spattered with paint. A woman arrived looking for a religious counselor to speak with. In the middle of August, few people were around, so she saw our open door and inquired after the rabbi first of all. She followed by asking who we were, and when I identified myself, she looked incredulous but asked for an appointment to see me. We met for the first time the following week.

Rosa (not her real name) was a graduate student who also worked at the university. Tiny and attractively plain, she had few relationships on campus and a reputation for being very organized, even obsessively so. In our counseling sessions, she revealed some difficult personal history but concentrated mostly on her relationships with various professors, both in the past and in her current position. In the meantime, she had become a regular at Sunday Mass, also volunteering in a number of programs, and increasingly circling in for her move. I made a number of suggestions for mental health referrals, but she was adamant that she needed to counsel with a religious figure—Where was the rabbi when I needed him the most?! Somewhere in my early forties at the time, I had begun to go gray but clearly did not include myself in the category of "older men" who were the object of her fantasies. In short order I was disabused when, as I questioned why she would be content to be some older man's mistress, she popped the question. Wouldn't I be interested? She promised that she would be the soul of discretion and make no real demands. I declined and started thinking more seriously about terminating as soon as possible. The opportunity arose when I received a call from a staffer at the athletic department, who told me his wife worked with Rosa. She had begun to receive phone calls from Rosa in which she actively fantasized performing sexual acts with me. Upon making some further inquiries, I discovered she was dragging my name all over campus, sharing her delusional sexual tales with all who would listen.

The next time I met with her I had my Presbyterian campus ministry colleague with me. Scott had agreed to do some short-term counseling in my stead (he was younger than I, and so probably safe). I told her our sessions were over and that she could not frequent our community Mass or activities.

"But I intend to become a Catholic. You have to instruct and baptize me," she desperately gambled.

"No, I don't. Not here either. There's a parish three blocks from here. They can meet your spiritual needs," I responded. I had decided on a ban as my best recourse for dealing with a woman who, though frail on the surface, had a steel will within. The next Sunday, she showed up for Mass with a law school student involved in a human rights clinic, whom she had enlisted to advocate for her. Luckily, my reverend friend Scott was in the environs and knew the law student, so he vouched for the reasonableness of my decision, and subsequently her advocate advised her to withdraw. But she poured out her story of exclusion to every soul who would listen, causing some members of the congregation to withdraw from the chapel community without ever speaking with me. Next came a signed complaint from Jacoby and Meyers (a burgeoning storefront firm), which alleged not only discrimination but sexual harassment and named Father Paul Dinter, Columbia University, and the Archdiocese of New York as codefendants. The next day, the *Columbia Daily Spectator* blazoned the looming scandal in a headline. At first, I thought it a ploy meant to pressure me to readmit Rosa into the congregation. Stubbornly, I declined to hire a lawyer and when the suit was actually filed—Columbia had been dropped as well as the claim of sexual harassment—relied on the diocesan lawyers to handle the matter.

The court threw the case out on the constitutional grounds that the government could not interfere in questions of religious congregational membership. At the receiving end of a harassment charge, I was genuinely grateful for the support I had gotten from my new supervisor bishop, Edward Egan, in his first stint with the archdiocese, who called me to determine how to proceed with the suit. But in retrospect I can see that his handling of the case was inadequate. All he did was ask me over the phone whether there was anything to this complaint, and he readily accepted my account of the nonaffair. Had there been grounds for Rosa's complaint, he could hardly have determined the facts of the matter by merely asking, "Is there anything to this?" When I explained my history of contacts with her, he readily accepted my words over the phone: "Good. As Cardinal Cody taught me long ago, if they get you into court, you don't leave till there's blood on the floor." I guess I was glad he was on my side even if I thought the sentiment unsupported by either Scripture or any reputable theological source.

The emotional force field that was the campus occasioned a regular string of minicrises that only occasionally rose to grab headlines. Like atmospheric white noise, the charged intellectual and sexual energy that thousands of students carry around with them has an explicit spiritual or religious counterpart that too easily can be passed over. Religious ferment definitely exists in young men and women but is best in moderate amounts. When heated beyond that, it is volatile and dangerous. Tempted as they constantly are by the threat of identity diffusion, students in late adolescence and early adulthood often succumb to sincere but dangerously narrow-minded religious hucksters. Associating their way with the "narrow road" to salvation of which Jesus speaks, groups like the official Catholic cult Opus Dei, the fundamentalist Church of Christ, the Unification Church (or Moonies), and other sects prey upon students' insecure sense of themselves. They also market simplistic religious solutions to complex issues of personal and sexual identity. Recruiting the sincere but wobbly young, selling their brand of religiosity as *the* answer ("But what is the question?" a Jewish student once called out from the crowd, to an evangelist), the religion hawkers always tried to portray the mainstream clergy as part of some soulless establishment.

Crossing the campus one day on the way to say daily Mass, I noticed a small crowd gathered on the main campus plaza around a man who was declaiming his version of the truth, holding what I presumed was a Bible in his hand. On my way back within the hour, he had migrated closer to my regular route, so I joined the somewhat larger group standing in a circle around him. As I listened to his rantings, which had taken on a decidedly anti-Semitic edge, a student standing nearby urged me, "Say something. He's giving religion a bad name." When I stepped into the circle, a small cheer went up. Seeing my collar, the preacher went for the jugular. "Have you been saved?" he yelled at the top of his voice. Matching his pitch, I shot back, "Yes, many times! That's what this stands for"—pointing to the same collar that had grabbed his attention. "Don't you realize that you're turning the Gospel into bad news?" I quietly asked him. As I engaged him, his assistant, who was hiding in the crowd, jumped into the circle and continued the barrage of screaming Scripture passages that this benighted sect took to be the equivalent of preaching. Refusing to debate him, I turned to the crowd and called out, "As it says in Scripture, 'Go to your homes!' " and left.

I guess I responded to the student's plea out of some annoyance at the perversion of preaching that was taking place out in the public square. As a priest, no other task so energized me, exercised me, or tested me as much as preaching did. The campus setting only took to another level my already heightened sense about what is at stake in preaching. It exercised my emotional intelligence and energy at least as much as counseling, programming, and interrelating with needy young people or heavyweight academics. It really held the key to the community-building task I wanted to engage in. Real preaching no more resembles sermonizing than it looks and sounds like those would-be missionaries' shouting out the words of Scripture as if they contained some magic totems that would latch onto people's souls and transform them willy-nilly. Yet the Scriptures remain the entry point of preaching, spurring on and also braking the fertile imagination of the minister of the word. Their authority lies in their being exemplary, not in their saying everything there is to say. They demand being searched and cross-referenced, not only with themselves, but with lived experience as well. For they become the catalyst for a graced encounter only when the page illumines life and when life is reflected on the page. At the same time, all of life is not reflected on every one of the pages of the Bible. Nor does every passage chosen for the lectionary readings illumine our dilemmas the way we might like it to do. For all of the years I spent at Columbia, I was fortunate enough to be able to share the job of discerning where the Scriptures might lead on a particular Sunday with interested members of the congregation. We did it formally, on Monday evenings at a meeting with our talented musicians, volunteer lectors, and other ministers who had signed up for the following Sunday's celebration. The group, which changed often over the years, served as a sounding board, a source for feedback, an anchor of reality in a sea of possible platitudes, a direction finder, and a building block for shaping a community response to issues in the narrow world of the campus and the wider world beyond. It wasn't all magic and required a commitment to get through dry spells, but it was also a deep well that gave me a thirst for setting a new and broader agenda.

In my ongoing personal search, as part of the continuing task of peeling the onion of my self-awareness, I regularly went on retreat to the Benedictines of Mount Saviour Monastery outside Elmira, New York. There among the cows (later sheep), the wild turkeys in the woods, the quiet, the monks' chanting the hours, and Prior Martin's conferences, I prayed for the insight necessary to integrate my considerable energy, my inner struggle with my own restless sexuality, and my commitment to a ministry worthy of a world-class university. Searching for an agenda or program that would enliven a campus ministry too often spent dealing only with the most emotionally broken students had preoccupied me for some time. Discovering the seeds while on retreat for growing a different product in the campus soil helped me deal for some years with my other issues. I still lacked the inner peace of a settled celibate sexuality, but it didn't seem to matter so much as I worked to bring my retreat vision to fruition.

In Thomas Merton's *Conjectures of a Guilty Bystander* he asserts that, in the life of grace, "there are no coincidences." So I might be tempted to consider my reading *The Seven Storey Mountain* in June 1977 to be some part of a larger intentionality. Up to that time I was only glancingly familiar with Merton's writing. What I discovered in his autobiography was that just over a hundred of the four-hundred-plus pages of Merton's work covered the period when Columbia and New York City made up his immediate world. As I would find from reading his many other writings, for anyone making a journey inward, he makes a fine companion. In the last days of his life, Merton would write that the journey inward is the only real journey we make—even as he fulfilled a dream and traveled to the Far East. But in the rush of discovering the power of his Columbia story that spring at Mount Saviour, I didn't leap deeper into solitude or self-awareness; I started mapping a strategy for reshaping the work I did on campus. By the time I returned to the city, I had drawn up a schema for a series of events to be held between the fortieth anniversary of Merton's (re)baptism at Corpus Christi Church, near the campus, and the tenth anniversary of his death in Thailand at a monastic conference. Within the year I was visiting Merton's own Abbey of Gethsemani to secure the imprimatur of Brother Patrick Hart, Merton's secretary, now editor, and unofficial chaplain to the burgeoning interest in the life and writings of his mentor.

In many ways, for the next decade, my search ran on an axis between Mount Saviour and Gethsemani, but I mainly pursued it in work undertaken in and around Manhattan's Morningside Heights. All the while, my struggle to make sense of a ministry becoming richer and richer took place as I rode an emotional roller coaster. But in the first flush of planning and organizing the Merton Commemoration at Columbia that brought over two thousand attendees to conferences, lectures, and services—and figures like Louis Dupre of Yale, Brother David Steindl-Rast, Father Henri Nouwen, feminist scholar Carolyn Bynum, and Catholic peace activists—the monastic solitude coupled with worldly engagement that Merton had struggled with at Gethsemani seemed a model for what a community of faith at Columbia could strive to emulate. My first visit to his monastery fueled that dream for me. When I arrived, Mass was just finishing, so no one was around to greet me. Making my way into the chapel visitor's gallery (like a choir loft), I saw the last monks just leaving, as were the guests from the gallery. The plastered Gothic kitsch I had seen in pictures of Gethsemani's chapel had vanished. Iron girders jutted up from the apse and the nave's ceiling was held up by naked wooden beams. Light played through nonfigurative stained glass. Only two images called out: an enormous tapestry banner of the risen Christ draped in the apse and an icon of the Virgin and Child off center where the choir and sanctuary met. As busy as my eyes were taking this all in, my ears were flooded with the silence. It literally rushed into me, not like the absence of sound, but as a windlike presence reaching out and greeting me. Later that silent welcome was matched by Brother Patrick's own warm embrace of me and the project. The auguries were good and the event was taking on the force of a spiritual juggernaut.

One of the reasons I had the time and energy to add event planning to my pastoral agenda flowed from my having recruited a priest colleague to work on campus with me. Nick and I had known each other since our first day at Cathedral. He had been sent to Rome to study and I had attended his ordination there. But I lured him away from teaching in high school when my yearly reports of the activity on campus convinced the chancery that, between my counseling load, interfaith work, and Ford Hall, the position warranted a second priest. We had worked well together for a year and a half, when, in the middle of my planning the Merton Commemoration, Nick resigned to marry Heather, a valued staff member who had begun to carry some of the counseling load. Stung and saddened, I could not share his newfound happiness and instead redoubled my level of activity. Turning away from the implications of his decision for my own dilemma—as I had after my first pastor's resignation only five years earlier—I buried myself in all the tasks of pulling off the commemoration. When the whole event had ended, I had begun recasting the campus ministry, but by the end of the year, I was emotionally drained and my office was financially spent. I closed up for the summer and supported myself by saying four to five Masses on the weekend in parishes up and down the archdiocese. Two factors saved me from the combined weight of my unfunded entrepreneurship and my fear of running out of steam. I found an unexpected donor in my aunt, who was staying with my parents as she recuperated from a cancer operation. She paid the leftover bills, which allowed me to return to campus in the black. Then the new semester produced a crop of students whose fresh enthusiasm for the work on campus demonstrated that I had some collaborators on tap to help in what had become a seriously lonely task.

Having the opportunity to invite these and other students to the Sunday evening celebration of the Eucharist in Saint Paul's Chapel on the campus proved an important catalyst for their deepening involvement. In fact, it would be hard to gauge the real value which the renewable gift of that space has had for Catholics, in particular, for the last thirty years. A severe, Anglicanized version of San Vitale in Ravenna, the building's domed serenity calls individuals out of themselves and incorporates them into a body-at-praise. For students raised on the thin gruel of postconciliar parish liturgy, the campus ministry offered a combination of familiar fare and an enhanced diet of rich music, intelligent use of symbols, and preaching that had to be able to stand up to comparison with hours of classroom lectures. Even during the crisis that I would soon face, I think I managed to remain up for the challenge. The full-flavored character of good worship respects the sacraments not as manufacturing grace but as in-between spaces where an interplay between the time-bound and the transcendent occurs. At any rate, our worship in common displayed a robust appeal across the board to graduate students, inquiring jocks, a small core of faculty, alumni, members of the wider community, and undergraduates up for a challenge. (Eventually, I took a "low Mass" liturgy into the dorms on Sunday night, developing a feeder system that sought to get students more comfortable with chapel liturgy.) As I had hoped, the "public work" of the liturgy became the common experience of grace that birthed an extended community of interest and of action. The seeds I discovered at the monastery found a fresh opportunity for increase back on campus.

Then another catalyst entered the mix in the fall of 1979 in the person of the pope. The vigor with which John Paul II hit the ground running after his election the previous year is worth recalling. When it was announced that he would visit New York, people sat up and took notice. Blocks of tickets to his Mass at Yankee Stadium were distributed to campus ministries, becoming hot items. I held a free raffle for the first group of tickets that I got, but when a second bunch came my way, I distributed them to my best volunteers, who included guys from the wrestling team who had taken responsibility, the week before, for hauling all the equipment to and from our post-Eucharist Oktoberfest, which kicked off our community organizing each year. It was the smartest investment I had ever made as they brought some of the same intensity they showed in the gym to putting John Paul's message into practice. Taking New York by storm, the pope's person and his message had an equal impact on students who had a residual, but predominantly cultural, loyalty to the church. His words about the United States coming to the aid of "Lazarus at the gates" had particular resonance on a campus at whose gates some of New York's dispossessed began to appear. Real estate reinvestment after the fiscal crisis of the mid-1970s had literally displaced thousands of occupants of single-room-occupancy hotels on the West Side of Manhattan. They started appearing on Broadway as beggars, a good number of them mentally ill and homeless. Because the university was a big player in the real estate market, some students grew discontent with studying global economics while ignoring the local consequences of market forces every time they went shopping at Mama Joy's for late-night snacks.

Taken together, the pope and the poor moved the campus ministry in a different direction, and eventually it launched its Diakonia Service Project. In no time, the project allowed hundreds of students to spend significant time and energy running a weekly community lunch (which expanded to three days a week when the Presbyterian congregation and students at Union Theological Seminary pitched in—and it is still in operation), staffing an emergency shelter at Saint John the Divine, distributing food and clothing, and partnering with primary schools to mentor young boys and girls from the neighborhood. Twenty years ago and more, what has become the "volunteerism" or "community service" agenda on American campuses was in its infancy. As an effort to redirect student energy to build up rather than tear down, it has been a real boon. Our huge annual Oxfam Fast Day and superstars competition did as much, channeling the efforts of hundreds of off-season athletes into fund-raising for hunger relief. But as enjoyable and productive as efforts like these were, the community that grew up around our service work came from a different source.

The texture of that difference could best be sampled in the music that helped firm up the community's identity. Arising normally at our celebration of the Eucharist, for which our talented musicians regularly provided new settings, those songs and settings of the psalms as well took the group from a room at Notre Dame rectory, where we prayed vespers every Thursday night, to as far afield as the Pantex nuclear weapons facility in Amarillo, Texas, one summer, at the end of a sixteen-hundred-mile peace walk. The music we played and sang at worship became the poetry of our social engagement, putting the heart and mind in touch, giving emotional depth to faith and charity in action. After first hearing "The Lord Hears the Cry of the Poor" at the papal Mass at Yankee Stadium, we turned it into a virtual anthem, knitting together our prayer, protest, and programs on behalf of New York's poor. In a similar way, "One Bread, One Body" became a theme song, moving many individuals to dedicate themselves to a community endeavor, vindicating what Cardinal Newman had written about faith affirmation and the way it makes use of our emotions, employing our hearts as the very instrument of worship.

Spurred on by all these developments, a large core group then came together and, after months of deliberation, formed a lay community that took on an explicit commitment to simple living, service, and peacemaking. These were also the years of the nuclear buildup that had spooked the Federation of Atomic Scientists to move the arm of its doomsday clock several minutes toward midnight. Since I had included the national meeting of Pax Christi USA as part of the Merton Commemoration, that peace group's agenda—disarmament, the nuclear freeze, and opposition to draft registration, which had been reinstated to oppose the Soviet intervention in Afghanistan—in addition to civil disobedience at a local weapons laboratory, all became part of this community's active concerns.

At the center of much of this organizing sat a goal that I had once thought was a specifically priestly one: living together with other ministers of the gospel and supporting one another economically, affectively, and unselfishly—the monastic trio of poverty, chastity, and obedience transposed to New York City in the

1980s. But despite much lip service to the idea, priests in general were not prepared to change their lifestyle. (Across the river in Brooklyn, some really smart guys realized something of the ideal by opting out of the diocesan structure through joining the Oratory of Saint Philip Neri, working in the diocese but escaping from its personnel deployment by their forming their own canonical association.) In my continuing struggle to make daily sense of the celibate commitment I had wagered on twelve years earlier, the community acted upon my soul as balm in Gilead. The lay members made no explicit personal commitment to be other than normally chaste, thereby shunning the two-tiered morality that has afflicted the church's "official" ministers. In fact, to the extent that many members of the community practiced temporary celibacy, they engaged in perhaps the most valid form of the discipline. As in Buddhism and its parent faith, Hinduism, celibacy plays a role for the believer either as a spiritual practice undertaken for a time or aspired to as a final state of spiritual growth. Young people, in particular, should be encouraged to adopt it as a discipline because it helps hold in check the identity diffusion that can occur either when they engage in serial mating or when they lose themselves in intense love affairs that blot out a person's individuality. So, having such a committed group at the heart of a much larger community (our Sunday Mass attendance regularly topped five hundred) gave our efforts resonance on campus, in the Harlem–Morningside Heights area, and, through an informal alliance with other campus and activist groups, in New York City itself.

When I realized how serious this core community had become, and that it needed a home, I made the decision to transform Ford Hall from an undergraduate residence to a graduate one open to members of this newly forming community. This change caused some serious dislocation for some students, but it had been long in the coming. In addition to our community home, Ford Hall then became a distribution center for food and clothing, and a sometime shelter for neighborhood home-less. Taking up a community lifestyle energized the group, maybe neurotically so, and created a unique venue for regular worship, intense discussions, endless community meetings, great meal gatherings, and activist planning sessions. Among others, we hosted Father Dan Berrigan, whose magnetic presence shaped the community's response to the host of crises that advanced capitalist societies in love with their own power create as a matter of course. But the greatest crisis we weathered occurred when one of our recent graduates, working as a tenant organizer, and pouring his heart and soul into all our outreach efforts, died of long undiagnosed endocarditis. David Joyce had been recruited from Columbus, Ohio, for Columbia's Ivy League championship wrestling team and had made the trip to Yankee Stadium with us. Short of stature, wiry, quick, and funny as hell, he possessed a confidence honed on the mat. Previously known on campus as a stuntman and an occasional brawler—he'd take on football players twice his size at the student pub if they started throwing their weight around—he had taken up nonviolent protest and enacted it with Gandhian guts. Outside the gates of Electric Boat in Groton, Connecticut, where Trident submarines were made, he waded into a lunchtime crowd of metalworkers to discuss their complicity in the arms race, looking every bit like them in his flannel shirt, jeans, and work boots, but disarming them with the broad smile that shone beneath his blondish mustache and his missionary swagger. They may not have beaten their swords into plowshares that afternoon, but they had to think differently about who was promoting reconciliation rather than armed blackmail against the USSR.

On another occasion, stopped by a line of police in front of the French mission to the UN, he and his buddies Joe and Pat adopted a novel tactic to reach the doors and deliver our protest note by executing simultaneous shoulder rolls past the surprised men in blue. Somehow we managed to avoid arrest that day, though the wrestlers had gotten dragged around a bit until the police were convinced that their athleticism was part of a nonviolent protest. When the nuclear freeze campaign heated up, Dave set up a table for collecting signatures every lunchtime outside the office where his tenant-organizing project was housed—the Catholic Center of the Archdiocese of New York. As the national office of Pax Christi regularly publicized the number of Catholic bishops who had signed the nuclear freeze petition, Dave particularly sought to recruit the men in black suits with the telltale gold chain across the chest as they came and went from 1011 First Avenue. After some months, his boss was told the tenant-organizing project had to find alternate space, for which Dave took a little heat.

But some of the roughest waters Dave had to negotiate involved his family's expectations of him. In particular, his heavy commitment to the chaplaincy's broad-ranging work and its activist brand of Catholicism occasioned some conflict with his father, to whom he was very devoted. This happened with other students as well, whose parents became wary and distrustful of me, believing that I was either trawling for recruits or distracting their sons and daughters from the career choices that an Ivy League education was meant to provide. I am grateful that I was not suspected of any darker motives, and no such accusations surfaced then or since. But the subtheme of rivalry for the loyalty and affection of their sons, in particular, remained one of the bevy of interpersonal issues we sought to work through in those formative years of the community. As a result, when Dave's parents came to New York for his graduation, I remained discreetly in the background. But on the night of the ceremony, as I was about to turn in, my phone rang in the rectory. It was Dave insisting I join him, his dad, and some friends at the local watering hole, where they were celebrating. He was trying to clear the air, I guess, and to introduce these two men who seemed to be playing tug-of-war with his future. Sharing a pitcher or two probably helped lessen the tension. When, after midnight, we said good-bye (he was leaving early the next morning to return to Ohio, having not made the decision to stay in New York as yet), we paused on the corner of Broadway and 114th Street. Hugs were exchanged all around, but Dave's came last. Smaller than I was, but stronger, he grabbed me in a wrestler's body lock, looked me straight in the eyes, and unabashedly declared, "I love you."

It may have been the first time in my almost forty years that anyone ever broke through to me with that particular message. My own father finally got there years later, saying it just as I was about to take a sabbatical leave abroad. As he would be dead fifteen months later, it helped to make up for many years of silence. But Dave's hug that night awoke a longing in me that I had tried to set to rest for years. Thinking that I did what I did because I was a priest working in ministry, I submerged my feelings for the people who validated my work under cover of a general religious fervor. With that spontaneous gesture, Dave blew my cover and planted a seed that he would also water as unwittingly only a few years later. When he moved to New York in September, the work that led to the formation of the community began in earnest, taking shape in September 1982 when twenty of us moved into a reconfigured Ford Hall. But nine months after we had gathered and committed ourselves to an alternative form of daily living the faith, Dave grew ill. He fought the unknown pains, sought medical help to no immediate avail, and was finally hospitalized. Just before Holy Week, a cardiologist who became involved in his case almost by accident had finally assembled the pieces of his pain into a diagnosis. Massive antibiotics were prescribed in preparation for replacing the defective heart valve that had hosted a viral infection. On Good Friday, much of Dave's own work as an organizer and newborn peace activist had reached fruition, when six hundred people enacted the Stations of the Cross as we processed across Forty-second Street in the heart of Manhattan. It was the first Pax Christi Peace Walk and would not have happened without the energy and enthusiasm Dave had had to "make the connections" (as he would say) between poverty, violence, exploitation, and politics as usual. Gathered near the steps of the New York Public Library, we had prayed for Dave, who was laid up in the hospital after months of living with shooting pain and weariness and was only now being treated for his not-very-exotic disease.

We visited him that afternoon and reported on the success of the walk, before leaving to prepare for the evening liturgy at the chapel, where his roommate, Joe, would carry the same cross that we had paraded through Manhattan that day. Dave's fiancée, Sue—they had met at a peace rally in D.C. some months before—left the hospital just as we were finishing up at Saint Paul's, but when we got back to the house, the phone rang with the devastating news that Dave had suffered a brain aneurysm. Sue, Joe, and a third friend, Mark, and I rushed to his bedside in time to have the worst of our fears solidified. Standing by his handsome face, so distorted with the futile tubes the doctors had inserted, I glanced at his best friend and the woman he was to marry and began to withdraw behind the mask that my collar always allowed me to wear in the face of death. "I have attended the dying before," I said to myself. "I can handle this. I need to be strong for them." Wordlessly, the answering horror on Joe's and Sue's faces peeled away what was left of my priestly armor, and my studied emotional reserve collapsed like a house of cards. An hour later, the monitor flatlined, and as Joe desperately tried CPR to revive his roommate, Dave left us.

The community, only recently named Cor Jesu (Jesus' Heart), flew to Columbus to bury him and returned to New York to memorialize their brother and friend. At the service back at Saint Paul's Chapel, Dan Berrigan poetized mightily and provided us all with the seeds of some hope in our loss. Amazingly, the community lasted for three more years, during which new people joined, sustained by a sense that they were participating in something larger than themselves. But then it came time for people to move on. The ministry knew much fruit from the community, as did the university, which today hosts a nonprofit organization that has sustained the work that Dave, and all those who were part of Diakonia, began. Community Impact, as it is now called, bestows the David Joyce Award annually as a tribute to a recipient involved in volunteer service. But within two weeks of Dave's sudden loss, financial trouble struck as well. The secretary at the Campus Ministry office was caught embezzling funds to the tune of over thirty thousand dollars. I should have caught it sooner but wasn't paying attention. So I presumed that I would have to pay with my job. Among others, Cardinal Cooke came to my rescue, signing the necessary papers to make the insurance company pay up within days of his own death from cancer.

This time, I tried to get a grip on things not by working harder, but by taking time to work out. I had dabbled in exercising with weights for a few years but hadn't made much progress. But when, in the middle of the investigation of the theft in my office, I heard that Joe, who worked in the office with me, was himself going back to the gym in the wake of his friend's death, I joined him. I have often said it saved my life. Facing forty, still struggling to make a go of it as a celibate, I had decided I needed to do something different. Reshaping the way I looked and felt about myself held out some hope. Some of my priest friends had also taken to the gym over the years, but we had never talked about it or worked out together. Even weight training was too charged a topic, especially since at least one of them had also joined the gay cruising scene as he buffed up. So, as in all of these matters, a gutless silence was maintained. As I also had taken up racquetball, I then got up the nerve to compete in some campus tournaments, generally developing a healthier sense of myself, which, I thought, could compensate for my being sexually frustrated.

But it was a two-edged sword. Not working out would have

kept me on the midlife clerical trajectory, becoming yet another Pillsbury Dough Boy in black, disdaining the body's claims, but not like the ascetics of old. Working out, and competing with college athletes—I, who had walked away from sports as an insecure adolescent—only changed the tone of my celibate frustration. That's when I took my first and only step outside the circle. Elena was a friend who was my age and had briefly been a graduate student ten years earlier. We had stayed in touch and gone to dinner maybe twice a year. Elegant, sophisticated, and successful, she had invited me to visit her place on the shore, and in front of the fire after a good dinner, I was far more sexually intimate than I had ever been. The bad news was that I hurt her, handling the aftermath of our evening together poorly. The good news was that I had *desired* her—not just entertained some idea of a woman or yet another masturbatory fantasy that I could get big but had wanted a live, lovely woman who would spend time with a male me. Yet after that evening, as confirming as it was, I still was not prepared to jettison my work, and because I would not play two sides of the street, I went on retreat some months later, wept over my mistake, and tried to recommit myself to living among others, for whom intimacy was real, as a gospel eunuch. The clock was ticking, but as yet I could not detect its distinctive sound.

Along about this time, the archdiocese announced a mandatory overnight conference that all priests had to attend on issues of wellness and physical health. If a boost to my self-esteem would do the trick, this was a place to get it. The group of several hundred that gathered at a retreat house was an actuary's nightmare. Overweight, most of them smoked, and many resented being called together to examine themselves and their habits of life. They sat through the doctor's slide show and its color pictures of a smoker's heart, a drinker's liver, and the like, making derogatory and defensive comments. The other focus of the meeting, of course, was drinking, and one of the sessions featured a psychiatrist from Saint Vincent's Hospital in Harrison, New York, where priests were sent to dry out or get psychiatric help when they needed it. In his talk, he tried to enunciate both the reasons for and the mechanics of reporting fellow priests who engaged in alcoholic behaviors. Perhaps no less than with a group of doctors or lawyers, his calling on a group of priests to police themselves, and to be frank with one another about detected failings, went over like a lead balloon. But he pressed his point about peer-to-peer responsibility, emphasizing the dangers of leaving the problem of priests' alcoholism or antisocial behavior unaddressed.

Because he was so insistent about the good we could do by being frank with one another, I raised another case with him. What if one priest became aware of another's having an affair, not with an underaged person but with an adult female who was otherwise free to have a relationship? The behavior wasn't pathological, just outside the normal rules. What would he advise? It was the only time in the course of the two days that the issue of sexuality was broached. Sweating, the doctor sidestepped the issue completely. For all his psychiatric credentials, he was not going to step into the minefield of mandated celibacy or even allow the question of sexual acting out to come up at the meeting. Out in the hallway afterward, I met an older colleague known for his straight-and-narrow approach to things, and was surprised when he thanked me for raising the question. "But they just won't let it be discussed. They don't want to hear about it," he said with some disgust. The issue of sexual health was not on the agenda. Neither was sexual acting out, which was still hidden away. Nor were there any prophets among us who had foresight about how badly the reputation of priests would suffer in the next fifteen years because of the sickness of some few priests who were given cover by a strategy of denial, cover-up, and evasion whose seeds had long since been sown.

My personal struggle with celibacy did have its emotional and sexual components, but it was not so buried in my psyche that it didn't get downright theological on occasion. As it happened, the catalyst for my most explicit argument with God (as opposed to my acting out with Elena) came one Sunday when the second reading for the day came from First Corinthians 7. I had always adhered to homiletic preaching, that is, addressing the scriptural texts designated rather than pulling sermon topics out of the air. But I probably avoided this particular text that Sunday because it took me to the edge of my tolerance for reading passages out of the original context in which they appeared. Paul wrote in that chapter the most explicit recommendation of celibacy in the New Testament, but it was clearly given in the light of what the Apostle called the "impending distress," the "appointed time" growing short, and the "passing away" of this world. Using himself as a model, he commended remaining unmarried but refused to impose on anyone his personal solution to the world change that he awaited. My own doctoral work guaranteed that I was no stranger to his letters, and to his mode of interpreting everything in the light of his own, overwhelming experience of Christ. But a close reading of Paul in his own, end-time context made it clear to me that Christians had read his Jewish messianic affirmations as if they were timeless moral teaching. In fact, despite the renewed liturgy's efforts at presenting far more of Paul's writings, the passages we read on Sundays are almost uniformly excerpted from his letters to make it sound as if Paul was always presenting moral or legal rulings that were not time-bound at all, but eternally valid: "Wives, be subject to your husbands"; "Let everyone be subject to the higher authority"; "Women should keep silent in the churches"; or "Live by the Spirit and do not gratify the desires of the flesh."

The crisis I endured on that Sunday was induced by a collapse of my sense not that I could interpret the words of Scripture, but that the words themselves were still reliable. It was as if, like the naïve evangelists I had once confronted, part of me still wanted the words themselves to heal my wounds or assuage my pain. But reading Paul's words didn't work that way at all:

> The unmarried man is busy with the Lord's affairs, concerned with pleasing the Lord; but the married man is busy with the world's demands and is occupied with pleasing his wife. This means he is divided. . . . I am going into this for your own good. I have no desire to place restrictions on you, but I want to promote what is good, what will help you to devote yourselves entirely to the Lord.

Though I was intellectually convinced that the historically conditioned statements of the Bible cannot be fobbed off as timeless truths (as church authorities still tend to do), the insight got me only so far. Because the world had not passed away, celibacy had become for me an ironclad rule of deprivation. So the passage felt like a lie. I understood that Paul meant his celibacy to be an anchor of hope that everything was about to change, but the truth of his words had become covered over by their being unnaturally forced to say something else two thousand years later. For some months, I found it hard to stand and deliver a homily with anything like the confidence I had brought to the task till then. What my head knew and what my heart could act on diverged, but I soldiered on, pushing myself yet again to find the key that I felt had to be missing for me.

The year after Dave died, I finally went into counseling and from there tried psychoanalysis in order to answer the question whether the celibate priesthood and my emotional health were long-term compatible. It would take a third try and another ten years before the question was finally answered. In the meantime, the diocesan landscape had shifted significantly. Being the spokesperson for Pax Christi in New York had put me in a tenuous position when my boss, Cardinal Cooke, as Archbishop of New York, was also head of the Military Ordinariate, in charge of Catholic chaplains during the years of Reagan's military buildup. When Bishop John J. O'Connor, himself a former admiral in the chaplains' corps, was elevated to the archbishop's job—even though a separate Military Ordinary was appointed after Cardinal Cooke died of cancer—I had a foretaste of doom, but that doom was a few years in coming.

In spring 1987, I arranged to have now Cardinal O'Connor invited to deliver the address at the university's interfaith baccalaureate service. I had hosted him once before as Merton Lecturer, in the series I had inaugurated back in 1978, on which occasion he delivered not a lecture but a rambling personal discourse mainly about himself. But inviting him back seemed the politically expedient thing to do, as Community Impact had been put together with explicit support from Catholic Charities, and I was laying down my role with Pax Christi to concentrate on building this new organization. Having tangled by now with gay activists and overcommitted himself to a press conference a week, at which he raised the hackles of many New York constituencies, the cardinal arrived on campus with protesters at the gates and a reputation for ornery notoriety. Ascending the high pulpit in the full-to-the-brim chapel where I had been celebrating Mass for fourteen years, he began graciously and proceeded to deliver a very credible address highlighting Alan Bloom's *The Closing of the American Mind*. But only a line or two into the address, he put me on notice. He said that he wanted to say how pleased he was before the service to meet all his "brother and sister clergy" (a surprisingly inclusive note). "But I was especially pleased to see Father Paul Dinter," he continued, "because he's the only one whom I can fire." Amid the general laughter, President Ellen Futter of Barnard College turned to me and asked, "How does that make you feel?"

Had I responded, I would have said, "Vulnerable." Within the week, I received a phone call from the cardinal's vicar for education, my immediate boss, Bishop Egan, who had come to my defense in civil court the previous year. When I visited with him, he told me he had a plan for campus ministry, and I didn't fit in it. He wanted a more intellectual tenor, not my socially active brand of campus ministry. I would have another year, as he had enough on his hands removing the chaplain at NYU, who was far too accommodating to the gay community. Perhaps most galling was the sham "evaluation" process that he had already put both of us through when his plans were a foregone conclusion. He said I should take a sabbatical and go to Rome, and then maybe I could return to the archdiocese to work again—but "I can't imagine your ever having a job as challenging and fulfilling as this one again." At first trying, then reconsidering, an appeal of his decision to the cardinal, such as he had granted to my colleague at NYU, thwarting Egan's plan, I spent my fifteenth and last year on campus preparing for a transition and a move away from a ministry that had taxed and delighted me to the max. I requested and received permission for a sabbatical year, which I did choose to spend in Rome. If I was going to make a continuing go of this life and work—having thrived, relatively speaking, in a very secular environment—I wanted to test myself among the institutions of its polar opposite, at the center of the Catholic world, in the Eternal City. In my own way, I was riffing on the song "New York, New York": if I could make it make sense there in Rome, I could make it make sense anywhere!

Perhaps I should have taken the hint and started looking for another career back then. Instead, I turned down efforts to recruit me to apply as chaplain at Catholic University in Washington, D.C., and at Thomas More House, the Catholic chaplaincy at Yale. As grateful as I was to be considered for those positions, I guess I didn't want to start all over again at another campus. Plus, I thought that trying to shape a worshipping community composed of multigenerational families, not just students, would be an appropriate challenge after my study sabbatical. The Columbia Campus Ministry I left behind was a very different animal than I had found. I could count as well how much I had changed, and in my farewell Mass, I credited that to the lay community that had collaborated with me so magnificently. My swan song to the campus came with the privilege I received to deliver the baccalaureate address a year after Cardinal O'Connor's had shortened my career. Challenging the graduates to integrate their competence with compassion as they went forth into the world, I tried to draw upon my own struggle for wholeness, one that I knew still had a way to go. One gushing parent approached me afterward and, surprisingly, put a monetary value on my message: "Thank you! You made the whole eighty thousand dollars worth it!"

But what hadn't changed in me took me one last time to Mount Saviour in an effort to sum up how far I had come and to prepare myself for the separation and potential isolation I expected to find abroad. By choosing to leave my family and friends, the community I had helped form, and the familiar pastoral scene of New York and head to Europe for a year, I was choosing a kind of classy exile. By spending most of that time in Rome, I would be running toward my problem, not away from it. I would be heading into the belly of the beast.

Five

The Men's Club on the Tiber

*B*ECAUSE JUNE WASN'T the time of year to be heading to Rome to start a sabbatical, I contacted a Dominican I knew at Blackfriars in Cambridge about staying in England over the summer. Asking around, he got me a two-month stint helping out the parish priest in a church on the outskirts of the famous university town, where I would also have time to write and travel. At the last wedding I had performed for a couple at Columbia, I had been introduced to the groom's brother, who had a bachelor flat in London. Peter welcomed me to stay with him on my way down to Cambridge and whenever I came up to London, so my summer was set. I could begin my sabbatical exploring sites in a physical and ecclesiastical landscape that had long fascinated me.

Oddly, the interlude proved more of an orientation to ecclesiastical Rome than I would have ever imagined. My stay in England inaugurated my effort to broaden my own base by contact with the center of the universal church, enriching my sense as well of ways in which local churches could fruitfully interact with it. At least, that was my hope at the time. Unlike the Catholic church in the United States, English Catholicism has deep roots and its own long and complex story. It shares with Irish Catholicism a history of persecution by both the Anglican and the Calvinist wings of the British establishment. But English Catholics have, by and large, managed to be loyal to the catholicity represented by the Bishop of Rome without fawning before Rome's pretensions to being the norm of universality. There is an Italianate wing of British Catholicism, represented by the Brompton Oratory, which, like the expatriate *scorpioni* led by Dame Maggie Smith in *Tea with Mussolini*, contemns its own native, British sensibility, preferring the more emotive atmosphere across the Alps. In the nineteenth century, Cardinal Newman acknowledged the extravagances of Italian piety, and he found room for a little over-the-top *romanissimo* because he understood that true religious worship is inevitably hedged round by superstition, which is some measure of faith's presence, perhaps even a necessary by-product of it. But he was equally clear that the regulating role in Catholicism remained its theological sense, not its devotional fervor or its authority structure.

So, while I did meet some *romanissimi* in England, I also encountered English members of international religious orders—Benedictines, Dominicans, Jesuits—who helped round out my grasp of the church scene. These orders, being international in scope and diverse in their work, have given enormous depth to Catholicism's clerical bench. They have also balanced the normal parochialism of diocesan bishops and their clergy, who were tied down to their localities by the reforms of the Council of Trent. Rivals, in some ways, of one another and of the diocesan clergy, orders like the Jesuits have thought of themselves as the papal cavalry, or special forces, which made the diocesan or secular clergy the church's infantry. One seminary rector once opined that if you wanted to teach, you should become a Jesuit; if you really cared about liturgy, there were the Benedictines; if you wanted to be a preacher, become a Dominican; but if you were ready to follow orders (and do nothing that special?), then you were meant to be a diocesan priest. I recognized the value of specialists but held firm to the role of the knowledgeable general practitioner of ministry for the local church.

But one of these men, whom I met at lunch at Blackfriars, though he was every bit a Brit, turned out to be a dyed-in-the-wool Romanizer. Father Nicholas Hadrian was a man with a sharp intellect, a severe demeanor, and an agenda to awaken Christendom from the kind of assimilationist thinking that he saw weakening Catholicism as the bulwark against society's alien influences. A noted fan of the current pope, he shuttled back and forth to Rome, as a member of a shadow network of traditionalist (right-wing) groups with all sorts of direct access to influential Vatican offices. The popularity the traditionalists enjoy, both at the Vatican and with politically conservative funding sources, stems from their following closely the script for theologians first laid down by Pius IX and reiterated right up to Vatican II: theologians were to "discover" support either in Scripture or tradition for the positions already arrived at by the official organs of the papacy. They were to be apologists for the "living" *magisterium*, or centralized teaching office.

The semioracular function of the papacy, itself an inflation of Vatican I's decree on infallibility, had a ready fan in Father Hadrian. His devotion to renewing Christendom led him one day to jump a jet for Vienna to lead the procession at the funeral of the Empress Zita, wife of the last Hapsburg claimant to the title of Holy Roman Emperor. A firm monarchist as well as an infallibilist, he could do no less for a woman who had upheld the old order late into the twilight of the twentieth century. Through my conversations with him, I learned of the kind of issues that kept people up at night in the Eternal City. We were within a year of the twentieth anniversary of *Humanae Vitae*, the papal birth control letter, whose teaching was as close to John Paul II's heart as it was far from the Catholic laity's. "There are some theologians," Father Hadrian assured me that first day over lunch, "who say that the pope holds that the teaching on contraception is infallible, but only in his capacity as a private theologian, not as the Holy Father." Breathing a sigh of relief, I replied, "Well, let's thank God for small favors" before I realized where he stood on the matter. The rest of lunch that day we spent uncomfortably avoiding a rematch.

My interlude around Cambridge was filled with many more delightful pastimes: punting on the Cam (I never got the poling technique down, so we tended to zigzag from bank to bank down the river); visiting the chapels and colleges; walking in the pastures called the "backs" on the other side of the river; roaming the bookstores; cycling back and forth into town. Celebrating Mass for the congregation at Saint Philip Howard, Cherry Hinton, was familiar and enjoyable, though the music, which derived from the English music hall, made "Kumbaya, My Lord" seem profound. On weekends, there were outrider Masses in two neighboring villages where the RCs rented the now Anglican parish churches for one weekend Mass. Both of those churches had been built before the Black Death in the late Middle Ages, and celebrating there certainly strengthened my sense of the deep roots of Christianity in England. Still, I was in Cambridge for over a month before I met any other priests, because the parish priest who engaged me to assist him lived like a recluse. The rectory was a modest brick structure at the end of a row of semidetached suburban homes, on a scale several degrees poorer than rectories in the States. Our social life was nil, and my few attempts at sitting with the P.P. in the small common room and watching cricket—the matches go on for days—made a game of solitaire seem exciting.

One evening, he was watching an old war movie on the telly—*Desert Fox* with James Mason as General Erwin Rommel of the famed Nazi Afrikacorps. Entering and sitting down, I ventured the question, "Was your father in the war?"

"Most certainly."

"My father, too. He served mainly in the Pacific. Where did your father serve?" I pushed farther into an effort at conversation.

"In North Africa," quiet Michael responded.

"He was *there*?" I thought I had a hit a vein we might mine.

"Yes."

Silence. I waited till a lull in the action and tried again. "Was he in any of the battles?"

"Captured. Spent the rest of the war in a prisoner-of-war camp." Conversation concluded.

Shortly afterward, when a young seminarian from the diocese arrived for a brief internship, things changed for the better. Within a day, we were sitting outside a riverside pub with pints and I was meeting some of the local priests, who had not heard that I was in town. Quiet Michael could not have been more different from sociable Jonathan, who took me on a tour of Nor- folk and its churches, showed me the re-creation of Julian of Norwich's hermit haunt (the original was destroyed by Nazi bombers), and generally revived my hopes that my time in En- gland would not all be spent as if I had entered a monastery. When I finally rented an auto, I managed to find my way up and back from London, which for a New York motorist feels like tra- versing Brooklyn and Queens completely on local streets. I also set out on a day's pilgrimage from Cambridge to Oxford, not to visit the rival university as such, but to spend time in venues mainly associated with John Henry Newman (1801–1890) in the period that led up to his becoming a Catholic in 1845.

At Littlemore, the semimonastic community where he gath- ered like-minded young men around him, and at Saint Mary's in Oxford (where he preached the sermons that made up some of my sabbatical reading), it is still possible for a person of fertile his- torical imagination to sense his impact. When he resigned from Saint Mary's and abandoned the Reformation's claim that Prot- estantism represented a more primitive form of Christianity, he declared, "In a higher world it is otherwise, but here below to live is to change, and to be perfect is to have changed often." This meant that the articulation of Christian belief "changes . . . in order to remain the same," Newman wrote. Ironically, he chose Catholicism as the more dynamic faith tradition only one year before Cardinal Giovanni Mastai-Ferretti became Pius IX, and just three years before the political revolutions of 1848 scared the pope into his increasingly reactionary stance toward modernity. But like someone looking through a telescope, Newman understood that corruption in religion was caused by a "refusal to follow the course of doctrine as it moves on," when "an obstinacy in the notions of the past" was preferred over change. These convictions made him a contentious figure in his own time but have secured for him the title "Father of Vatican II."

Driving back on that long English evening, I zigzagged along the only roads that ran through Buckinghamshire to Cambridge, stopping to have a solo dinner in a restaurant that had all the markings of a Tudor inn. For years, I had avoided solo dining. Better to snack or even skip a meal than cook one for myself alone or, even worse, sit alone and eat a meal, staring across at no one in a public setting. Though known as solitaries, even monks ate together—cenobites living in common—supporting one another in their disciplined inner searching. But sitting in that cozy corner of English country comfort, I was trying to condition myself to feeling at peace with being alone—again. All of a sudden I was an altar boy once more, kneeling in adoration in my parish church back home, feeling alone but working hard to find a purpose to my aloneness. Could I be both alone and whole? This was the question I had come on sabbatical to answer. Back at Cherry Hinton, I felt some sense of accomplishment that I had navigated the visit solo and managed to touch holy ground.

While in Oxford, I had also managed to visit Blackwell's bookstore. In that famous book-buyer's haunt, I had a chance encounter with a theologian whom I had not previously known. Along the back of the store, along a wall ceiling-high with bookshelves, I was thumbing through a £32 ($50!) theological tome when he approached me and we struck up an acquaintance. Tall and bearded in monkish fashion, he was in civvies as I was, but the book I was perusing had given me away. As we talked, the topic of my sabbatical and my Rome destination came up. Since we had interests in common, he promised to meet up with me there, offering me some hints about negotiating the baroque landscape of overblown theological claims currently in fashion.

Packing up in early September as autumn made an early entrance, I was met in London by friends from the States. We took the boat train to Paris, rented a *voiture*, and drove through an increasingly damp month via Rheims, Heidelberg, and Stuttgart down into Luzern, Switzerland. Paying a small fortune for a cable car ride to the top of Mount Titlis, we arrived at a summit totally enveloped in bright white fog. Visibility: ten feet. Glad to be off the mountain, we headed south and, after enduring a claustrophobic eleven-mile drive under the Alps, emerged in a flash of bright sun on the southern flank of the mountains, turning the clock back to summer in a mere eleven minutes. No one was minding the Italian border when we arrived on a Sunday at the dinner hour, so we continued driving south, overnighting at Parma, and detouring around Rome for several days at Positano, on the Amalfi coast. We then reversed course and, heading north, fought our way through Rome's traffic nightmare and located my sabbatical quarters, the Collegio Maryknoll, via Sardegna 84, a few blocks east of the via Veneto.

Rome remains a city of enormous contradictions that has physically survived by living, first of all, in the imagination. For more then six centuries after Alaric the Visigoth's sack of the city in A.D. 410, Rome shriveled, its monuments sinking into the soil. But Rome sustained its mental hegemony in western Europe, based on its glorious antiquity and Christianity's engrafting the legend of Peter and Paul onto the older legend of the city's mythical founders, Romulus and Remus, even as the city became a back-water. Still impressive enough centuries later to host the crowning of Charlemagne on Christmas Day A.D. 800, it was a wispy shadow of the earlier *urbs*, the city that had dominated the Mediterranean for centuries. The city's revival took almost the same amount of time as its decline. Accompanying Europe's slow rise out of the morass which we call the Dark Ages, the city reached a population of thirty-five thousand by the year 1200. By then, a resurgent economy had created both agricultural and trading riches and had contributed to the wealth and influence of church institutions as well. Money pouring into Rome and the papal curia had the temporary effect of refurbishing many churches with magnificent mosaic work and the highly stylized marble carving and inlay that came to be known as *cosmatesque*. But Boniface VIII's death in 1304 was followed shortly by the transfer of the papacy and its patronage to Avignon. After the Great Plague devastated the continent in midcentury, revisiting Rome every so often, the city's population had shrunk again—to about seventeen thousand.

Papal Rome per se came into its own only with the jubilee year of A.D. 1600, itself an amazing accomplishment because the second great sack of the city had occurred in 1527, as the result of a dispute between the Catholic emperor Charles V and the Medici prince-pope Clement VII. Charles's troops were largely Lutheran and so carried out random pillaging and looting with newly found religious zeal. Rome's resurgence, and its determina-tion to turn back the tide of Protestantism, demanded its own artistic and architectural signature: thus the baroque era was born, shaping a city of papal propaganda that endures to this day.

Securing a berth at the Collegio Maryknoll was a stroke of good fortune. The Maryknoll Missioners, headquartered not far from where I grew up in Westchester County, had been sending

Americans abroad since shortly after their founding in 1911. As a society of men who had all needed to find a home away from home, they knew how to play host to guests. Things got a little strained here and there when the guests were female, but Brother Peter took the heat and applied the Gospel norm of hospitality even to them! Built in an area that had been fields and vineyards of the Boncompagni family until 1870, the residence occupied the former palazzetto of some deceased cardinal. In a space that accommodated one prince of the church and his servants, at least twelve residents and guests lived in reasonable comfort. I received one of the student rooms on the top floor in the old servants' quarters, with a window looking out over the enormous magnolia tree in the rear garden and beyond to some not-so-distinguished-looking rooftops pierced by TV antennas. In Rome, unlike in England, I was among other priests all day every day except when I went off to a local gym, which I discovered buried under the Borghese Gardens.

We were, of course, a mixed group. The Maryknoll Fathers and Brothers had not been adding many new members of late, the reason they had rooms for us guests. Only four of the residents were Maryknollers, two of them in the student quarters: Neil McGuire, who had worked in Tanzania, constantly had long, loud conversations in Swahili on the antique phone in the common hallway, and seemed to covet a position with the Roman Congregation in charge of mission countries, and Ned Galtner, who had worked in Egypt and was finishing a degree at the Pontifical Biblical Institute and was one of the few Arabists at the Biblicum. He had always appeared to me skeptical of some of the normal arrangements in the all-male world of the clergy. Today he is a married professor of the Bible and far more relaxed as a result. Of the other guests, Larry Brown had resided at Maryknoll the longest, having been plucked out of the diocese of Fargo, North Dakota, and sent to study canon law at the Angelicum, or "The Lazy A," as it had been dubbed by students across town at the Jesuit-run Gregorianum. Last to come that year was Tony, a former monk working as a priest in the diocese of Santa Rosa, California, a *sabatista* like myself.

Life at the college followed a very normal routine. Daily Mass was concelebrated by all priests who cared to do so at 7 a.m. I wondered at first at the dispatch with which the liturgy was carried out. In a house full of priests, only some of whom vested every day to concelebrate, I guess I expected the liturgical menu to contain a richer daily diet—no one ever preached; there were no prayers of petition. But the imperative seemed to be to finish in time to let everyone grab a light breakfast downstairs and get back up to the TV lounge by 7:30 for the rebroadcast on a Swiss network of the *CBS Evening News with Dan Rather* from the night before. So while watching the news remained a daily feature for me, I only sporadically attended the "quick-and-dirty" daily Mass.

Since we were in Rome, we did what the Romans did and sat down to *pranzo* every day at 1 p.m. Sensibly, our evening supper only consisted of soup or sandwiches or a combination of both, coming after daily cocktails, which took place at a genuine social hour. As good a men's club setting as it gets. The table was graciously laid, and we were free to invite guests, many of whom marveled at the cuts of meat that Brother Peter secured from the Vatican butcher on weekly shopping trips. Conversation rarely lagged or turned clerically negative, as the general human carnival which is Rome and the Vatican always kept us in fresh topics, rumors about who's in and who's out of favor, reports of celebrity sightings, and so on. One of the other sabbatical guests that year, Jake Rideau, had the habit of taking a daily constitutional across the Veneto, down the via Francisco Crispi to the del Tritone, across the Corso, through the viali of the Campo Marzio, out along the Tiber, past the Castel Sant'Angelo, and up Mussolini's broad via della Conciliazione to Saint Peter's—at least a mile and half. There he would consult the schedule of events, hoping to make his day by seeing the pope cross the square, or celebrate a Mass, or appear at his window. Months into his stay in Rome, he would return at lunch and, if fortunate enough to have gotten a glimpse and a pause in the chatter, would announce, "I saw the Holy Father today. Oh, it was so wonderful!" and proceed to narrate the details, like a boy at his first Macy's Thanksgiving Day Parade.

Father Rideaux seemed to have as bad a case of papal fever as one runs into in the Holy City. Its symptoms affect many visitors to Rome, as well as millions of people who have encountered John Paul II on his world missionary travels. Contracted via a wicked transference, it causes people to bundle a host of conscious and unconscious expectations that they have had of significant individuals (perhaps even of God) and direct them toward the person of the Holy Father (the name is no accident). Because Papa Wojtyla believes he *is* the Holy Father, he strives to mirror those expectations and beam them right back where they came from. Remarkable things can happen. At Yankee Stadium, I'd seen him charm sixty-five thousand people like a good politician working a small roomful of constituents. It caused one of the first "waves," already popular at soccer matches, to be introduced to the House That Ruth Built. As John Paul's gaze, working in tandem with the patented papal wave of the hands upward, circled the stands, the beamed-back waves of transferred emotion made the circuit of the stadium as well. Section by section, the crowd in all three decks rose and fell back with frenzied cheers and cries of "Viva il Papa." Standing no more than three hundred yards away from him, I swore he saw me in the crowd of priests where I was cheering him on, looked into my eyes, and knew who I was! Hundreds, if not thousands, that night felt the same thing, and literally hundreds of millions have experienced his amazing presence around the world.

As a rare peak moment, the exchange of vicarious emotions involved here can be exhilarating, though it is rife with possibilities for exaggeration. My friend Elena, who visited me in Rome, had never seen the pope before. So she took herself off to the regular Wednesday audience. An urbane sophisticate who lost her father when she was young, she came back from the event a basket case. Elena thought that she was going out of curiosity as much as devotion but discovered that she was looking for someone she had lost a long time ago, and for a brief moment, she was in his presence. She wept the whole time she was at the audience, not knowing quite where her emotions came from or what they meant. Experiences like the one she had at the Vatican are sacramental in the sense that, like all significant human interactions, they signify far more than can be said about them. No less is this the case with the papacy. But trading on this idealized exchange of love—asking people to accept the pope's every word and action as divinely inspired—cynically abuses it and turns the moment into a program for subservient fealty.

One day, crossing the Piazza Navona, I had a chance encounter with one of the papacy's perfervid supporters whom I had met back at Columbia. Propriety dictated we speak, or rather that I listen as Father Silver expounded on the pope's agenda in moving the church to the center of public life so as to challenge the "culture of death" he found so pervasive in modern life. Concluding, the priest questioned me catechetically: "Don't you hold that a genuine loyalty to the person of the Holy Father is constitutive of Catholic faith?" Surprised to be flung back into an apologetical debate from circa 1870, I countered modernistically with the question "Would you ask that if the pope were Alexander VI or Julius II?" (The first was the father of the famous bastards Lucrezia and Cesare Borgia; the second, the della Rovere enemy of the first, enamored of warfare, whose mania for rebuilding Saint Peter's as his own tomb triggered the Protestant Reformation.) The priest was bewildered by my effort to separate the person from the office and to understand the office itself in a more nuanced way than papal monarchists want to do; he rested his case for John Paul's personal authority on a kind of baroque enthusiasm, like the nineteenth-century Salesian Don Bosco, who declared the pope to be "God on earth."

Meanwhile, at the Collegio Maryknoll, creeping infallibilism had continued to overcome Father Jake. When the opportunity came for him to put his name on the list of priests who got to concelebrate Mass with the pope in his private chapel, he could hardly contain himself. He was antsy for days beforehand, leaving that morning for the Vatican way before the cocks crowed. Afterward, at lunch, he went on at length about how moved he had been to be in the same room, how happy he was to have had his photo taken with the pope afterward, and how the purpose of his stay in the Holy City had been fulfilled. The whole episode, and his description of why the Mass was so special, suggested what can happen when symbols, even sacramental ones, are mistaken for the Reality. In practice, the opportunity for priests to celebrate the Eucharist together with their own bishop, the way an abbot does with his monks (and nuns *don't* get to do with the abbesses), is rare enough. Perhaps in smaller dioceses, a bishop plays a humbler role as primus inter pares (first among equals) and will risk a celebration with colleagues, even taking the opportunity to remove his miter and speak man-to-men. But most big-city hierarchs operate only on a big stage with supporting cast in place. As a result, few priests have had the kind of collegial experience built into the very architecture of the old Roman basilicas.

In the rounded apses of those churches, under the mosaic of Christ in glory, or the Lamb of God, or the Tree of Life, the bishop sat center with his elder-advisers (what "presbyter" or "priest" really means) to his right and to his left, like arms enfolding the congregation. Every celebration of the Eucharist in those churches enacted the shape of the presbyterate, for the bishop had come from among these men and led them as the head of a college, not as a prince set above them. But as the pope's private chapel was built much later, no such symbolism operates there.

This is the pope's Mass, shared according to the rubrics with concelebrants and whatever lay faithful are admitted, but it is the pope's personal expression of daily religious devotion.

Oddly the Mass seems to reach its apogee only after the celebration of communion, when the pope retires to his kneeler for his "thanksgiving" reflection. At any rate, that's what impressed Jake the most, and he effused on the moment this way: "And it was so wonderful being so close to him and watching him pray so intently. I felt so close to God at that time above all. And then he spoke to us all afterward and asked us where we were from, before he left. Golly, I can't get over how lucky I've been to celebrate Mass with the Pope himself!" Jack ended near tears.

Larry, our canon lawyer with an interest in good liturgy, was the first to speak: "But, Jack, you celebrate Mass every day. Isn't God as close to you then?"

"Well, yes, but it's different, you see! There's lots of us, but there's only one Holy Father, who we know is guided directly by God! I don't think I'll ever feel like I did today for as long as I live."

Larry countered, annoyed, "So who's being worshipped here? God? Or the pope?"

Poor Jake was in over his head and avoided a confrontation, but down the table, Ned frowned at me and whispered under his breath, "That guy drives me crazy. He's like a boy in the body of a man."

Ned was onto something which I had been wrestling with all over Rome. I had started feeling comfortable getting around the city by myself, coming and going from the Gregorian University to sit in on a seminar in Hans Urs von Balthasar's theology and making occasional trips to the Vatican, touring the other basilicas and museums dotting the city. Rarely would I wear clerical garb—even black suits are a compromise, full dress cassocks still being the norm with the locals. Surely there were entirely too many priests on display here already. Both in the city and at the Vatican, especially, the ratio of clergy to laity seemed all wrong, an inversion of the idea that the church is the People of God whose servants are the ordained. There at the hub, the pope and his robed minions are a ruling class, the center of a tourist industry and a prosperous little economy, but masters as well of a spiritual universe. The first time I sensed the minihigh that comes from being one of them, I was following careful instructions from another priest, arranging for a tour of the Scavi, the excavations beneath Saint Peter's—one of the most fascinating sights in a city full of them. Very careful about these rituals, Jason was familiar to me from years before, when I would attend Mass in his parish the year I taught high school. As a seminarian home on the weekend, he would prance around the altar fussing over details a little too fastidiously—good training for the vice-chancellorship he now held in his diocese. Now he had instructed me to wear my clericals to ease the transaction and had given me directions to the office beneath where the sacristy juts out from the marble mass of the Renaissance- and Baroque-era megachurch. So I dressed on that occasion and headed across town to the Vatican, walking across the immense piazza and heading to the left of the basilica's entrance through the vehicle-accessible archway opposite the Scala Regia. The entranceway was manned by a Swiss guard in full regalia, halberd at arm's length and anchored against his Renaissance-era boot. I was composing a brief request in Italian for permission to proceed on my way when he snapped to attention, clicked the heels of his boots, and drew his halberd before his face in salute. I passed through the gate and out of tourist land into the sacred enclosure and accomplished my errand in no time. It was enough to make me believe that I was somebody important.

Ostensibly, the world's most ornate shrine exists to memorialize Simon bar Jonah the fisherman, promoted to Cephas, or Peter, the Rock, who was almost certainly buried here near the site of his crucifixion in Nero's Vatican gardens. But, of course, over the centuries this tomb site of so many popes—saints and scoundrels—has become a shrine to the papacy itself and to its pretensions to a putative "universal ordinary jurisdiction" over the whole Catholic world. That's what creates the magnetic attraction that draws certain types of church people so powerfully. It's the center, and every other place is on the periphery. But to the extent that the trappings of this jewel of a ministate inspire such awe, they function like painterly trompe l'oeil, fooling the eyes of the beholder to misconstrue beauty for truth and goodness. Yet the "simple faithful" who come in their multitudes to see the pope and cheer his appearances are not the most likely people to swallow the appearance for the reality. Vatican officials tend to see the masses as evidence of support for the pope's brand of leading the church. But the crowds who throng ceremonies at Saint Peter's, as at the recent canonization of the fanatically beloved Padre Pio, are not that gullible. They come as much for a stamp of approval on their own religiosity as to make any statement of their fealty to the one, holy, catholic, and apostolic church and its headman. In Rome there are always more layers at work than the most obvious one.

In many ways it is the papal officials themselves who are needy of what the Vatican, as a society dispensing spiritual favor, bestows. Long before they achieve their insider status, they can be found clustered in the literally countless religious houses and seminaries that keep the specter of the worldwide vocation crisis invisible at the center of the Catholic world. Because Rome is the center, it is also a listening post where even small religious orders and national hierarchies keep a presence so as not to miss out on the holy action. Being a big and wealthy church, the U.S. hierarchy has several establishments and U.S. religious orders have dozens. Even our small Collegio Maryknoll functioned that way, filtering information to the Vatican gathered from its contacts in China and trying to keep abreast of the latest moves by the pope and his enforcer, Cardinal Ratzinger, to stamp out what was left of the liberation theology and the base community movement in Latin America.

Despite having colleagues at the North American College (NAC) and at its graduate affiliate—the Casa Santa Maria, on the via dell'Umiltà—I rarely ate in either place or socialized much in their rarified atmosphere. The latter, called "the Casa" for short, was a converted convent located not far from the Trevi Fountain in a central but noisy location. I often hooked up there with another New York priest whom I'll call Daniel, who was a friend of a friend back home. We became friends, too, that year, having a lot of common interests, but dining out when we got together to escape the oppressively clerical air on Humility Street. It was a shame, in a way, because the house's cloister, its garden, its baroquely marbled chapel, and even its refectory, where Napoleon had stationed his horses, were museum quality and made for an interesting setting where I would have enjoyed spending more time. NAC had been built only in the 1950s on land suborned from the poorer Urban College, providing an opportunity for postwar American riches to erect an enormous, fortresslike gated compound with magnificent views overlooking the Vatican. Its style might best be characterized as sterile grandeur. It houses seminarians sent from dioceses all over the States (despite its name, I never met a Canadian or Mexican there), and even Dunwoodie in 1964 did not exude the self-satisfied smugness one sensed at NAC. The familiar spectrum of clerical types displayed itself a quarter century later, even if the numbers and ratios differed. Out-and-out jocks seemed far fewer, and the ones there were seemed much more determined to stand out. Because the bar for masculine types in seminaries had been significantly lowered, there was a small coterie of young men who stood apart in the softer environment by doing enough weight lifting to look like bodybuilders. Far more prominent than these few, though, were the young men I kept experiencing as overeager, overwrought with emotion at ordination ceremonies, and seemingly ready to audition for a runway turn in the clerical fashion show in Fellini's *Roma* at the drop of a pizza-shaped black hat. Attending a reception at the big college after one ordination, I was struck by just how much gushing and hugging went on, and not mainly with family members visiting for the occasion.

Spending time one evening with one of these gushing young clerics only made me warier of the impact of the Roman clerical scene on the health of the priesthood worldwide. The occasion was a formal dinner when Cardinal O'Connor came to town. A regular visitor to the Vatican, where he sat on several high-level committees of cardinals, O'Connor would at times bring a group of clergy with him if the occasion warranted it. On those occasions, tradition dictated that all his clergy in the city gather with him for an evening meal in one of the city's many great restaurants. Getting the invite meant "Show up." Not getting it meant "Don't show your face." I never figured out which was worse. On this particular occasion, dinner was to be preceded by drinks in the apartment of Cardinal Baum, the former Archbishop of Washington, who—Roman rumor had it—had received his hasty summons to a position in the papal curia after the police back home raided an off-hours cinema in the District. His Eminence's apartment topped what I had taken to be an office building. It opened onto the Piazza Pio XII, facing the great open-armed colonnade Bernini designed as the gateway to San Pietro in Vaticano. It had an extensive rooftop terrace with a spectacular view of the basilica and Saint Peter's Square in one direction and the cityscape of Rome in the other. But we were there only long enough for me to wonder about what a comparable piece of real estate might cost in New York, before the dozen or so of us were ushered back downstairs and across the boulevard to the Hotel Columbus, where a private dining room had been booked for the cardinal's party. It was not ready on time, and the delay may have made the Eminence a little testy.

At the base of the U-shaped table sat John O'Connor with

two curial officials, Archbishop Justin Rigali (now in St. Louis) on one side, and Archbishop John Foley of the Pontifical Commission on Communications on the other. Next to Foley, in a fourth chair, sat Father Eager, a newly ordained priest, who seemed to make a point of trailing along at such events. He was a convert whose father had been a Pentagon official during the Reagan years, which must have been his connection with our Eminent Admiral since he was not from New York. He stayed chipper throughout, engaging one of the Big Men in conversation whenever he could. I sat next around the corner with my friend Daniel on my right elbow ready to join in the general conversation that such a table arrangement fostered. Except that there wasn't any. Restless with playing the gracious host, the cardinal would aim random barbed comments or questions to one side or the other, then resume brief exchanges with his fellow prelates. Soon Daniel's turn came. He was finishing his third year in Rome with the Benedictine faculty at Sant'Anselmo, where he was qualifying for his doctorate in liturgical theology—a degree that made him suspect in the eyes of any good Gent. "So, Daniel, what have you been doing here?" the Great Man boomed.

Wary, he responded, "I'm finishing my dissertation on the reformed liturgy of the Paschal Vigil, Your Eminence."

Without batting an eye, O'Connor shot back, "Well, I'm sure that will play well in the South Bronx!" So much for Daniel's study of the most central celebration of the entire church year.

I knew that, when among priests, O'Connor rarely turned down an opportunity to belittle or weaken the position of someone who might rival his own preeminence. To me the dinner felt a little like being back in the Hayes dining room, where large dinners often played out like something of a spectator sport. So, awaiting the next course, we all sat around the U waiting to see who of us would next be skewered for the general entertainment. My turn would come soon enough. During another lull when O'Connor was sufficiently bored with normal conversation, he looked down the table in my direction and asked what I was up to on my sabbatical.

"I'm writing a book, Your Eminence."

"On what?"

"On how believers today can overcome their sense of loss . . ." But he had turned away already and was engaging in some repartee at the other side of the table. Meanwhile Father Eager was discoursing at some length on how hard it was going to be for him to leave Rome: "Oh, I'm sure there will be a lot of interesting things that they'll ask me to do in my ministry back in the States. But it just won't be the same. Here, you feel so close to the church, to its inner dynamism. I'll miss the chance to go to Saint Peter's so often—I can see part of the dome from my window at the college. It's just not going to be the same."

Coming away from such clerical soirees, I invariably felt as if I had been to Boys' World, an amusement park for stunted emotional male souls. Within its confines, life remains premodern in its affective arrangements, lacking none of the modern conveniences, but decidedly backward nonetheless. Many men who answer its siren call compensate for the Gospel's softer side (boys aren't big on compassion) by developing a hard external shell that, combined with a certain kind of charm, prospers them in the very male society of the clergy. Other clergy, who do not develop their defenses, out of a commitment to humbly serving, are easily victimized by those who lord it over them from the seats of power. Neither position is a recipe for maturity. Neither ever requires men to develop emotional autonomy or the ability to enter into genuinely mutual relationships—certainly not with any adult living women, who remain in the shadows of ecclesiastical Rome.

For, despite all the prominent feminine images in Rome of Mary (as God-Bearer, as Queen, as Sorrowing Mother), of Veronica, of Teresa, of the Magdalene, of Agnes and Cecilia and the other female martyrs of the church, the City on the Tiber remains the most exclusive men's club of all. Yes, there are religious women there in abundance, some in respectable jobs in the curia, some managing their own orders' works of charity. But women, as human beings made in the image and likeness of God, appear at most as auxiliary helpmates, not actors in their own right. In her role as wife and sexual partner of the husband, as reality principle and ground of both his posterity and future, as recipient of his sexual gift and bestower of her own love gift, as coagent of his maturity, she is wholly absent.

The formula has worked for centuries, and despite the present pope's efforts to redress the worst of the silence surrounding women, he has been adamantly opposed to changing the chemistry between men and women and among adults in their sexual relations with one another. He trusts only himself to give voice to the highest aspirations of women, believers and nonbelievers alike. In this effort, he seems to be taking his cue from a now famous episode that sent panic echoing through the halls of the Vatican when, for the one brief shining moment, the voice of women counted. The panic resulted from the final report of the papally established birth control commission and led to the sneaky publication, two years later in 1968, of Paul's VI's disastrous encyclical. Robert Blair Kaiser's *The Encyclical That Never Was* (the English title; the American one, *The Politics of Sex and Religion*, did not help to sell it) details the story of that commission and its potentially revolutionary impact. Though starting off, under John XXIII, as a typically Roman men's discussion group, the commission was expanded, by its own members' insistence, to include women—not academic feminists, but Catholic mothers active in the Christian Family Movement, whose input complemented the testimony of doctors and who reflected on the regulation of birth from an experiential rather than a philosophical base. Slowly, like the *Titanic* making a successful turning maneuver, the commission listened. Loosing its anchor from the philosophical analysis that acts follow preordained ends, it moved to develop the teaching on the role of sexuality in marriage. The groundwork for change was laid. Amazingly, an additional Commission of Cardinals signed on, but as Paul VI dithered, the theologians in the minority (and perhaps the young Cardinal Wojtyla as well) fought a ferocious rearguard action. Their logic was airtight and gave no room for the Spirit to blow so much as a whisper. If the teaching against every single act of artificial contraception changed, then it would be argued that its prohibition in the past, by Pius XI and Pius XII, was in error. And while error might have been granted a right to exist at Vatican II, the new candor did not extend to papal error!

So *Humanae Vitae* locked the gates against change and development of Catholic moral teaching on sexuality, and the issue eventually became a test of who would make it into the upper reaches of leadership. Under Paul VI, a small movement in the direction of democratizing the choice of bishops had taken place. Instead of the process being completely stage-managed from Rome, priests from the actual dioceses were nominated after discreet, local inquiries were held. Their appointment resulted in a more diverse and pastorally sensitive episcopacy in the United States, one capable, into the 1980s, of challenging the political establishment on both nuclear weapons and the economy. As a fledgling expression of the ancient practice of collegiality, revived by Vatican II, it gave a livelier shape to the checks and balances that elevate church governance over mullahlike tyranny. But as an experiment in picking leadership "from below," it was short-lived. Under John Paul II, who novelly insists that he has been given by the Lord Himself the office of directly appointing bishops for the whole church, before a man is to be ordained a bishop he must take an oath that he will not raise his voice on the issue of birth control or women's role in the church. So stasis has been canonized in the corridors of power, and men sworn to uphold the moral perspective of a sexually neutralized class of males retain their humorless hold on official Catholic teaching about issues over which they eschew any direct experience.

While in Rome, I got to witness just how humorless the Roman clerical position in these matters remains. As spring deepened and the academic year drew to a close, I attended Daniel's
doctoral defense. In general, the Roman universities were fascinating to me because it seemed that much of the theological
drama lacking at the papal court took place in them. Any interplay that survives in Rome among the remnants of the "schola of
theologians" that Cardinal Newman saw to be the true guardians
of the faith actually takes place here on the various faculties.
Though no academic free-for-all, the university scene has im-
proved from the days before the Vatican Council, when, if a professor displeased a high-ranking Vatican bureaucrat, he could be
banned from teaching and publishing for being insufficiently sup-
portive of the *integriste*, or intransigent, party. Even now, being a
Roman academic takes a certain amount of playing-along-to-get-
along. Theologians must learn how to use the academic idiom to
the full to disguise critiques that are devastating at the level of the
footnotes.

At the universities, doctoral defenses are not closed interviews,
as they are in the United States, but open colloquies at which a
candidate must demonstrate proficiency with the material presented in the written thesis. At the clerical colleges, they are major social events. Friends come from near and far to listen (if the
previews are favorable) and prepare to support the candidate and
celebrate with him afterward. So on a glorious Roman spring afternoon, a party gathered to listen to Daniel's Class A defense of
his dissertation, in which his own access to the manuscripts in the
Vatican library had corrected a misreading of an ancient text by
a noted authority. After initial congratulations, we gathered for
drinks at the Casa before retiring to the neighborhood trattoria,
Da Sciarra, for a festive dinner.

Aside from his professors, who included the noted European
scholar of liturgy Father Adrian Nocent, as well as a priest and a
nun friend from New York, the crowd of twenty or so included

other students in liturgical studies and the New York clergy who were students in Rome. Just before the dessert course, during a brief period of speeches of appreciation, the priest visiting from New York—where jokes about HIV/AIDS had become part of the way the epidemic swelling there was dealt with—began distributing a bunch of small "favors" in little white packages. Too shy to make a fittingly grand presentation, he passed them around the table and then watched each of us take one and pass the rest. Receiving one of them, I saw that it was labeled "Daniel's Defense." There were only puzzled looks, then a hearty laugh from Father Nocent, then grim faces. A personal souvenir condom! To me the humor resided less in the disconnect between a doctoral defense and a little latex shield than in the grumpy response of the priests, for whom condoms signaled nothing but sexual immorality.

Just how grim the Roman ecclesiastical perspective on male ejaculation of sperm is became clear to me during some of the more interesting conversations I enjoyed over afternoon coffee at the Bar Sant'Eustachio, just off the piazza of the same name. That's where I met up again with my acquaintance from Blackwell's, once we got in touch in Rome. These were my equivalent of Tuesdays with Morrie, postsiesta coffee and conversation with an older and a wiser man who had negotiated the theological back alleys of the clerical culture for decades. As the twentieth anniversary of *Humanae Vitae* drew near, the Vatican planned a conference to note its significance and celebrate its vision, an affair staged even more carefully than a production of *Aida* at the Terme di Caracalla. As such, it excluded people such as my conversation partner, who, though of international renown, was still persona non grata in the Vatican Congress hall. For Morrie (as I'll call him) had pointed out that Paul VI's own anguish in issuing the letter, its apologetical tone (so unlike the easy certainties of Pius XI's *Casti Conubii*), and the emotions and reactions set off by it had revealed the pope, the curia, and the church to be composed of ordinary human beings. But John Paul's Vatican had set out not just to restate that teaching more positively, but also to banish any uncertainty about its divine inspiration, and voices like Morrie's were not welcome.

His life and work were evidence for an equal and opposite reaction theologically to Rome's pull toward the center. But because all roads lead there, they take traffic from all directions and create a fruitful mix despite the tendency to homogenize thought. The global reach of the religious orders, in particular, brings to Rome thinkers who can put real flesh on the bones of the Christian body, pluralizing or diversifying the totality of experience on which faith reflects. Though, on the surface, the principle "don't make waves" reigns as supreme as the pontiff, significant stealth theological work takes place, waiting for an opportunity to help the church make an evolutionary leap forward before the house enforcers rush in again. Lucky enough to meet some of these unsung servants of an ongoing but underground aggiornamento, I was very encouraged by their ability to plug away at fulfilling the Gospel mandate of being learned enough to produce not one single product, but the right combination of "the new and the old" (Matthew 13:52).

And none seemed more capable of doing so than my ecclesiastical Morrie, who carried on his scholarly work discreetly despite the pressures to conform. Having learned the topics of the talks being given at the Vatican's twentieth anniversary fest, I was angered enough by one of them to bring the matter up one afternoon over coffee with him. One speaker not only blamed the contraceptive mentality for the world's evils—abortion, euthanasia, in vitro fertilization, and so on—but did so based on his insistence that contraception itself was murder and needed to be named for the crime that it was. How, I wondered aloud, could such a biologically uninformed perspective possibly be advanced, let alone inflated into a blanket moral condemnation? I told Morrie of the look of horror on the faces of Daniel's dinner guests.

For them, perhaps, and certainly for the outraged Vatican spokesman, the sperm contained the actual homunculus, or minihuman being! Spilled seed did not participate in nature's exuberance, its overambitious, evolutionary efforts to guarantee successful procreation against the odds. Rather, it contained the equivalent of a little silver bullet with a name on it, meant to find its way to a womb and gestate. If it is frustrated from that predetermined end, evil wins the day!

Morrie was always patient with my disgust, and full of insight. The issue, he reminded me, was as old as Aristotle, who created the system of analysis first adopted by the medieval Scholastics and then revived at the end of the nineteenth century. In that way of thinking, each human capacity was seen as having an inbuilt purpose or "end" without reference to its interrelationship with the body (much less the person) as a whole. Sexual behavior did not relate to the whole human being—it was determined, rather, by the "natural" end or function of the sexual organs. "People who think that way don't take things as a whole," Morrie told me. "They view people only in their component parts," so much so that the whole morality of human sexual behavior has been "deduced from its connection with the male emission of semen." As a result, official Catholic morality has not been able to find any context large enough to contain nonreproductive human genital activity. Nonreproductive sex—every single act of it—is branded as disordered and labeled hedonism.

"But," I objected, "what about female sexuality? Women don't emit semen, and nature ensures that their wombs are fertile only periodically and for a time. Where do they fit in?" He looked at me, a little impatiently this time, and the answer was obvious: From Rome's perspective woman's position is completely derivative of and dependent on the male as sexual norm. What is more, he pointed out, "No one in official quarters has been able to deal with the simple fact that science has discovered that the relationship between lovemaking and conception is statistically variable.

It has its own intelligibility beyond any absolute norms that renders one form of regulation of birth as 'natural' and others 'artificial.' Their whole position comes down to wish fulfillment. It doesn't depend on any form of 'right reason,' ancient or modern. So even their claims to teach based on 'natural law' are overdone and exaggerated." I shared with Morrie my own dawning recognition that, for many of the clergy, sexual activity played in their imagination the way money beguiled the fantasies of the poor. They idealized it out of all proportion and didn't know how to use well the little they had. He regretted, in turn, how sad it was to see the return of the expectation that theologians should be relegated to the task of "discovering" how what the papal *magisterium* teaches is found, either explicitly of implicitly, in Scripture or tradition: "That makes theology nothing more than apologetics," a poor cousin of the genuine effort of faith to seek understanding; "I prefer to see the relationship between the hierarchy and theologians differently. Like that of a patron and artists. The patron commissions the work, but the artist's final product may not quite be what the patron had in mind." That leaves real room for the Spirit to enter the conversation, for fresh insights and new light, for teaching to develop as it must if the church is to fulfill its mission to be *semper reformanda* ("always reforming"), in the words of Vatican II.

Coffeetime was over. As I ambled back up the via della Porta Pinciana, I once again was struck by the tendency of those in authority in the Catholic church to call a spade a club and to insist that reality cannot be otherwise. And my season in Rome taught me how grand are the illusions that they surround themselves with. The Eternal City's over-the-top architectural displays can stand as a symbol of these even grander mental creations. Baroque churches, in particular, do not pretend to be assembly places of the faithful, who come apart from the world in order, ultimately, to sanctify it. They are sacred miniworlds that ape earth and heaven and mimic how easily the veil between God and humanity is supposedly pierced—via the ministrations of the official church. In contrast, none of them can touch the holiness of place one experiences in Saint Francis's tiny hermit cave on the mountain overlooking Assisi. But even that holy site is only a place. In Rome, the all-male ethos of the religious establishment inflates the sacrament of created beauty out of all proportion, substituting a religious aesthetic in place of truth claims that they cannot demonstrate. Roman ecclesiastics participate in a self-confirmatory culture that censures outside influences and contrary opinions as those of "the world" against which they are defending the church. At least that is the impression this priest visitor got over and over again.

Early in my stay in the city—I hadn't yet learned my low tolerance for such events—I attended a gathering of clergy at the Villa Stritch near the Vatican. There I met up with a familiar spokesman for the kind of ecclesiastical positions that masquerade as intellectual apology among the men of the club. The villa houses American priests working in the Vatican bureaucracy and lies within an easy commute, one of the comfortable residences where in-house gossip flows as freely as the food and drink. Unbeknownst to me beforehand, none other than my ex-supervisor from New York, Bishop Egan, who was visiting, was attending the gathering. Conversation with him that afternoon was unavoidable, but while it was cordial, it brought me back to an earlier gathering in New York and an earlier encounter with him. At a must-show event for campus ministers, our new bishop boss had seized the occasion of a homily at the NYU chapel, to throw a shot across our bows by waxing eloquent about the glories of the *First* Vatican Council (1869–1870). It was a signal of what New Yorkers should expect in years to come.

Vatican I had proclaimed—against those who argued that faith alone could convince us of God's existence—that human reason, even without God's gift of faith, could attain to knowledge of God's existence. The bishop grabbed at that theological straw and ran with it. With the puffed-up grandiloquence he has become known for, Ed Egan took a grain of truth about human reason in the Vatican Council's 1870 decree on faith and turned it into a mighty oak supporting the position that "man can know" all the truths that the universe has to offer. The corollary he drew from stretching the decree so far then covered the issue of moral ambiguity. If "*man* can know," then it followed that certitude in moral actions was possible; and if that was possible, then it was necessary for man to follow the course of actions that were set out for humanity in the clear teaching of the papal *magisterium*. It followed as the night does the day.

The bishop's tendency to inflate religious knowledge, and to assert dubious truth claims as a certainty, ignoring both historical developments and critical perspectives, is completely at home in the Roman Curia. The pope and his teaching assistants regularly do the same in the name of holy religion. No one has ever accused Ed Egan of not keeping august company! After I left Rome and sought to take up work as a priest Stateside, the habit drove me both to distraction and to the periphery of the ordained ministry. Within a few years, Cardinal Ratzinger's Congregation for the Doctrine of the Faith (the CDF, or the Office of the Inquisition by any other name) issued a letter on the "Church as Communion" with the express purpose of informing ecumenical dialogue with a "correct" understanding of the mystery of the church. In it, he claims, contrary to what any normal historical investigation yields, that the universal church did not result from a coming together, or communion, of particular churches but existed on the level of being and in time (the big words are "ontologically and temporally") before any individual, particular church came into being. As evidence, the letter first cites claims in "the fathers" (i.e., two citations in minor early Christian authors) that the church "precedes creation," then offers an interpretation of the Pentecost scene in the Acts of the Apostles that requires enormous credulity to be accepted. In Chapter 1, Mary appears, we are told, as "the representation of the one unique Church" and the Twelve Apostles as "the founders-to-be of the local Churches." But the interpretation lacks cogency because it depends not on literary or historical evidence, but on a mythological notion that a centralized, universal church existed *in nuce* in the figure of Mary. Like Venus emerging a mature woman from the brow of Zeus, this interpretation portrays the church as being born from the mind of God (for who or what else existed "before creation") and thus avoids having to explain factually how, as a human institution, it grew and developed. But the poetic truth in an icon of Pentecost (used principally by the Orthodox, who would hardly cotton to the CDF's interpretation) cannot be used to justify a medieval notion of a community governed by a universal, juridical authority that is then read back into the New Testament. Yet it was enough for Cardinal Ratzinger to state a dubious claim boldly and authoritatively. Once put in a curial document, it must be so. So the controlling issue behind these magisterial interventions is not the "symphonic" character of religious truth (Cardinal von Balthasar's criterion), but the authority of the conductor and his first violinist, Cardinal Ratzinger.

A second example of the same wishful-thinking style of doing "theology" took place at another Vatican conference in the early 1990s, commemorating the Holy Thursday Letter of John Paul II's *Pastores Dabo Vobis*. At it, then-Archbishop of Denver James Stafford gave a paper entitled "The Eucharistic Foundation of Priestly Celibacy." Now head of the Pontifical Council on the Laity, Stafford was clearly staking out a position destined to win him friends in influential places. In the paper, he first had to work his way around the long history of married priests in the Eastern churches and around recent "exceptions" to the rule of celibacy in the West, both of which he personally found "difficult to understand." So, in defiance of the historical fact of married, validly ordained priests existing for centuries side by side with celibate ones, Stafford aimed to discover an "inner intelligibility" that strictly associates celibacy and priestly ordination. He found the necessary link in the practice of purity, or ritual cleanliness, that Jewish priests were held to before offering sacrifice. Then, building upon this analogy, he likened the notion of a priest's marriage to that of an adulterous affair: "His attempt to marry must be a profanation of his priesthood." Why? Since "the husband institutes the freely irrevocable bond between the spouses" [!], he must "pay his debt" (immolating himself) either to a wife or to the church in the offering of sacrifice. He cannot be husband to both wife and church, the archbishop affirmed, bringing together all the elements of a tendentious, preconciliar, Neoplatonic position: sex as contamination or sacrifice of self, women as inferior, virginity as superior, and the "flesh" and the "spirit" as absolutely distinct.

Let me offer a last example of Rome's assertion of questionable absolutes, this time from the pope's own statements on the priesthood. John Paul has clearly taken great pains to reinstate the mystique around the priesthood and around the authority he wields on its behalf as well. In so doing, he has assiduously asserted—contrary to the lived experience of the faithful since Vatican II—the existence of an "essential difference" between ordained Catholic priests and ordinary baptized Catholics. When the Second Vatican Council confirmed, for the first time in Catholic history, the principle that Luther had championed as "the priesthood of all believers," it also affirmed in passing that the difference between the status of the baptized and that of the ordained was one of kind, not of degree. But since then, the Vatican's favored theologians have sought to undo the breakthrough, which enhanced the role of the laity in the life of the church, by ratcheting up the difference. The material for constructing a wall comes from the Middle Ages, a time when the laity almost never received communion, a practice now seen as a degradation of Catholic worship. To justify the laity's abstention, which he merely took for granted as normal, Thomas Aquinas employed a distinction between the priest's "sacramental" and the laity's "spiritual" participation in the Eucharist.

Seizing upon this convenient distinction, the pope raised it to an essential difference. He claimed that priests are somehow "inserted" into the sacrifice of Christ sacramentally as a matter of personal identification with Christ—an identification that the laity do not share (*Dominicae Cenae*, 1980). And this essential difference between a layperson and a priest has yet another strange gradation. For the priest's personal identification with Christ is possible only because of the priest's maleness (*Ordinatio Sacerdotalis*, 1994). All this, according to the pope, is part of "a plan to be ascribed to the wisdom of the Lord of the universe." Hence, laywomen (there are no other) remain at a *double remove* from their Savior: different from Him by way of both sex and status! In the priesthood above all, biology is destiny. Male and female, instead of being relativized by Christ's resurrection, now totally determine how Christ can be manifested in the ministry of the church—a clear contravention of Saint Paul's vision of a new humanity in which there is "neither Jew nor Greek, neither slave nor free, neither male nor female, but all are one in Christ Jesus" (Galatians 3:28). According to John Paul, when a priest says the words of consecration at Mass, Christ is present in his person, not merely instrumentally or sacramentally, but in the same "realist" way that Christ is present in the consecrated bread and wine. The literalism here is staggering and completely novel to Catholic thinking, a virtual statement that there is a Real Presence of Christ in the priest. Ordination is no longer analogous to baptism—it shares in the mystery of transubstantiation. Not only are the elements of bread and wine changed into Christ's Body and Blood, but the priest, too, as a male human being, is made into a real "other Christ" (*alter Christus*). According to this bizarre way of thinking, just as the bread at Mass must be made of wheat to be valid matter for the sacrament to take place, so also the priest must have external genitals to represent Christ in the flesh.

Preparing to take my leave from Rome, I faced the future in about as sanguine a fashion as Boccaccio's Jew in the *Decameron*. Having himself gone to see the City for itself, the man, one Abraham, returned home and announced that he would seek baptism. Pressed for a reason, he replied that the actions of the cardinals and other members of the pope's retinue were so outrageous that he had become convinced that, were the Catholic church not divine, it could not have survived the likes of them. For me, the issue was not the gluttony, luxury, and lasciviousness of the curia—though they may exist—but their puritanical convictions and their fanatical narrowness. Still, I reasoned that not even the pious exaggerations of the sincere yet overreaching leadership could trump the good sense of the body of the church. For, despite all the efforts they have made to instill such a guilty conscience in matters of sexuality and the body in members of the church, the Catholic laity was surviving and, in some sense, even thriving.

Whether they like it or not, the pope and the Vatican "have a history." Even at its historic center, the Catholic church is not exempt from the passage of time and the changes that all societies must engage in if they are going to continue to thrive and not just physically survive. And even the least observant tourist is confronted with Rome's layered history just by strolling around the city. A person who looks a little deeper in places like the church of San Clemente, or who tours the Scavi beneath Saint Peter's, will recognize that what exists on the surface has a history buried beneath it. But what is not immediately obvious is this obscured truth: like all Christian art and architecture, Rome's basilicas and, even more insistently, its shrine churches exist to fill a void for human beings created by the hiddenness of God. Even Christians who profess Christ to be the Word of God made flesh know His presence incompletely "until He comes again."

But the void that believers face is more than a spatial one; it is temporal as well. We use the word "history" to describe the way humanity fills the temporal void caused by a God-with-us, present in sign and symbol, not immediately. And history remains the record of humanity's woundedness, the body of evidence that displays our common inhumanity and that records the advances and struggles that we disputedly call civilization. Into this would-be void, theologians and teachers seek to insert words and images that render history, or the passage of time, tolerable for a faith founded on the message that "the time is at hand," and that "the world as we know it is passing away." In a real sense, then, history and the body-in-time are affronts to the Gospel's promise. That is why believers are tempted to suffer time's passage in one of two inadequate ways: either they sanctify history, making it the map of God's own footsteps, or they deny that historical change really occurs in religion. Likewise, they are tempted to make the human body other than itself. Either they pretend that it is a sacred instrument removed from base purposes, or they try to neutralize its sexual potential in the light of the eventual promise that we will one day escape time and decay.

Between these two extremes, preachers and teachers have another option: to make sense of the woundedness of the body-in-time. Since Catholic history presents us, as the theologian David Tracy has noted, with a "strange mixture of great good and frightening evil," church teaching must grapple with the whole "canon" of historical experience. Instead of glossing over the sin and error of the church, or attributing them as the present pope does to "her children," but not to her fathers (or, God forbid, her Holy Fathers), we must take courage from the paradoxical teaching that even sin occasions grace (the "happy fault" still proclaimed in the Easter liturgy). Rather than pretend that the Catholic church, as the so-called spotless bride of Christ, perdures mystically unmarred by its priests' and people's crimes and misjudgments, the church must newly encounter its guilt in matters of sexuality and mourn its partly arrogant, partly desperate efforts at avoidance. Coming to terms with a collective bad conscience, or feeling guilty for the body's unruly feelings, will mean for Catholics outgrowing both Augustine's fatalism and Aristotle's analysis of sexual function and moving toward a more mature understanding of sexuality than official teaching insists is for all time and all cultures.

Packing up my room at the Collegio Maryknoll, a little weary of a city where cars were parked on the sidewalk and pedestrians had to take their chances dodging traffic in narrow streets not meant for autos, I met Daniel for a few last dinners at La Pigna and the Vecchia Roma, before we caught separate flights back to the States. Within six months, both our fathers had died, mine suddenly, his after a long illness. At his father's wake, I mentioned to his mother how curiously coincident their deaths were, and how neither of us could have guessed at them that spring in Rome. Sagely, she told me, "It's good we don't know the future. It would make us crazy!" For his part, having performed admirably in his academic assignment, Daniel found no job awaiting him. Fortunately he was able to go into exile to teach in a faraway diocesan seminary anxious to benefit from his expertise. My fate back home was to be internal exile, living in various rectories and vesting in multiple sacristies of the archdiocese, but not officially assigned anywhere, not quite "free at last" but headed in a direction away from the men-only club where I had spent the better part of thirty years.

Six

Grace Abounds

*L*ANDING AT JFK on an Alitalia jet from Rome in early June 1989, I was anxious to pick up where I had left off, determined to continue in priestly ministry and looking for a fresh opportunity to serve. In an effort to round out my experience, I had applied for a large parish in the northern suburbs of New York, anxious to prove myself in a setting very different from the campus where I had spent fifteen years. But I found myself hobbled by my own history with my bishop bosses and the bureaucracy. At first I received no assignment, until I had satisfied Cardinal O'Connor personally that a letter written by an aide in support of Governor Mario Cuomo's accepting my invitation to speak at Columbia—at a time when the cardinal had forbidden the governor to speak at Catholic colleges because of his support for legal abortion—did not contain evidence that I was disloyal to him. When we met, the cardinal dismissed the incident as insignificant and assured me that I would make a fine pastor— when a parish opened up. The personnel director, my contemporary from the seminary, informed me, in a private conversation, that there were other reasons why I had not received the assignment I had applied for. The priests on the board that advised him felt that, by applying to be pastor of a parish in the suburbs, I was trying to waltz from a cushy campus job to a well-to-do parish without doing any time in the trenches.

None of them had bothered to look further than their noses at the kind of ministry I had practiced, working with homeless and marginalized people around the campus as well as with a diverse community on it. So the deal I was offered involved my being a circuit rider for a year or so, filling in when the clergy's shallow bench left a parish without a resident pastor for a time. I agreed—What were my options? Ten years earlier, I had done similar duty in an upstate parish during the summer I had closed the campus office for lack of funds. I had found then that my biggest problem lay in curbing my energy and leaving things the way the pastor wanted them. Upon reflection, it was not a lesson that I profited from the second time around.

Both in Milton, New York, where I had replaced a sick pastor in 1979, and in the Bronx, where I did the same in the summer of 1989, I found parishioners who had adapted to deenergized pastors and expected little from them. In a classic reversal of roles, they really were taking care of the pastor sent to care for them. For their part, both of the pastors I replaced had been protecting themselves from excessive contact with people long before sickness took its toll on them. On my first Sunday during that earlier summer, a woman leaving Mass asked if I would mind if she made me some food and dropped it off at the rectory. When I replied that I'd be happy to eat the food with the family at their house, I was told that the pastor never took meals outside the rectory, lest he seem to favor one family in the parish over another. Because he did not employ anyone to prepare meals for him and neither cooked nor entertained, dinner for him amounted, at most, to a foil-covered dish. All my rehearsing to be good at priestly solitude hadn't prepared me for eating a warmed-over care package in a dimly lit kitchen in an old clapboard house with faded wallpaper, down a road off Route 9W north of Newburgh,

New York. But after years of adapting to life with a semirecluse, the parish was unprepared for me when I started putting out plans for a youth mission leading up to Pentecost and suggesting other activities. So I backed off, contented myself with saying Mass and preaching, doing some marriage preparation counseling, and escaping the rectory to visit friends whenever I could. That summer in Milton also helped me realize to what extent I engaged in pastoral activity as much to stay busy and keep my sanity as to build up the Body of Christ. Work fended off the specter of what I feared more and more: becoming a lone priest, left to himself in a rectory, with not even a housekeeper to talk to, eventually deforming and becoming a mere shadow of his own unlived life.

Faced with this prospect or something similar to it, other priests, such as the pastor I would briefly replace in the Bronx after returning from Rome, preempted the threat by adapting very differently to rectory living. They spent as little time there as they possibly could. Big Tom, a man of forty-nine on his fourth heart attack, had never lived life sparingly. In the seminary he had gotten the nickname Saddlebags from his habit of stuffing the ample pockets of his even ampler cassock with what goodies he could find in the kitchen. In parochial life, he had perfected the clerical art of attracting parishioners willing to take care of Father—their name is Legion—and to make sure his needs were met. The other half of the trick was finding others, including the parish's permanent deacon and a hired hand, usually a foreign priest studying in New York, to do the lion's share of pastoral work. This allowed him to enjoy being a pastor like the benefice holders of old, living in a condo in Westchester (when he was not spending time in a second abode he shared with some priest friends in Puerto Rico), and making cameo appearances on enough Sundays of the year to escape the judgment that he was an absentee shepherd.

Trying to figure out my new role as fill-in pastor (technically, I was a temporary administrator), I had to confront the extent to which the dynamics at work in the life of the average diocesan priest partake of certain "laws" that are endemic in the Catholic clergy. Cross-fertilizing peremptory authority with unaccountability, the clerical system promotes personal behaviors that tend to follow a standard repertory of action and inaction. The way things are now set up, all priests benefit, to some degree or other, from their assuming the mantle of mandated celibacy. Though there is a personal loss involved, many priests cope by making up for it by what psychologists have dubbed "secondary gain." Priests receive approbation, personal devotion from those who idealize them, loyalty from people struggling with their own self-worth, patronage gifts and behests from lay fans, and are cut many breaks—all as a result of their assuming a public role as a "white martyr," or committed celibate. What is more, many priests sustain their personal self-idealization by clinging to the notion that their lives are a public sacrifice—they are immolating themselves for the Bride of Christ, in Cardinal Stafford's image. They are dedicated to the service of others, just by virtue of waking up alone in bed in the morning and wearing their vocation in the shower, even before they put on a black shirt and tab collar or vest for morning Mass. If the uniform does not make the priest, it still bathes him in a relentless identity that can protect him from seeing himself in the mirror anything like the way he appears to others. Any internal disparity between this professed ideal and the way a priest feels about himself remains beneath the vestments, unless he actively seeks to achieve some insight into his condition. If he does not, those disparities will be acted out— through sex, booze, or money. His feelings will never have to be tested in the cauldron of a monogamous relationship with a partner whose needs are quite different and at least as great as his own. Because this test is not even an option, priests are set up by the system to fail internally—ascetic giants are the only exception—even as they continue to make an external show of their spiritual purpose.

When this internal failure begins to take over, priests often revert to forms of external piety and older modes of clerical manners than they propounded for the first few decades of their ministry. They begin to promote devotional forms of Catholicism that have always been a refuge for people with special needs for approval—ostensibly from the Blessed Mother or certain saints. After years of being comfortably informal in manner and dress, they will begin to insist on being called "Father" and appear in clerical black when in the presence of layfolk. No longer content to promote the public worship of the church, or to extend the ancient forms of public prayer to which Catholics have been minimally exposed, they begin to schedule novenas or holy hours, install more statues in their churches, and build a reputation for adherence to "traditional" Catholic piety. The more the internal fissure grows, the greater the need for external evidence of obedient adherence.

As part of these dynamics, priests are further tempted as creatures of flesh and blood by a deep need for approval from a transcendent source. Though faith tells them that this kind of approval (called "justice" by Saint Paul) is a grace freely given by God, the source of all good things, the actual feeling that God approves of me cannot be packaged and delivered by FedEx. The reason: Catholic faith teaches that this grace is always mediated. It comes through middle persons or events in the course of everyday living. Grace does not arrive like light through a pane of glass, an insubstantial seeping into the soul, but, as Saint Thomas said, "through the senses." Unmediated grace is but another name for the divine. But virtually all our human experience of grace is *mediated*, coming via temporal, local, circumstantial, and personal instruments. This is not a "law of nature," but the law of the spirit: that divine grace "builds upon and perfects" the natural. Now, in this divine dispensation, celibacy as an ascetical discipline certainly has an important place. It can help an individual to collect the disparate pieces of the self that can be split off and to seek gratification in passing sensual thrills. It is also "natural" as a time-honored, but temporary, mechanism for personal consolidation and part of the discipline that any mature individual must practice to protect the exclusive relationships in his or her life. But the picture gets murkier when celibacy is a permanent condition of ministerial solitude, because then it acts internally like a missing limb. Hence, permanent celibates who don't cheat are like disabled persons, who still feel ghost limbs where the real ones once were, their loss an everyday nagging presence.

I have the highest regard for the way disabled people struggle to be whole by compensating for their loss, by making up for what's missing in some adaptive way. Watching wheelchair athletes compete in a marathon or seeing otherwise disabled people fighting it out in the Special Olympics never fails to challenge my own complacency or self-pity at problems I am facing. The danger, of course, comes when a person so challenged adapts by overcompensating. Then the tail begins to wag the dog, and the person, though seeking to mask the disability, becomes his or her disability incarnated. In the life of diocesan priests, celibacy is supposed to be a lifelong integrative strategy, but too often, the longer it goes on, the less there is to integrate. The exception is the person genuinely energized by being in a state of suspended sexual animation. There are such celibates, but they are few and far between. I mean no disrespect to the thousands of priests out there who struggle daily to do it right, but the nature of their dilemma is inexorable: remaining celibate in order to hold spiritual office leads men to overcompensate in order to survive. They make up for what's missing in their lives instinctually, employing unconscious mechanisms that twitch inside them like ghost limbs doing a Saint Vitus's dance.

When priests secretly see themselves on a career track, then celibacy becomes even more ordered to spiritual power than it is to self-emptying. The dynamic interplay between internal need and external posture then becomes even more complicated. Covert careerists (the only kind in the priesthood, since ambition for higher office must be masked) compensate more blatantly than most priests, acting only in ways that court approval from those set as father over them. They learn how to mirror the needs of those in authority, bringing all their learned skills as compliant sons to the challenging task of pleasing the omnipotent spiritual Father. It can be a roller-coaster ride of a life, kowtowing to em-purpled and scarlet egos convinced they are doing God's work even while they sleep. One poor priest I heard about, who was in charge of liturgy at the seminary, got hoisted with his own petard one day after arranging a ceremony of eucharistic benediction with Cardinal O'Connor presiding. Summoned afterward to His Eminence's suite of rooms, he rushed there to find the cardinal on the phone with Fidel Castro, discussing some political issue in-volving the church in Cuba. The following exchange ensued:

"*Perdona, Fidel. Yo tengo una problema aquí.* . . . Come here, son. How come we didn't sing 'O Salutaris Hostia' at Benediction tonight?"

"According to the latest norms from the Congregation of Di-vine Worship, Your Eminence, the rules for—," he stammered.

"Rules! Don't tell me the rules. I *make* the rules. From now on, we'll do it my way at my seminary. That will be all. . . . *Yo estoy aquí, Señor Castro.*"

As in eighteenth-century Versailles, so in late-twentieth-century Dunwoodie, one mistake like that could cost an otherwise dutiful priest his whole career and get him sidelined to Roscoe, New York, in the outermost regions of the archdiocese.

Another well-placed cleric unwittingly told me his tale of sub-tle humiliation when I met with him to discuss his taking my po-sition at Columbia. The chaplain's job was being combined with that of pastor of one of the local parishes, an expanded pastoral position I had promoted and hoped to fill, but the authorities thought differently. When Monsignor J. Christopher Maloney came to see me to discuss the scope of work on campus, he was still clearly in shock from his visit to the neighboring church of Notre Dame, where he found much that needed repair and fixing up. He doubted that the positions of pastor and campus minister could be successfully merged or that he would be the right person to accomplish it. His shock and doubt loosened his tongue, and he told me frankly that he had not been expecting to be reassigned from his position as Cardinal O'Connor's second-string secretary: "A few months ago, the cardinal came to me and told me that he wanted me to be clear that he did not think of the secretary's position as a stepping-stone to higher office. He thought of it as a three- or four-year assignment, after which a man would cycle out to a pastoral assignment. So I presumed that Jimmy McCarthy, the First Secretary, who had been in the job longer than I had, would be leaving soon and that I would be taking his position. Then this came up!"

I listened empathically to his dilemma, noting that he seemed clueless about being misled by his boss, the cardinal. No clerical wag worth his salt would have believed O'Connor would jettison Monsignor Jimmy, who, of course, stayed on for years and was promoted to auxiliary bishop, following the career track of so many members of the hierarchy. As the infamous Gent Jack Barry had noted decades before of Terence Cooke, "He fed Spelly his Post Toasties in the morning and tucked him in at night, and now he's the archbishop!" So there really do seem to be some laws of success and succession operating among the normally sonless members of the hierarchy, but they didn't include Monsignor Chris, who was not allowed to turn down the plan, and who labors on in the Heights to this day.

Most priests, of course, don't aspire to the career track and avoid the greater risks of humiliation with which that higher road is littered. They compensate for the loss of personal autonomy more individually, adapting reclusively like the pastor in Milton, who shrank his life to fit his own expectations of himself, or moving in another direction entirely. One of those directions was the path taken by Big Tom in the Bronx, who enlarged his sense of self-importance until he finally burst. On this path (where one finds the most Gents), priests find comfort in the status they enjoy, becoming convinced that they deserve every perk they can collect. My method of compensating overcommitted me to making a difference in the brief time I had in that Bronx parish—how brief I didn't know. I organized the teenagers to pitch in and clean up 212th Street from the refuse of the auto shop on the corner; attacked the years of neglect of the convent property, mowing more grass than I had seen in the previous fifteen years; contracting out other landscaping repairs to damage left by an auto accident years before; setting up an office where the clergy could meet counselees (the parish had lacked one); working on the parish budget; and meeting with the school principal to prepare for the opening of school, and with the music ministry to beef up the liturgical celebration. But while working hard worked for me, within seven weeks, Big Tom couldn't take it anymore. From his convalescent repose, he sent word to the diocese that I was spending too much money—cutting down on the money he weekly took under the table—and would have to go.

When I was on my way to meet with the personnel director to dispute the decision, word came of my father's heart attack on the parade ground of the Naval Air Station in Pensacola, where he had gone for his grandson's, my nephew David's, commissioning. His passing several hours later punctuated my journey far more than moving out of the Bronx rectory would. For the third time, the death of someone I loved—first Sister Frederick, then Dave Joyce, and now Dad—spun my internal compass in a direction I would spend a few years catching up with. Their separate deaths all acted as paving stones on the path to my liberation from the prison I had constructed so many years earlier. But I was not yet through running the race I had set out on. For weeks after I buried my father and moved in with my mother to help her with the abrupt transition to widowhood (and mine to clerical unemployment), I waited for word about another assignment, was told to attend an orientation program for new pastors, which I did, waited some more, and again telephoned Monsignor Connaughton at the chancery.

"No, nothing's come up yet. I'll let you know."

"Can I apply for Saint Clare's Parish in the Bronx? That's open, isn't it?"

"Oh, some Italian will get that one. You'll just have to wait."

I put down the phone, and for the third time in my life, the internal Jiminy Cricket–like voice said to me, "Your father's dead. You'll never work for them again." And I knew that it was true.

In the next few days, I picked the phone back up and contacted two pastors in southern Westchester County who might have a room and a parking space, as I wanted to be able to look for some teaching work and be able to drive upcounty to see Mom, help her pay bills, and so on. One begged off; the second, my classmate Pat Carroll, rolled out the red carpet, and in short order I was collecting my things from storage at my old colleague Bob Lott's parish, where I had had temporary space before I left for Rome. Somewhat helpfully, Pat had a bunch of eighth-graders move my boxes upstairs, so I was days finding out where things were and sorting them into a very livable little apartment in Yonkers, within easy shot of my friends on Manhattan's West Side as well. Soon I was doing regular "supply priest" work at a nearby parish, also filling in at Saint Gregory's on the West Side, and teaching a course on early Christian literature to undergraduates at Fordham University. The following fall I secured a one-year appointment teaching religious studies at neighboring Manhattan College, through the instrumentality of my Pax Christi colleague Joe Fahey. I was in as good a place to form an independent perspective on my life and work as a priest as I could

ever expect to be, and far freer than if I had received an assignment as pastor, as I had requested. In part, I had Cardinal
O'Connor to thank. He wasn't really firing me, as he once had
said he was glad to be able to do, but he was putting me on a long
leash. It would not be the worst thing that has been said about
him that he acted as coagent of my freedom, giving me time to
reflect on what was happening inside me and around me, and
keeping me off the treadmill of another pastoral assignment.
And I had the opportunity to take anew the measure of the
diocesan priest's vocation as it continued to resist any ongoing development twenty-five years after a general church renewal had
begun.

Remembering those first years of my freelancing ministry
mainly entails my recalling the faces of the parishioners I met
and served, if only briefly. Though none of these congregations
were as intense or demanding as that at the Columbia chapel, the
people I preached to both in the city and in the close suburbs—
an increasingly diversified and educated laity—were easily as
hungry for verbal and sacramental nourishment as my campus
community had been. Coming to them as a "visitor," a cameo
role without the day-in and day-out contact with parishioners, I
sought to use my quasi-independent stance as an opportunity to
invite my listeners into a wider conversation about God's self-
revelation today. Some parishes will not welcome the words of a
relative stranger. Many will, which facilitates "catholic" worship,
where people feel deeply connected to the church of the martyrs,
of the poor everywhere, of those for whom some experience of
grace will help them either survive or die with some peace. On
occasion, unexpected faces showed up, as happened one Sunday
when the late actor Raul Julia, whom I admired for his passionate
portrayal of the martyred Archbishop of San Salvador in *Romero*,
spoke with me outside Saint Gregory's and thanked me for the
homily and the celebration.

I will be the first to admit that the kind of communion I experienced with those parishioners motivated me to work at the task of preaching a good deal. Clearly, I delighted in and needed the kind of attention I got from people who expected me to say something that mattered to them. So in the pulpit, I worked at reading their faces, holding secret minichats with individuals whose lively looks or noncommunicative stares broadcast a message to a perceptive preacher. Out of the pulpit, I was able to sustain the dialogue when I was invited to give some formal educational talks and informal courses at the parishes as well. Now that I sit on the other side of the preaching exchange, in the pews, I know what it feels like from what was the people's perspective then. Too often it means being ignored while being preached at as part of a faceless mass expected to digest spiritual formula spoon-fed like pablum to babies. Less frequently, I encounter a preacher who tries to be the catalyst that connects me to some word rumbling around in my personal depths or to a challenge hovering over me like a bolt ready to strike. "Lord, make me an instrument of your peace, or of your disturbance, or of a little bit of both," comforting the weak, and discomfiting the comfortable. All those variations are present, often in the same "message" that resonates very distinctly in the ears of different hearers. The preacher is the mere instrument, not the divine Potter, and the principle of understanding articulated long ago by Saint Thomas Aquinas still holds. "Whatever is received," he wrote, "is received according to the mode [of understanding] of the one receiving." This means, too, that preaching must be a vernacular sport, translating idioms crafted long ago in foreign tongues into words that penetrate here and now. Even then, a preacher's conscious word-framing matters less than the way he is present to his listeners.

The average priest spends far too little of his time attending to this conversation, one that takes place in all interactions with his people but that takes on a performative aspect when he takes to the pulpit. Too many merely instruct, crafting "lessons" that sound as if they were developed from vignettes in *Reader's Digest*. Even some of the most diligent still have not learned how to risk a dialogue with the men, women, and children they are staring at Sunday after Sunday. Because it presumes some ability to be intimate while in public, that kind of preaching requires much of the preacher. The priest (or deacon or whoever) must climb out on a limb and not use the pulpit defensively—or perhaps a greater danger, use it opportunistically, claiming more wisdom or more authority than the preacher has earned.

If I took uncommon pleasure in the challenge of preaching—a task I never passed up except for the time I said Mass in my cousin's parish in Zagreb, Croatia, and maybe on one other occasion—I took equal displeasure in hearing run-of-the-mill confessions. The worst were the confessions of parishioners who were offered the opportunity every day just before the scheduled daily Mass, and of children required to have a confessional one-on-one before making their First Communion. The issue arises in my memory of my final years of priestly ministry because, so often, the confessional exchanges in which I was involved were, by any serious moral measure, just plain silly. It's not that the adults, the children, and what they were speaking about were silly. But what was silly was the clergy's understanding that sacramental reconciliation remains the appropriate forum for what the adults or children end up talking about in confession.

Some of these confessional exchanges took me back to an earlier time, when I was first ordained, hearing Saturday confessions in the claustrophobic boxes stuffed under the gallery at the back of Saint Joseph's Church in Greenwich Village. Back then, overcoming my fear of having some psycho come into the box and stick a hat pin into my ear—it happened once, we were told—I would lean my ear on the mesh screen to one side and then the other and repeatedly listen to men whispering to me their admissions of illicit sex with other men. Initially convinced that I needed to respond in my best counseling fashion, I was more than once told, when I tried to engage them in a dialogue about the state of their souls, "Shut up and just give me absolution!"

Since then, most boxes had been replaced with slightly more welcoming spaces and most people had stopped padding their way to church, Saturday after Saturday, to repeat over and over their habitual reactions to problems in their lives. It's not that the confessional setting did not make available a valuable opportunity for genuine spiritual unburdening. It's just that, in the twenty-five years following the Vatican Council's close, the Catholic faithful had already decided, in a spontaneous and inspired expression of the *sensus fidelium* (the faithful's sense of belief) if there ever was one, that their participation in the Eucharist would now normally suffice as the way they would celebrate the forgiveness of their sins. Despite the continuing insistence of the hierarchy that individual "auricular" confession of sin to a priest was the normative, properly judicial way that sins are forgiven, the people had voted with their feet and vindicated a much more ancient tradition, still expressed in many of the prayers of the Mass, that "our sharing in this mystery frees us from our sins."

While church officials were fighting a rearguard action (and continue to do so), insisting that the old discipline prevail, it just wasn't working. Rome has not had the last say, and in this matter, it won't. Yet, it is important to appreciate why the pope, in particular, has continued to bemoan the loss of a "sense of sin" and to insist on the normative nature of individual confession: the issue is spiritual power, who wields it, and how much the clergy can continue to dictate to the faithful the terms for graced encounter with God. But in the light of many developments—not the least of which are the clerical sex scandals here and abroad—the Catholic laity are far less willing to accept the judgment of either the "upper" or the "lower" clergy in such matters as what constitutes serious sin and what are its consequences. Rome knows what is at stake and can be counted on to uphold its right to call the shots—though in this matter its authority is waning by the day.

The background to the Vatican's resistance to change stems from what became the classical definition, from the Middle Ages onward, of priestly ministry. It focused on the twofold power unique to the priesthood: the power to effect a change in the bread and wine at Mass and the power to forgive sins. Beneath the first was raised the philosophical superstructure that focused on the act of transubstantiation. Beneath the second lay a theory of confession as an adjudication of sin and a meting out of the appropriate penalty, or penance. Centuries before Gilbert and Sullivan had the Mikado sing about letting "the punishment fit the crime," books called penitentiaries had been compiled to describe the appropriate penance that a priest would assign for each and every possible sin a human might commit. If a penitent did not accept the priest's judgment regarding the appropriate penance, absolution would not follow. Because Saint Augustine's understanding of the human condition as radically corrupt had so infected Western theology and penitential practice, the premise was that human beings stood before God desperately in need of grace, which could come only through the mediation of Christ's church. While ordinary men, and even women in extreme cases, could act as God's instruments of grace in some circumstances (most notably in emergency baptisms), when push came to shove a unique mediation was required to accomplish the "miracle" of the Eucharist and to tender forgiveness, on God's behalf, for a person's sinfulness.

All but missing for centuries in Catholic theology was an adequate grasp of the Paschal Mystery: the scandal, as Saint Paul calls it, of the "once-for-all" nature of the forgiveness of sins won for all humanity by Christ's "trampling down death by death"— his breakout from the tomb and his return to the realm of God, dragging us in tow. Many of the pieces of this mystery survived in some form—the incarnation, atonement, sacrifice, forgiveness (understood narrowly as "satisfaction" for sin), and grace—but they were viewed together through the lens of a metaphysics that saw all change as a link between cause and effect. If the effect of penance was a supernatural bestowal of God's life on a mere mortal for all eternity, the presumption was that only a truly sanctifying cause, or agent, could make it happen. That's where priests came in. Priests, as understood through Old Testament and pagan rituals of satisfaction, formed a unique link in the chain of supernatural causality, so much so that bishops were reduced to "high priests" and the pope was the "maximal" priest (*pontifex maximus* was taken right over from pagan Rome) because it was the power of the priest, wielded on behalf of God the Judge, which alone kept Saint Augustine's "damned mass" of humanity from all going to hell. But most people, it was presumed for centuries, would suffer damnation. Only those human beings who received the ministrations of priests validly and licitly could even hope to be saved. This belief eventually gave the church a monopoly over eternal life and made it an important economic sector in its own right, enriching monasteries and cathedrals, turning the papacy into a tax collection agency and an instigator of the Crusades, and eventually spawning the indulgence controversy and the Reformation to boot.

Those Christians who became Protestants did so by denying the necessity of priestly mediation, and the most radical of them threw the baby out with the bathwater, doing away with the sacraments as well. In response, Catholicism firmed up its insistence on a system of seven sacraments, at the heart of which was set (at least in theory) a reformed clergy. But the church in the period from the Council of Trent to Vatican II so emphasized the role of the clergy that it flirted with making priests into figures right out of Harry Potter's world of wizards and sorcerers. Like the graduates of Hogwarts Academy, the ordained clergy had their own secret codes and training schools, played by different rules, and were ruled by their own hierarchy, which was unanswerable to any power in this world, certainly not to any Muggles or unbelievers. But Vatican II's reform affirmed the theological recovery of the New Testament's perspective on God's reconciliation of the world in Christ. As the reform began to be lived from day to day, even members of the segregated clergy, used to wielding extraordinary powers, began to rethink their roles. As a result, many priests who had been ordained before the Council resigned. Because they no longer could view their ministrations as an automatic "effecting of grace" in people's souls that saved them from hellfire, the priesthood they had been formed for had lost credibility. Other priests tried to regain their balance and readjust to the changes overtaking ministry, while a solid majority of those remaining in the ministry sought to adapt to the new style while keeping the substance of clerical power intact.

Those of us ordained after the Council were armed with at least the rudiments for understanding priestly ministry in other than medieval categories, but we ran into resistance both from the Gent establishment and, increasingly, from the leaders of the church, for whom the challenge of reimagining the priesthood as other than a link in the spiritual chain of being was overwhelming. But the catalyst for their greatest panic, as I narrated in the last chapter, was a reconceived vision of marriage (and its sexual underpinnings). For these fearful men, the papal ruling against "artificial" birth control served as a great dam holding back a flood of change that the church had to contain for the clergy to continue to play their old role.

This is the case because any alteration in the way Rome understands fertilization—as following God's unchanging rules for human behavior—would challenge all the rules of human sexuality. A new perspective would dissolve the metaphysical substructure of the Vatican's naïve theology of cause and effect. If making moral judgments about sexuality were based on something other than Aristotle's metaphysics (and its naïve account of human biology), it would be necessary to rethink the entire framework of how sexuality integrates human beings, body and soul—John Paul's philosophically personalist approach notwithstanding. And that would mean changing our evaluation of what sex says about human spiritual potential as well. So Rome's inflexibility about birth control, like its overvaluation of clerical celibacy and of an all-male priesthood, represents the hierarchy's own instinctual sense that their entire worldview is at stake. But the pressure to change remains inexorable because it arises from a fundamental shift in human perception—at least in developed societies—regarding why things happen the way they do, in other words, a shift in understanding the supernatural physics of the spiritual life.

Today we all understand that events are shaped not merely by acts of human free will but that genes, chance, environment, statistical variability, and randomness play a crucial role as well. (Earlier thinkers relied on less complex grids on which to map happenstance: either fate, or God's will, or the stars, or karma.) Sexual fertility illustrates nature's randomness in a significant way. We know that some couples conceive a child as easily as they plug in a toaster, while others try for years and, even with no medical counterindication, keep missing the boat. Some couples, who have been told by doctors that they cannot conceive, adopt children and then become pregnant naturally without even trying. Either a capricious God is casting lots, using billions of sperm and ova, or there is a *natural* random chance at work in human fertility, the same random chance that underlies many of the harshest realities humans have to deal with: drought-induced famine, natural disasters, accidents caused by human error, and the shape of a human personality, including sexual identity. Causes still have effects. But random evil and random good do not follow the naïve organization imposed on them by the kind of "natural law" cited by papal teaching. The claim that God's law in nature directly confirms the papacy's restrictive positions on a whole range of sexual issues just doesn't hold water.

Wrestling with these issues, as I did in the years when I combined pastoral and academic work in an enviable mix, I was struck by how insightfully they were addressed by—of all things—a sugar-coated Hollywood fable. Though it tells its story agnostically (at most, Hollywood pinches incense at the altar of the Unknown God), *Forrest Gump* showed in bold colors how grace occurs serendipitously in a world characterized by randomness and threatened at every moment by chaos and meaninglessness. God has only one cameo in the movie, playing the role of a storm in the Gulf of Mexico that—serendipitously—lays the foundation of Forrest's unlikely wealth as the purveyor of Bubba Gump shrimp. But Unmediated Grace is most certainly a character, instrumentally present in a smothering mother, a handicapped son, a gentle girl, a Vietnam casualty, a mean drunk of a veteran, and one random act of intercourse.

Wandering in seemingly aimless fashion through a pockmarked landscape of disasters, Forrest Gump is Everyperson caught between chaotic happenstance and some overall economy of grace that we can hardly guess exists. The controlling metaphor of the movie is the feather that floats as aimlessly on the wind in the opening and closing scenes. By itself, it is an image of the ineluctable nature of fate, demotically noted in the expression "Shit happens." But the role of the feather is explicitly interpreted by Forrest himself at the graveside of his wife, Jenny, who has died of AIDS after giving birth to an unimpaired son. In a monologue to his dead spouse, the challenged hero wonders aloud, "Are we just blown around on the wind or . . . is there some plan for us?" In refusing to opt for either blind fate or run-of-the-mill providential design, Forrest describes the horns of our dilemma in pretty profound terms: "It must be a little bit of both."

In other words, there are laws in nature, but they encompass randomness, statistical variability, and seeming chaos; law and randomness are not opposites. For those who say that life is too statistically hit-or-miss and fate too indeterminate for Providence to exist, the figure of Forrest points beyond any easy resolution using either blind chance, on the one hand, or "God's will," on the other, to explain cancer, accidental death, and the like. God's overarching design and will are best understood as a series of divine improvisations that respect the freedom of the expanding cosmos to be its flawed self, a mystery Saint Paul hinted at in the paradox "Where sin increased, grace abounded all the more." In this curiously flawed garden, God does not, and humans cannot, impose an "order" that does not respect the undetermined realms where matter and spirit, necessity and freedom, intersect. Efforts by church leaders to insist on "laws" of God or nature that don't fit the human experience of nature in all its complexity are futile in the extreme.

This is all the more the case when it comes to human sexuality, which participates, perhaps more than any other created reality, in a riotous admixture of randomness and design that human freedom seeks to negotiate. What is more, our sexual drives also saddle us with overly generous opportunities to fail at transcending the chaotic inner world that Freud named the id. But just as God exhibits infinite patience with the rebelliousness of created nature, so humans better emulate God's design by accepting the openness of human sexual response to wider possibilities than requiring that "every act of intercourse be open to the transmission of life" (as *Humanae Vitae* insisted).

Grace helps us to weave together a greater cohesion from our actions, to close the gaps that naturally appear between our capacities and our inclinations to selfishness. But in the final state of nature, which is still unfolding in God's eyes (our sight is limited), the tapestry of creation will not look so monochromatic as the repressed desires of the clergy would paint it. Until then, God will always be perceived, as Woody Allen named him in *Love and*

Death, as something of an "underachiever," threatening us on occasion, but mainly content, as my adviser Morrie once remarked, to "woo the beauty that had gone forth from his hand." As always, created things become the instruments of God's self-manifestation and the occasion for humanity's spiritual progress. But nature's own randomness is itself an instrument of grace as we stumble along life's uneven roadway. God's graciousness does not pick and choose who wins at blackjack or who dies in a plane crash but is present in the face of either fate, a coefficient not of the physical fact but of the larger, moral outcome of it. For just as nature is "free" to follow its own creaturely impulses, risking chaos but somehow also ordered, so human freedom enters into the picture when, having been dealt either a victory or a blow, we can respond graciously in the face of happenstance, whether it is beneficent or tragic. Jesus' scandalous teaching in the Sermon on the Mount confirmed as much when he called on his followers to be "children of your heavenly Father, who makes his sun shine on the good and the bad, and causes rain to fall on the just and the unjust."

Pursuing what I hoped would be an alternative ministry of teaching, preaching, and staying involved as a board member with Community Impact, while I fostered the friendships that I had counted on to keep me emotionally afloat, I also stayed connected with my ordination colleagues—we still used the term "classmates"—with whom I had gotten together on Tuesday nights for over two decades. Coming together in the beginning as a gathering to discuss Scripture, in preparation for preaching the following Sunday, we had loosely become a "support group," complaining, laughing, trading gossip, and staying connected. At most weekly gatherings, we were five to twelve men, now in our forties, roughly half of the group ordained in 1971, with a straggler or two from other classes as well. Most of the others in the

class would join in the annual anniversary celebration of ordination but not participate regularly; some people more easily became the butt of jokes than others, and we weren't good at
policing ourselves in these matters. Over the years, we put a lot of
stock in our not becoming a gathering of Gents, never serving alcohol on Tuesday nights, though our get-together could become
somewhat raucous anyway. The commonest bond that we had
was our being hard workers—by and large. One guy was a big
golfer with the kind of ministry on the links that I never understood; another seemed to spend an amazing amount of time fixing his hair. But one would have to look very hard to find a group
of priests as firmly rooted in the tasks that had brought them to
ministry some thirty years earlier. None of the core group had
moved into central administration, though one of our natural
leaders had done a stint as director of the archdiocesan CYO. He
did not stay and was again a priest in the inner-city parish where
he had lived since ordination, for a good number of those years
in a room in the basement of the rectory. We had nobody among
us who wore French cuffs under his clerical rabat (shirtfront)
when he went to work, and we tended to be inordinately proud
of it.

So the camaraderie I brought to and sought from the group
meant a great deal for me, and it was the rare Tuesday that I did
not head out at 9 p.m. and drive up to a half hour to get to whatever rectory we were meeting in. I had even made sure I got to
the group the one week I was back in the States in my sabbatical
year. At the same time, as the years passed, what the group had to
give filled less and less of the emotional hole that had been opening up like a fistula inside me. There seemed a terrible sameness
to our gatherings. At times it felt as if we were all waiting for the
same bus, which never arrived at our stop, week after week,
month after month, year after year. So, while living in Yonkers
and teaching religious studies to undergraduates at Manhattan
College, I rooted around and found a therapist—my third—to

guide me up and out of the series of purgatorial circles where I seemed to be wandering. Dr. Richard Billow is as empathetic a hard-ass as one is going to find in a therapist's office. Smart, intuitive, at times abrasive, but always on point, he pushed me almost to the point of breaking off with him when I moved north to Croton-on-Hudson in 1991.

After a year at the college, I had secured a position at a small graduate school of theology at Maryknoll, farther upstate, finding refuge once again among the missionary fathers and brothers I had sheltered with in Rome. Moving gave me the opportunity to terminate with Dr. Billow, but I didn't do so. In fact, after resisting his suggestion for a year, I had finally joined one of his group sessions. He had become convinced that some of the issues I needed to deal with would best be done in a group setting. Resistant as hell at first to exposing my clerical underbelly to mere layfolk, I found myself very engaged in the process and much more connected to the women in the group than to the men, especially the one Catholic in the group, a cranky lawyer who had the hardest time of all when I revealed to the group after some weeks what I did for a living. This man played the role of my superego, holding me to standards that he had long ago abandoned. Most of the time we got along, but one evening, I spoke of having had dinner with my friend, Elena. As I related being back in her apartment afterward, and having the most powerful urge, which I told her about, to make love to her, he couldn't handle it at all.

We hadn't wound up making love, but through no fault of mine. Elena had held her own, and I was not so horny as to risk forcing it—I remained controlled even if beset by longing. She was the same friend with whom some years before I had enjoyed the briefest of sexual encounters, an indiscretion that our friendship had survived, but only with some effort. When I was in Rome, she had visited the city, staying at the Hotel Excelsior nearby on the via Veneto, and over the several days she was there, we had met often for dinner and some touring. But I never got beyond the front desk. I think that was her way of maintaining a boundary that she had no confidence I would respect. Nor had I, so we met and said good-night in the lobby. Back in New York we continued to see each other as friends until the fateful night I got to talk to my group about. But nothing sexual happened, as she refused to enter helter-skelter into an arrangement in which we were both not free. Demurring, she told me that she wanted a relationship with someone who could be there when she came home, not with a guy furtively sneaking in and out and assuming his other life after a brief encounter. I saw her point and told her so. I always admired her for her good sense, and talking about it in group—confession was easy next to this!—helped me sort through my frustration.

I had no one but myself to blame for that frustration. Like many priests, I had bought into the whole shtick about sublimating my sexuality for a greater good, had sold my birthright for the promise of meaningful work, had dreamed a dream of standing apart from the crowd. Though expressly turning my back on the old clerical mystique, I still counted on an internal version of it to keep me going. As I saw my forties begin to wane, the prospect of becoming another unlived life seriously haunted me. My resolution never waned to remain a celibate priest, if, and only if, I could somehow throw the emotional switch that would ease the pain of my solitary life. But the more I got to know myself, the less likely it seemed that my solo act was going to receive any more rave reviews to keep it a long-running show. Multiplying prayers or begging God to make me someone other than the vicissitudes of life and love had made me didn't seem to work. Grace, I came to believe, had to build upon and perfect *my* nature, not some idealized embodied soul I had imagined myself to be. Throughout the years, I had always clung to the practice of praying the prayer of the church, the Divine Office or the Liturgy of the Hours—never all the daily offices or hours, but almost always some portion. The psalms and readings that are at its heart represent the voice of Christ and the church in dialogue, expressing pain and joy, sorrow and peace, in equal measure. They're not "feel-good" prayers, and so I prayed them as a way of opening myself to a larger drama than the one I was at the center of—though they clearly spoke of my own needs and struggles as well. There were other words of Scripture that I called upon in my prayer as well, begging God, with Paul the Apostle, to remove the thorn from my side, and with Jesus on the cross, questioning God about my fate. The answers I got, such as they were, sent me deeper into my own internal struggle. For when the apostle put God on the spot, the words he heard were full of paradox: "God said, 'My grace is sufficient for you. For in [your] weakness, [my] power reaches perfection.' "

So where was my weakness? In my seeming need for sexual communion? Or in the self-image that I had harbored for years and that had sat me on the bench, a reserve player not meant to get any time on the field? No magic answers here, or in the very real dialogue I had had some years before, after a very difficult analysis session. Filled with anguish about my emotional fragility, I was walking south on Central Park West, not my regular route, and the words of Psalm 22 that two of the gospels put into the mouth of Jesus on the cross came to me: "My God, my God, why have you abandoned me?" Here was the second occasion that a voice spoke back to me. The reply came in my voice, entirely inside my head, but it spoke an unbidden response in a way that made me sit up and take notice: "So that you will know who *you* are!"

The final chapter in my shedding of the celibate mystique unfolded in the village of Croton-on-Hudson among a community of believers where I still live and worship. I moved there, after getting the appointment at Maryknoll School of Theology, in response to an invitation from a classmate who had become a pastor there some years earlier. For the two years and some I resided at Holy Name of Mary rectory, Henry (as I will call him) did much to make me comfortable, give me a role in the parish, introduce me to many new friends, and help restore my sense of having a community, which I had lost three years before.

But there were more than two of us residing in the rectory, and therein lies a sad tale. Henry and his assistant pastor, Don, mixed like the proverbial oil and water—a wanton extrovert and a painful introvert, a workaholic and a sensitive musician, two ill-fitting peas in a small pod of a priests' house. At first when I moved in, Don was convinced the move was a conspiracy to create an indomitable force of two against one, and he clearly resented my presence. As Henry sought to accommodate me in every hospitable way, grateful for the company I provided and counting on at least my moral support, his assistant remained surly and rarely joined us at table for dinner. But after some months, as I weighed in on some pastoral issues in a way that supported Don, he mellowed. When I then contributed my Mass stipends for six months to the new organ fund, he warmed considerably, and I was no longer treated like the interloper.

The lessening of tension in the rectory was welcome as I was dealing with enough of it at Maryknoll. Walking into a twisted clash between the old guard, the old new guard, and the new new guard—a clash that involved more parties than the faculty of the school, few of whom were Maryknollers—I turned down a feeler about becoming acting dean even before I had arrived. Members of the society could bring pressure to bear if they didn't like what they perceived to be going on at the school, and I had no confidence I would be politically astute enough to manage the melee. The Maryknoll society had, in essence, contracted out what had been their own seminary and then had withdrawn their few seminarians, leaving it something of a rump school for laity and a religious pining for something different from the standard clerical fare in many Catholic graduate schools. The old guard had a few right-wing nuts in it but largely consisted of retired missionaries of the cross-and-flag variety and a former progressive grown defensive of movements he had not mastered. The old new guard had a left-winger or two but mainly consisted of those who still felt that historical and critical investigation of the sources of theology had a role to play in shaping how faith seeks understanding. The new new guard brought the concerns of feminist and liberation theology to the fore, filling out the theological spectrum with a forward-looking agenda, but displeasing enough of the missionaries at home and abroad to loosen many Maryknollers' commitment to the school's survival. Most of the time, I straddled the line between the two new guard positions. What I appreciated most about the school was its form of "engaged" theology, which promoted the link between thinking and doing (although sometimes not in that order). But its activist reputation had attracted some students not patient enough to deal with the sources of Christian theology before crafting their agendas for social change. All of the territorial struggles took their toll, and the school's receiving only provisional accreditation from the American Association of Theological Schools dealt a blow that it never recovered from. It closed in 1995.

But by then my own life developments had put me on a different course. After Maryknoll, I would teach only part-time, mainly as a slave-wage adjunct professor at several colleges. Some of my best work I did as a volunteer, teaching a course on women in the Bible at a women's maximum-security prison, where I also directed a college program for almost two years. Any college professor weary of trying to engage undergraduates should have the opportunity to teach incarcerated women or men, who recognize how privileged they are to have a shot at higher education and who bring a life experience to the task second to none. But before all this took place, while I was still teaching, resident at Holy Name, and helping in the parish, I had gotten involved with another group meeting that complemented the rough-and-tumble of my weekly therapy group. The men's group, as we called it, paved the way for my eventual decision to abandon enforced celibacy and take my place with the married men whose quest for spiritual self-discovery and commitment to the inward journey I was fortunate enough to share.

Our meetings contrasted starkly with what I found among my long-standing priest colleagues. For even after thirty years together, we ended up leading guarded and essentially private lives, seeking out close friends (and sometimes more) outside our clerical circle, and sharing our common lot only within safe parameters. Inside the circle, fear of gossip or of being shamed if the old self-ideal no longer held true seemed to require us to build up a reserve of defensiveness and kept us from getting beyond the old style of celibate male bonding that we originally had tried to reject. Were we becoming Gents in spite of ourselves? I feared as much. When Brian, a Tuesday-night regular who had been a class fixture since high school, all of a sudden upped and left to marry in early 1993, he spoke with only one of the guys before disappearing. The rest of us were left guessing. As our anniversary approached, Henry and I wrote to the class, inviting them to celebrate at Holy Name and raising the issue of our need to do better at being frank about our lives and our struggles if we were really going to support one another. But when we gathered, the same jokes got told, the same stories circulated. No one spoke about Brian, and I found no opportunity or openness to talk about what was happening with me.

By contrast, in the men's group I could bring up my discomfort and the ongoing challenges I was facing and receive support for dealing with them. The range of life experiences—pain, loss, marital failure, struggles with our individual fathers, with childlessness, and with parenting—all proved far more fertile soil for brotherhood in Christ than years in the priesthood had given my classmates and me. What's more, against the background of the brutal kind of honesty that was the rule in my mixed therapy group, the men's group truly nurtured me and, taken in tandem, moved my priest peers to a distant third when it came to measuring how deeply I felt connected. Even with Henry, whom I at least touched base with in the evening before we retired, there was a line we did not cross, a clinging to a celibate ideal wearing thin with me that I could not and would not discuss until I finally threw in the towel.

When I was still living in Yonkers, I had made a fresh effort twenty years into ordination to summarize the condition of celibate ministry, and I published a piece in *Commonweal* magazine, entitled "Disabled for the Kingdom: Celibacy, Scripture and Tradition." It argued that celibacy, as urged by Jesus on the once married and divorced for the sake of the dawning Kingdom (the only context in which it is addressed in the four gospels), closely resembled what we called a disability. Celibates accepted their disabled condition for a variety of personal reasons, some of which matched up well with the explicit ideal, but many of which only aped it. Because the psychosexual context in which we lived had so radically changed (something that Rome, of course, denied), and the ideology of mandatory celibacy had so compromised the free gift of self that ministry required (not to mention deforming the episcopate into a collection of yea-sayers), I urged that married men be admitted to the ranks of the priesthood to begin to repair the damage. But at the same time that I was defending celibacy as a paradoxical condition rather than a heroic ideal—helping me hop better on one leg, as it were—I was continuing to fight my own sense of personal disability, my own personal "poor me" syndrome. Initially the young peer group I had at Columbia had acted as a kind of challenge to me, moving me to stay fitter and get emotionally healthier. So I had been trying to get better at traveling without a crutch, as it were. Then, having spent so damn much time in therapy dealing with my learned inner debility, I began to yearn for some psychological normalcy. And whenever I was among numbers of priests, at conferences or large meetings, I found myself reacting to the pronounced idio-syncrasies on exhibit there. By contrast, the men's group, whose members spanned a thirty-year range, modeled a more candid and forthright style of behavior. Some time after the celibacy-as-disability piece had been published, I shared it with my therapist but did not ask him about it. Months passed, and one day, when I alluded to it, he asked why I had not sought his opinion about it. Clearly nervous about his reaction (he was also a psychology professor and I was unsure my psychoanalytic understanding was up to snuff), I waited for his withering critique, only to hear him remark, "I just think it would be better if you were more energized by being a celibate, rather than disabled by it, that's all." A simple, subversive statement, its message rang like thunder down to my toes. I knew I wasn't "turned on" by being emotionally unattached and had grown suspicious of those who were. Even those priests who seemed pretty together only seemed to me to wear their celibacy with less brittleness than most. But many others were clueless about their own self-centeredness, which they looked to pass off as a professional hazard of ministry, not their actual emotional state.

Push finally came to shove just a few months later when I headed out to Notre Dame for a conference that combined some of my interests in interpreting Scripture in a culture imbued with science. I had been to that great center of Catholic learning and football only once before, to give an address at Saint Mary's College, contrasting the writings of Thomas Merton on peace in the nuclear age with the pastoral letter of the American bishops. But that was in the winter. Now it was April and students were everywhere, in the chapel, on the fields, in the gym (where I snuck in a workout), massed at the lake for a competitive race between dorms. The whole sprawling campus had a great feeling to it in the spring, and the conference lived up to its billing. I had dinner with some old acquaintances and met several notable theologians. I should have been one happy, academic camper. But everywhere I went I was shadowed by . . . no one. I was there alone, and never more so than when I went back to the motellike room at the conference center. Alone in another motel room. The trip home meant a lot of airport time, during which I distracted myself by finishing John Grisham's novel *The Pelican Brief.* If you only saw the movie version, with Julia Roberts and Denzel Washington, you won't understand how distracted I was by the ending of the book, which I consumed just as the plane was landing at Westchester County Airport. In the film version, there are only hints of a romance, but in the book the heroine escapes to a lonely tropic isle only to be found there by the intrepid reporter who's fallen for her big-time. It doesn't say, "They lived happily ever after," but it might as well have done so. A mushy, cinematically perfect, Grisham ending. Just what I didn't need rattling around in my mind's eye.

Returning to the rectory that night, I found the house dark and empty. But not so dark and empty as I was. My apartment was small, literally in the garret of a Tudor-style house, and the ceiling and walls pressed down on me. Pleading before an icon of the Savior brought from Jerusalem years before that hung on the wall of my bedroom, I came away uncomforted and alone. For over an hour I fought against a personal night that felt as if it were invading through my pores. There was no one to talk with; no one to call—what would I tell them? "Could you please stop over, I think I'm having a breakdown!" There were other nights in other rectories when I'd had a minor premonition of being a soul turned inside out, all raw and bleeding. Yes, I had then turned to the priest's self-soothing mechanism. No, not booze. Others might. Not me. I'd masturbate. But when your body feels this kind of external weight upon it, bodily distractions don't work. So I prayed some more, and the threat waned after another hour. Eventually I got to sleep, though I had spent a year's worth of nights lying awake, waiting for sleep, alone in my single twin bed. That was my last night, mentally and emotionally, as a celibate.

The next day I had a biweekly session scheduled with Rich Billow and poured out my tale from the night before. "What's keeping you from making a choice that you don't have to live like this?" he asked. For a brief moment, my father's ghost entered the room and I told him, tearfully, that I feared becoming a failure. I had imbibed a wicked work ethic from Dad and had transferred it here, thinking if I could only run hard enough or long enough I'd outrun his disapproval. But as suddenly as I halted and stared the fear in the face, I stopped running from it. That night when I got into my car for the drive back to Croton, I had come out the other side of my personal tunnel. No bells, no whistles, just a knowledge that I had given it my all and it no longer worked.

How many other priests had faced what I now faced? And yet there was no "how to" manual available: how to lay my burden down, how best to exit from the ordained ministry in a way that left the fewest people scarred, and how to find a job and put a life together for myself outside the confines of the clergy. As I began to plan, events around me framed my leaving more dramatically than I would have intended. It was 1993 and the papers began to fill with more stories of priests who had victimized young people. The second wave of sex abuse scandals was awash in the media and the credibility of the priesthood was being questioned, just at a time when I was preparing to take my leave from it. Anxious to distance myself from the clergy whose record around sexuality I found so dismal, I wrote a piece for the *New York Times* Op-Ed page that appeared under the title "Celibacy and Its Discontents." Nowhere in its seven-hundred-plus words did I announce my intention, but my claim that "most men and women are meant to seek holiness by enacting their sexuality, not by avoiding it" was patent. By coincidence, within a week or so, a priests' as-

sembly was called around the issue of sexual abuse. A few guys
approached me about the *Times* piece, but only a few of them,
and quietly. At the meeting, some men got very worked up when
Cardinal O'Connor admitted that, in a recent case in Poughkeepsie, he had followed advice of counsel and pursued an ag-
gressive defense of an accused priest. This meant impugning the
actions of a teenager—who charged he had been plied with alcohol and molested—accusing him of seduction. It would become a
standard strategy in some dioceses, where the pastoral and personal consequences to the victims placed far behind legal and financial damage control.

The meeting ended up causing a small storm in our rectory,
which set the stage for a tragedy after I moved out. Henry, the
pastor, had known the priest in Poughkeepsie some years before,
when he was still a seminarian. In fact, he told us that he had
reported the seminarian to the church authorities for showing
pornographic videos to teenagers in the rectory when he was in-
terning at Henry's parish. But the man was ordained anyway, at-
taining a platform from which he could act out his perverted
desires as an ordained priest. For his part, Don had himself been
the victim of sexual abuse when he was a teenager. The organist
in the church of his youth—he was a convert to Catholicism—
had abused him, something that he now spoke openly about. So
he was exceedingly angered by the cardinal's legal strategy and
wrote him a stinging letter, taking O'Connor to task for blaming
the victim and betraying insensitivity to the youth in question. I
supported his outspokenness, but I thought he went too far when
he told his tale in a talk on reconciliation that he gave to
teenagers at a retreat weekend. Making his own reported forgiveness of his abuser a moral example to prompt a group of fifteen-
to nineteen-year-olds to go to confession seemed like a form of
grandstanding to me—even of protesting too much. In the newly
charged atmosphere over the issue, a parishioner then called me
and insisted that I warn the pastor—whom she did not speak

to—that his habit of taking teenagers to his lake house would expose him to accusations as well. Though she was clearly no friend of Henry's, I conveyed the warning and concurred that he needed to heed it. Priests taking altar boys on trips was a long-standing practice—I had done it in the Bronx two years earlier—and I had visited a few times with Henry at the lake over the years. He often had whole families and young adult guys who had grown up in his parishes there as guests. But bringing younger teenagers there no longer seemed wise. The times had changed, and people were far more ready to be suspicious of behavior that had gone unquestioned for a very long time.

But clerical issues soon paled for me as I busied myself with catching up to the future that unfolded before me. Within a short time of my own decision, I witnessed a deathbed scene and a funeral that landed me in an ambiguous role in the parish, comforting the widow and family of a young husband and father who had died of cancer. I knew David Entwistle from making the twenty-eight-hour men's "Cornerstone" retreat with him eighteen months earlier at the parish. As moved as I was by the experience (it would help spawn our men's group), he had enrolled and participated in the leadership team for the following year's retreat. By the time of the next Cornerstone, he had been fighting brain cancer for four years. Now he staved off its deadly effects long enough to summon the energy to offer his story to the men who had gathered. But he declined rapidly afterward and died at home just over two months later. At the funeral liturgy and, afterward, at the cemetery, I got my first real look at his two girls, aged nine and five, standing by the grave next to their stricken mother. Caitlin, the older, was sheltering Tara, both appearing too small for the burden of grief they were shouldering. But I was watching Marilyn, too. It seemed immodest, crazy, an overwrought and weary celibate's fantasy, that I should reap what another man had sown. I shut up deep inside me any thoughts about inheriting a woman's love and a family, nestled right up against the secret voice that simultaneously assured me, "You're going to marry this woman."

In the coming days, I joined other members of the parish cadre who visited to console the family with covered dishes and sympathy. Marilyn had herself led the women's Cornerstone retreat the winter before and had become very connected to the parish community. She had a way of meeting your eyes with her own, her broad smile beckoning and her long wavy brunette hair framing her bright countenance. Tall and strikingly attractive, she wore long dangling earrings that laughed along with her when she conversed. As the weeks went by, I delayed my own visits to the family into the evening, arriving just before the girls would go to bed. When Tara called me in one night to kiss her good-night, I took it as a sign—as I also took Marilyn's candor with me and the play of her bright blue eyes. Once we had come together, on the occasion of her birthday the following year, I gave her a card with a line from a Shakespeare sonnet that expressed how mesmerizing I found those windows on her soul:

> *To me, dear friend, you never can be old.*
> *For as you were when once your eye I eyed*
> *Such seems your beauty still.*

Having such romantic thoughts and a woman to spend them on gave me a new lease on life. Needless to say, my therapy group—especially the women in it—cheered me on and urged me to declare myself, but I fought off an early declaration until I thought the time was right. When I finally did and got permission to come courting properlike and not under the guise of pastoral solicitude, I felt like Motel the Tailor from *Fiddler on the Roof* singing, "Wonder of wonder, miracle of miracles . . ." Actually, the song on my car radio when I left the house after the lunch at which I declared myself, by Huey Lewis and the News, was "If this is it, please let me know, if this ain't love, then just say so." Within a month, I

made an appointment with my boss the cardinal to ask for a leave
of absence from the priesthood. I had not spoken with him since
he had visited my mother's house on the long weekend between
my dad's death and burial. Surprised when told of his coming
visit, my family welcomed the important guest, who showed a
special regard for my nephew in his spanking navy whites and
warmly consoled Mom in her pain over Dad's sudden death. He
really could be a gracious man.

As he was when I visited with him. He made it all very easy
for me. The first thing he asked was about my mother and my
nephew and how they were doing. When I turned the conversation to myself, he told me that he knew how hard it had been for
me and granted me the leave I requested immediately. But when
I hit Madison Avenue a mere nineteen minutes after entering, I
got the impression that the skids had been greased for my exit.
Meeting Marilyn afterward to tell her how the visit had gone, I
reflected on the cardinal's overt pleasantness, relieved but irked at
the same time that twenty-three years in the ministry should end
not with a bang, but a whimper. I announced at the Masses the
weekend after that I had been granted a leave and that I was taking it specifically because I was no longer able to bear the burden
of the law of celibacy. The next Sunday would be my last.
Preaching at that final parish Mass I would lead as a priest, my
theme was that day's gospel reading about the second son (from
Matthew 21, not the Prodigal Son from Luke), who refused his father's wishes the first time around but got a second chance. The
applause and the hugs afterward, combined with my announcing
I was staying in the community, not running away, confirmed that
many of the laity harbored a lot of sympathy for my decision. A
year later, when I formally resigned, John O'Connor urged me
to request a papal dispensation from celibacy. After a fifteen-year
hiatus, dispensations had only just begun flowing from Rome
again, prompted clearly by the 1990s wave of sex abuse scandals.
And I got the dispensation, too, thanks to some string pulling that

Henry, our pastor, got a former curial official to do, just in time for our marriage (there was one canonical glitch, but it was handled by those who handle these things). The ceremony took place at the same altar where I had last celebrated the Eucharist twenty-one months before.

In leaving, I repudiated nothing and affirmed nothing that I had not already repudiated or affirmed as a priest. The changes I had undergone, in my self-image and in what I looked for in relationships, had taken place in order for me to remain my true self, dynamically speaking, to be "me" with a recognizably continuous ego function. Not to change would have exacted too high a price, feeding off lay friends and seeking to live their fuller lives vicariously. In moving to the other side of the altar, and moving as well into a committed relationship with Marilyn and struggling to parent Caity and Tara, I learned at least as much about the state of my soul as I had in years of self-reflection and therapy. The pure joy of being *solus cum sola*, as the old moral books would have named it, as naked as Adam was with Eve, provided me with more consolation for the years of self-involved solitude than I could ever have imagined. One day, at lunch, when I was still teaching at Maryknoll, a female student told an off-color joke that sent me into paroxysms of private laughter: "Why do men give nicknames to their penises?" she asked. Pause. "Because they don't want a stranger making all their decisions for them." For me, let's just say that it was good to befriend a former antagonist, one whom my wife could make friends with as well (the name will remain a secret).

The greater discovery that came along with the revelation of the mysteries of intimacy came as a real surprise to this old bookworm. I don't think I was as ignorant of them, mechanically speaking, as the seminarian dropout in David Lodge's tender novel *Paradise News*. But I had a lot to learn about how a woman's sexual experience of the whole shebang makes amazing demands on a man. How paradoxical that it offers him, as well, fun-filled possibilities for being focused outward and herward even at his biggest moment of bliss. Damn! This was news. It paupered the way sexual love was described in the moral literature, completely from a man's perspective, ignorant of the marvelous complexity I'm still discovering in coital harmony. When Freud wrote, almost a hundred years ago, that genital sexual union is always a victory over diffusing and dispersing sexual energy away from mainstream genital heterosexuality, he may not have gotten everything just right, and he probably didn't have me in mind, but it sure felt as if he did. It's clearly a victory with a generous moral payoff, one that Catholic moral teaching about real "natural law" should be celebrating rather than herding into the narrowest corral it can find. I will argue no further: Holy fathers! Get back to the drawing board and study nature's God-given designs before you pronounce so firmly about what you do not know and have not even begun to ask women about.

In my excitement and exploration of the new emotional and sexual horizon sprawling before me, I could easily have forgotten to tend to my friendships with priests, some of which were of almost thirty years' duration. I'll say that I tried. Refusing just to disappear, I paid visits to a number of the men I felt closest to over the years before I took the leave from the priesthood. A few of the visits went well, but the tenor of most of my friends' responses was that I was leaving them in the lurch. In the New York clerical culture, no natural or gracious way for a man to withdraw from the priesthood had yet developed after three decades of continual resignations. When a priest withdraws, there are no thanks for the decades of service, no funds to help a soon-to-be unemployed brother in his transition, no formal outreach from other former priests who might offer support, unless one is lucky enough to know a network of men who have resigned. Twenty-three years of pension payments on my behalf were absorbed and disappeared off my record. How different from the more generous reactions to my decision that I received from Jeanette, the parish secretary, when I informed her. "Well, cops and firemen get to retire after twenty years," she said. "Why not priests?" In truth, two older men, my mother's pastor and a colleague from Hayes years before, let me know that if I needed money I should ask them.

Telling Stan, my buddy from seminary days, was especially tough. I had often visited with him on vacations, and he clearly saw my going as a big loss for himself—as it was for me. He took it the hardest, finally asking as if in rebuke, "What did your mother say when you told her?" In fact, she had been a trouper. I had been nervous about telling her, choosing the moment in a restaurant rather than at home. When I stole a moment in the conversation and led with the line, "Well, I've been thinking a lot about my future," she shot back, "Are you going to leave and get married?" Not exactly sure of where she was coming from, I responded, "Well, I'm considering it." Without a pause—with her still raw experience of widowhood just under the surface—she replied, "Good. Nobody should grow old alone." As someone who's had to do that, she has opened her arms to my new family consistently and generously, easing the transition considerably. Marilyn's own parents—Bronx Irish Catholics both—were no less welcoming and supported us every step of the way.

On the home front, the daughters whom I have tried to help Marilyn raise are now teenagers, and Caity is in her first year of college. She and Tara acted as bridesmaids at our wedding, braving this new chapter they had been so unfairly dealt. We have all adapted to one another, the joys more than matching the challenges, which we have worked to confront head-on. We have always marked David's birthday and the anniversary of his death and made Father's Day a day of joint recognition. I have flattered myself that their father would not mind my picking up where death made him leave off. He hated dying young and leaving them, but he had reached a stage of acceptance late in his dying that overcame his anger and his youth. That, too, has been a life-giving legacy for his family.

The most difficult chapter in my postpriesthood life has involved our friend and former pastor, Henry, who lives today in limbo, ordained but not allowed to function as a priest because of allegations of abusive behavior. After I moved out of the rectory, Henry fell afoul of his own lack of good judgment and of his unhappy colleague Don's conviction that his parish boss was guilty of the sexual abuse of young men. As a result, Don pursued him first in anonymous letters, then in the media, and finally in tandem with an injured party into civil court. Our parish community, which had been so enlivened by Henry's leadership—his personality quirks and all—endured some years of strife over the accusations as some people withdrew and others supported Henry until his term as pastor ended and he himself went on sabbatical. Had he abused the young men to whom he had given back rubs with massage oil? None of them have accused him of it, but his attentions certainly made some of them uncomfortable and wary of him. Other stories emerged of his too insistent wrestling years earlier, and of inappropriate contact with an adolescent, and these were thrown into the mix, painting a picture of someone not always in control of his behavior. He certainly seems guilty of failing to grow up on time and of carrying too much undigested sexual curiosity into his adult years as a priest—as many of us products of the minor seminary did. Buying into some typically clerical narcissistic self-delusion that priests harbor about inhabiting a twilight zone of nongenital body contact, Henry made stupid mistakes and allowed himself to be targeted for spending the wrong kind of needy time with young men. For these mistakes—far short, it seems to me, of crimes, but far more than a member of a mature priesthood should have done—he is paying a price much higher than many malfeasant bishops, who have ignored far worse.

Standing on the other side of the altar, as I have done during this fourth phase of a now prorogued priesthood, I continue to be encouraged by the healthier state of the body of the faithful, even as I wonder at the debilitated state of the clerical establishment. On the positive side of the balance sheet, it was perhaps inevitable that Vatican II's monumental repositioning of the laity should lead to a devaluing of the formerly overvalued clergy in the Catholic economy of salvation. All demigods have clay feet, as King Nebuchadnezzar's dreams revealed. It was not possible to rediscover and publish the truth of the laity's priesthood through baptism without raising questions about the exclusive spiritual status that had surrounded ordained priests for centuries. But had the clergy actively and enthusiastically cooperated with the readjustment of expectations—like parents easing their adolescent children's growth into their adulthood rather than fighting it tooth and nail—the story of the priesthood and sexuality might be in a different phase right now. Instead, priests have codependently kept the official myth of Catholic sexual teaching in place, frequently compromising the strict and unreal teaching in private forums, experimenting privately as well with the limits of their peculiar (and forced) notion of chastity, turning their heads when things go awry, playing along, in many cases, because any hope of preferment comes only to those who, at least on the surface, march in lockstep with the Vatican.

For their part, laypeople have begun to take up the slack, providing both administrative and spiritual leadership, sometimes hindered by a lack of professional training, but often making up for it through trial and error. If my parish community is any measure, people feel deeply connected as members of Christ's Body by their participation in the reformed order of the sacraments. In them, the priest acts as a catalyst, energizing all the ingredients, rather than bringing sacred form to base matter and providing the essential magic. Through the sacraments, when they are fully celebrated, laypeople feel empowered to stand and serve, to bless and praise, and to bring their own experience to bear on the life of faith, not just to pray, pay, and obey as of old. Many priests have found it hard to readjust their understanding of how they fit into this new chemistry, especially the newer, re-clericalized priests who have been taught to assume the old hiero-phantic posture that no longer fits their instrumental role in the sacramental exchange. So the clergy's being humbled further by the terrible scandals the church has endured may well be part of some overall scheme where random evil and grace are interacting unexpectedly.

On the negative side of the balance sheet, while there are fewer of the clergy under forty than over seventy-five, the men who are being ordained seem to be largely a self-selected group of regressives. They do not lack goodwill, but successive witch-hunting seminary visitations by orthodoxy watchers have ensured that most men who survive to ordination these days rate high on the conformity scale. To complicate matters, if it is true, as almost everyone who watches these things says it is, that growing num-bers of homosexually oriented men are entering the seminary and being ordained, then a day of reckoning with clerical con-formity may be in the offing. Gay men have long sought and in many instances achieved an honorable place in the Catholic clergy, often being among the most creative and imaginative priests as they bring their natural gifts to bear on ministry. But gay people, in general, have today become a cultural, and some would say spiritual, barometer of a major change in human self-understanding regarding sexuality. So a higher number of gay clergy cannot help but tip the balance against Rome's own re-gressive stance on sexual morality. Gay sexuality can no longer be understood as the perverted opposite of "normal" heterosexual-ity; for all human sexual organization lies along a spectrum. Immorality remains an acceptable risk at any place along the spectrum, but only at the different ends of this spectrum does sexual activity spill over into pathology, either of the repressed or of the hyperexpressed kind. The great majority of men and women live their lives somewhere between the two extremes. Morally speaking we are all called upon to achieve a harmonious balance between sexuality as self-expression and sexuality as an instrument of faithful love, which may be an operative definition of chastity. It is an achievable ideal, but one that requires both self-insight and hard work. But how this underlying change will play out in an increasingly gay Catholic clergy, I cannot begin to guess.

An older priest, whom I had early on consulted about my growing unease as I approached forty, told me that he stayed in the priesthood because otherwise his life would be about smaller, daily matters. He didn't want that to happen. He wanted to be involved from day to day with weightier issues than laypeople get to deal with. Perhaps this is an element of the romance of celibate nonattachment that I've given short shrift to in this account of a priest's personal struggle. It certainly caters to the either/or model of the spiritual life: either the flesh or the spirit, either lightweight concerns or heavyweight ones, either time or eternity. Or call it "the cost of discipleship" mode of understanding the priestly vocation. And yet accepting the dichotomy necessarily devalues the day-to-day struggles of our mothers and fathers, of our sisters and brothers, and of the overwhelming multitude throughout the world who must fight much harder than the poorest monk in the meanest monastery just to live one day of a dignified human life.

Every day, as I ride the commuter train, or attend meetings about how better to serve New York's homeless people, or review my daughter's Italian lesson, or pay bills with my wife, I do so as a justified sinner struggling to redeem the time. These are all "secular" pursuits which either make sense or don't depending on how I engage in them. All of them get the best of me at times, but none of them are small in the overall scheme of a life of faith. Now I do them no longer armed with the totem of the Roman collar to imbue them with automatic significance just because Father is doing them. They are all near occasions of grace, reaching out to me as part of a life I seek to weave into whole cloth from the bits and pieces that I am dealt. Some moments do not rise to this level of opportunity, but most of those moments come when we are asleep and aren't free to respond.

These days, I also submit to the discipline of worship without the professional swagger and sense of importance that being an "officer" of the liturgy brings in its wake. Without the extra layer of clothing I wore when vested as a priest, no matter how else I am dressed, I feel far more nakedly me. Being unvested knits me more closely to my family and to the larger body of believers and makes demands on me now from which the uniform used to shield me. Am I holier as a result of disrobing? Only God knows, and God's not telling. But I know I am more whole and even freer betimes to let go, to be undone, to let grace be grace, and to grow in spite of myself.

I offer this story of my spirit and its decades-long dance with my flesh as a cautionary tale for Catholic Christians in these opening years of Christianity's third millennium. There is nothing necessary about the link between celibacy and ordained ministry. Despite the thinking of people like the Vatican's Cardinal Stafford, one of whose associates actually compared the priest's kissing the altar with a man's performing cunnilingus on his wife, sexual love does not obviate a man's, or a woman's, ability in Christ to minister to the Body of Christ. Selling the idea of a necessary connection between celibacy and priestly ministry, and of an even more essential connection between the priesthood and male genitalia, denies the very structure of divine grace. It segregates beforehand those whose nature prevents them from standing in the place of Christ from those whose nature allows them to do so. Pretending that the distinction exists because of some eternal, divine legislation amounts to an idolatrous self-establishment of the clergy as above the church, not in service to it. It promotes both fear and hatred of female sexuality and a phobia of most forms of sexual love that human beings practice. It distracts priests from the demands of overcoming their own grandiose notions of themselves and sharing in the whole people of God's struggle to discover deeper connections between sexuality and spirituality, *the* challenge of the new millennium.

Happily, believers have many resources that allow them to start all over again. Chief among them is the book of beginnings, the Book of Genesis that opens the Bible. There the image of God is first revealed to be both male and female. That's where the church can start to refashion its vision and to rebuild its trust once its leadership is no longer in love with its own self-ideal and deluded about one of life's central mysteries.

Acknowledgments

I HAVE MANY PEOPLE to thank for helping me with this book, not only those who walked with me at some time during the journey recorded here, but especially those who accompanied me in my transition from ordained priest to life as a resigned one and as a happily married man. While still in the ministry, I joined together with men in the parish where I was residing to form a men's group that has met regularly for the last ten years. Each in his own way has walked with me, talked me down, picked me up, and helped me keep my balance through some trying times. They have also contributed some of the wisdom I hope these pages hold, and I owe them much: Joe DeGenova, Tim Dinger, Mike Gaffney, Paul Landolfe, Rob Luntz, Greg Maher, John Shumway, and John Young. I wish to thank Thomas McCabe, Vincent Murphy, and Anthony Sucich for their openness and willingness to share their experiences and also Leo Wegeman for his constructive suggestions. I owe a particular debt to an esteemed comrade of almost forty years, Chuck Anthony, a linguistic artisan, who read my drafts and helped me make many improvements in them. I am also grateful to the priest friends whose stories I have adapted and whose names I have not dared to use. A word of appreciation as well to Thomas Cahill, historian and biographer, whose trenchant grasp of what is at stake in this era of reform and reaction I can only hope to emulate. And, most especially, my gratitude goes out to the many women who opened the eyes of the blind along the way and, most particularly, to Marilyn, my wife—who suggested this book's title—and to Caitlin and Tara, our girls. Their patience with this bachelor-priest, still blinking in the bright light of day, has been life-giving. My editor, Paul Elie, has been an important catalyst for this project and for what it hopes to say to a church in need of new leadership and in search of its real mission. A final word of thanks to Susan L. Neibacher, the executive director, and to my colleagues at Care for the Homeless, who have encouraged and accommodated me in bringing this project to a conclusion.